THE ARTS
AND
PSYCHOTHERAPY

THE ARTS
AND
PSYCHOTHERAPY

By

SHAUN McNIFF

Provost, Endicott College
Beverly, Massachusetts

CHARLES C THOMAS • PUBLISHER
Springfield • Illinois • U.S.A.

Published and Distributed Throughout the World by

CHARLES C THOMAS • PUBLISHER
2600 South First Street
Springfield, Illinois 62717, U.S.A.

© *1981 by* CHARLES C THOMAS • PUBLISHER
ISBN 0-398-04112-1 (cloth)
ISBN 0-398-06277-3 (paper)
Library of Congress Catalog Card Number: 80-24389

*With THOMAS BOOKS careful attention is given to all details of
manufacturing and design. It is the Publisher's desire to present books that are
satisfactory as to their physical qualities and artistic possibilities and
appropriate for their particular use. THOMAS BOOKS will be true to those
laws of quality that assure a good name and good will.*

*Printed in the United States of America
I-R-1*

Library of Congress Cataloging in Publication Data

McNiff, Shaun.
  The arts and psychotherapy.

  Bibliography: p.
  Includes index.
  1. Arts – Therapeutic use. I. Title.
[DNLM: 1. Art therapy. 2. Dance therapy.
3. Music therapy. 4. Mental disorders – Therapy.
WM 450.5.A8 M169a]
RC489.A72M32   616.89'1656   80-24389
ISBN 0-398-04112-1.— ISBN 0-398-06277-3 (pbk.)

OVERVIEW

TODAY'S arts therapists are practicing one of the most ancient forms of healing. They are in many ways reviving a lost art. Reinstated as a transmitter of curative activities, the artist is learning how to adapt proclivities for expression to the prevailing structures of mental health systems. Myth, ritual, and symbol making are entering the mental health clinic, not as objects of psychopathological analysis but as living processes. Clients are up out of their chairs and their couches, their therapists with them, and they are dancing, finding balance in kinesis. They are not only talking about conflict but finding it in their bodies, visualizing it, talking *to it*, and exorcising it. Theatre is returning to its point of origin, where dreams and emotional memories are enacted with sensitivity to affect life in the present, where we are distracted by our inability to see the obvious. We are learning again to appreciate the most familiar of our sensations, which are so taken for granted that they must be rediscovered together with the places we inhabit, our physical environments, and the people and things in them.

Those who have been convinced that unconscious forces rule their lives are believing again in *the will* and the life of the spirit inside of and between people. Empowered by a belief in themselves, people see that art gives form to changing outer and inner realities. Art provides a structure for being, for confronting what Keats called Negative Capability, the acceptance of ". . .uncertainties, mysteries, doubts, without any irritable reaching after fact and reason." The willful person has the power to focus, to concentrate and perceive selectively. Most importantly, however, this person can transform material existence. This is where the great power of the arts in psychotherapy lies. Throughout time, art has shown that it can change, renew, and revalue the existing order. If art cannot physically eliminate the struggles of our lives, it can give significance and new meaning and a sense of active participation in the life process. This is offered as an alternative to passive resignation to self-fulfilling forms of emotional "illness," which will ultimately cripple the strongest personality. The arts in therapy are the return of the folk song in all of us. In group song and dance, we transcend the isolation of individuality and participate in the oneness of community enchantment.

Many of the problems that we face today grow from the multitude of distractions that interfere with our penetration of the moment. In 500 B.C., Heraclitus proclaimed that "man is estranged from that with which he is most familiar." I would imagine that the complexities of contemporary life have made this condition significantly worse today. Even concepts such as "becoming" and "actualization" can be neatly integrated with the production values of our age. These psychological constructs are useful as long as they do not negate and take attention away from *being*, the pure present which is the timescape of art. The cult of becoming can be problematic if it sets up expectations beyond the immediate reality of being, and the notion of actualization can suggest for some that one will one day be something *more* than one is now. We give too much attention to consequences rather than to the process of action and hence interrupt the completeness of the moment, pregnant with possibility.

Life offers each of us the challenge of creating ourselves within continuously changing yet unchanging time, and within an environment that is moving. To the extent that we enact this movement in psychotherapy, we are approaching the fullness of life. We respond to each emerging moment through the physical posturing of our bodies, the intelligence of our senses, and the expressiveness of our spirit. Our sensitivity to process must somehow be aligned with a culture that does not share these conceptions of time and in which unrealized goals dominate the mind with thoughts of acquisition and retention of what is acquired. Many refuse to accommodate themselves to this dissonance of values and consciously work toward the changing of the social order. Others cannot cope and lose their ability to cohere and live a self-sufficient and balanced life within the complexities and social contradictions that surround them and confuse them.

Psychotherapy has grown to be a principal means by which the individual learns to reestablish the functional order of life with the help of one or more other human beings. The therapist fills the role of the listener/observer who helps people to hear, see, and feel themselves and the things around them. The therapist also assists in decoding the complexities of dreams and the cryptic or indirect messages people send to themselves and others. Perhaps most essentially psychotherapists strive to be present with their patients as completely within a given moment as is humanly possible. With their clients they learn to create an identity and a sense of who they are within the multiplicity of roles that they play within their work and personal lives.

The role of the therapist has grown as more traditional ways of finding support, self-validation, group inclusion, and guidance have either vanished or have become inadequate. With the integration of the arts and therapy, psychotherapists are harking back to the most ancient and time-validated methods of healing. Art allows for the expression of inner chaos and pain through a reassuring external order. The emotional scope of art is unparalleled by other modes of expression. The arts bring creative action to psychotherapy and break expressive boundaries. The full physical catharsis of the body and the more varied and far-reaching communication of artworks penetrate previously inexpressible places in people and further total expression and total perception.

By and large, the arts have been introduced separately to psychotherapy. Professional associations and the published literature on the subject have generally increased this separation. My own writing up to this point has been focused largely on art therapy because I had been trained to think of myself as a visual artist whose function was different from that of the actor, dancer, musician and poet. Work with clients in psychotherapy and artist colleagues has shown me that like most human beings, I have the ability to move forcefully within all of the arts and accompany students and clients in the varieties of their self-expression. Rather than refer to individual dance, drama, music, poetry, and visual art therapies, I will conceptualize them generically with the term "expressive arts therapy." If psychotherapists universally used expressive modalities in their work, this term would be unnecessary. My objective is not the creation of yet another hybrid mental health profession; rather, I am working toward the inclusion of the arts into the psychotherapeutic or healing process. The term psychotherapy might itself someday prove inadequate because it perpetrates a mind-body split with its exclusive reference to psyche.

When the expressive therapist introduces action to psychotherapy, there is an acknowledgement of the fundamental kinesis and flux of the life process. Action within therapy and life is rarely limited to a specific mode of expression. One form of expression tends to flow from another. Thus, the expressive therapies of art, dance, drama, music, and poetry have an essential unity and complement each other in practice. In our work as psychotherapists, we find that people have different expressive styles with strengths and weaknesses. One person will be more visual, while another will emphasize the kinesthetic or verbal modalities. By opening the psychotherapeutic experience to the full range of expression, we augment the clinical depth and scope of the arts. An integrated approach to the arts in therapy allows us to respond to the client's emotional state, and it facilitates expression in the most direct and forceful manner possible.

The separation of the arts in therapy is rooted in the product orientation of technological culture. We are trained from childhood to perceive individual artworks as commodities, audiences as consumers, and artists as people who follow specific vocations and master a sequence of skills that enable them to develop a proficiency which will earn them "a living." The very notion of life is conceived economically. Our language in turn makes these ideas about art and artists permanent through linguistic categories and terms that continuously specialize the art impulse. The tendency of professional societies to secure a defined and financially viable place for their members within our modern maze of human service job classifications continues the progressive alienation from the emotional wellspring that gave birth to art. External economic pressures and the mind set of society have isolated art from its healing powers.

There is an indivisible dimension to the practice of the arts in therapy, however. When the human organism expresses itself with complete authenticity, all sensory modes are in action. To perceive with total efficacy also requires this fullness of gesture, vision, sound, and touch. In ancient times and in societies not touched by modern mechanization, this integration of the senses in artistic expression was utterly natural. The arts were not only connected to one another but with life as a whole. A unified approach to the arts in therapy can begin to restore this forgotten balance.

Nietzsche, in his advocacy of the individual's power to trans-valuate and renew the meaning of life through art, anticipated the reemergence of the arts as the primary human healing experience. In his *The Birth of Tragedy* (1871), he predicted that when the omnipotence of science was pushed to its breaking point, thus exposing its limits in explaining human phenomena, there would be a rebirth of tragedy. Nietzsche felt that existence "and the world seem justified only as aesthetic phenomena." In this scheme the tragic myth integrates "the ugly and disharmonic" as comple-mentary parts of the eternal artistic context. Nietzsche's studies indicated to him that we reach exaltation through the full use of all our symbolic powers.

> We need a new world of symbols; and the entire symbolism of the body is called into play, not the mere symbolism of the lips, face, and speech but the whole pantomime of dancing, forcing every member into rhythmic movement. Then the other symbolic powers suddenly press forward, particularly those of music, in rhythmics, dynamics, and harmony. To grasp this collective release of all the symbolic powers, man must have already attained that height of self-abnegation which seeks to express itself symbolically through all of these powers. (Nietzsche, 1967, pp. 40-41)

Nietzsche would say that limited consciousness keeps this world of expression beyond our vision. He realized that through-out time not only art but the specific ritualistic and therapeutic uses of art have shown themselves to be an emotional imperative for all cultures with striking similarity. The actual behavior of today's expressive therapist parallels the methods of ancient predecessors in enacting and giving sensible form to dreams and conflicts. This book will attempt an integration with large conti-nuities of culture and thus provide an alternative to those stories of origin which see the expressive therapies growing from twen-tieth century psychology and psychiatry. From an anthropo-logical perspective, modern psychotherapeutic practices are but a tiny dot within the universe of humankind's efforts to renew and heal the psyche. We have so completely accepted contemporary notions of time, space, life, and death that we have forgotton how these ideas were themselves constructed. Artists are generally more sensitive to our power to define and maintain concepts of reality. Today's psychological reality is but one of the myriad theoretical constructs that have been invented through history to justify and explain existence. If one is unhappy with life as it is perceived, it rarely occurs to that person that one's perception of life can be changed and reconstructed in a way that offers personal meaning. Art's greatest power lies in its ability to create, change, and sustain value.

In his *Letter to a Young Poet*, Rainer Maria Rilke confronts the reader with the merits of the inward search through art.

> If your daily life seems poor, do not blame it; blame yourself, tell yourself that you are not poet enough to call forth its riches; for to the creator there is no poverty and no poor indifferent place. And even if you were in some prison the walls of which let none of the sounds of the world come to your senses – would you not then still have your childhood, that precious, kingly possession, that treasure-house of memories? Turn your attention thither. Try to bring up the sunken sensations of that far past; your personality will grow more firm, your solitude will widen and will become a dusty dwelling by which the noise of others passes far away. And if out of this turning inward, out of this sinking into your own world verses come, then it will not occur to you to ask any one whether they are good verses. . .you will see in them your fond natural possesion, a fragment and a voice of your life. A work of art is good if it has sprung from necessity. In this nature of its origin lies its judgment: there is no other.

Rilke's instruction should not be construed as encouraging emotional complacency. The person living under oppressive social conditions will hopefully always strive to improve the quality of life. However, during the period of change, that person still has the power to focus creatively on inner resources. The artist understands the importance of working with the subject matter of your life. Wealth for the artist is to be able to interact continuously with a sensate world and to have what Blake described as the freedom to create his own system rather than "be enslav'd by another Man's." Faulkner spoke of how economic freedom was not needed by the writer. He did not know of any good writing that came from gifts or money. To him people are indestructible when driven by the "will to freedom."

To the extent that the literature on the arts in psychotherapy subordinates itself to traditional principles of psychiatry as it is commonly practiced, this literature is derivative and often unoriginal. What is needed today is a theoretical and operational approach that comes more from the historical continuities of art. We must go back to and restore the early art-life integration of the first artists and healers. The constructs upon which contemporary mental health systems are based must be questioned. We should also look critically upon the concept of *art as an entity unto itself.* The conception of "art objects" and "artworks" as separate from the lives of the people making them is antithetical to the therapeutic functions of art. Art therapy does not accept the belief that the artist is only a vehicle for what is to be created. Within the psychotherapeutic art experience, what matters is the person or the group of participants. Art is a means through which they intensify, clarify, elevate, and share their personhood.

The fixed commodity definition of art is in opposition to the dynamic process and constant movement of nature. We have been so completely schooled to think of ourselves as people who acquire things that the problem of acquisition presents itself in the training of therapists. Psychotherapists come to think of themselves as technicians skilled in the application of specific techniques to specific problems. The construct of mechanical, replicable, and technical action permeates professional life. An alternative operational mode is offered in the role of the artist who acts within a more conceptually open-ended, changing, and fundamentally emotional universe.

As a result of the ascendency of mechanical science as a paradigm for existence, the influence of art has been steadily diminishing. Psychology has not yet incorporated the space-time relations of modern physics, and perhaps the arts can be helpful in this integration. Transpersonal psychology, as an alternative way of viewing phenomena, challenges the perfunctory rules of psychological science that are in conflict with Einstein's description of a "finite" yet "unbounded" universe with *no limits.* Freudian and behavioral theories of psychological determinism, with their chains of causation extending in a linear progression, are related to Newtonian principles of fixed positions in space as the measuring point of reality. For Einstein, "the fictitious rigid body of reference is of no avail in the general theory of relativity" (Einstein, 1961, p. 98). Our movement through, or more accurately *in*, life is nonlinear. The step-by-step principles of developmental psychology are distinctly western constructs. Humanistic psychotherapy and art have in common a commitment to give order to changing experience by understanding the relationship of one dynamic occurrence to another. Their field of reference is open, and all participants move in relation to each other. The illusion of the therapist as fixed to a constant position of observation is removed. With this unmasking the therapist's personal process and changing observations within the therapeutic moment are as vital as those of the client. Skill and experience come into play through an ability to maximize the healing potential of the relationship. Just as actors determine the form and intensity of expression through their interaction, so, too, the psychotherapeutic relationship is based on the dynamic of exchange.

The rigidities of psychological determinism have alienated us from artistic and mythic explanations of existence. A one-sided adherence to "empirical truth" would lead us to think that imaginative realities have no "validity." Through the use of the arts in psychotherapy, behavior does not necessarily fit into a dogmatic cause and effect schema but rather *participates in* a timeless human drama. The artistic mode of perception keeps the mind in touch with a world possessing both archaic continuity and infinite novelty. The arts offer a valuable operational polarity to the use of discursive language in psychotherapy, and they allow us to communicate with the emotions in their own language. Their multisensory rhythms must be kept intact rather than be absorbed within the more conventional verbal exchange of psychotherapy. The importance of emphasizing and supporting the distinctness of these polarities is reinforced by brain researchers who distinguish the more imaginative and nondiscursive hemisphere of thought from analytic and verbal thinking. Those of us engaged in the therapeutic use of the arts have learned much from the more established psychotherapeutic disciplines, but rather than place too much effort on adopting their style, expressive arts therapists should maintain an identity that is unique to them.

From a more practical standpoint, I have learned from my experience as an expressive therapist that within the context of psychotherapy there are many things that can be communicated more effectively through the arts than through a verbal exchange. I would like to provide an initial overview of the therapeutic concepts that will be discussed in the following chapters. I do not wish to downplay the importance of language in the expressive therapies. Spoken language is a unifying medium that is used to facilitate and clarify expression in other modes.

TRANSITIONAL OBJECTS AND THE THERAPEUTIC RELATIONSHIP

All of the art forms provide a focus for sharing between the therapist and client. Poems, drawings, dramatic improvisations, and the like are tangible representations that can be discussed with the goal of discovering the motivation for the expression and how it relates to one's life as a whole. Participants in an expressive therapy experience might simply wish to share how they perceived an artwork and the feelings it provoked. Preliminary dialogue of this kind inevitably brings up issues that can precipitate the further association of feelings. The stimulation of artworks supports the exchange of energy between therapist and clients. When the therapist and client are finding it difficult to relate directly to one another, the artwork may be a bridge between them, a third object, or what the psychoanalysts call a transitional object, which gives them a safe middle ground through which they can be together. For one person, the intermediary might be a drawing, for another a poem or perhaps a series of improvised movements. All of these principles are equally applicable to individual or group therapies.

Artworks might be first discussed from a formal point of view as a warm-up to more personal sharing. The analysis of color, sound groupings, the shape and texture of movements or the placement of bodies during a drama exercise will draw attention to the many different qualities of an artwork and expose different levels of meaning. Preliminary discussion provides participants with an opportunity to become acquainted and discover how they might best communicate what is on their minds without jeopardizing personal needs for safety. Trust, together with stimulation, can grow from this process, which helps to prepare the therapeutic relationship for the sharing of more private and conflict-laden feelings. When working with seriously disturbed or withdrawn persons, the therapeutic experience might be exclusively focused on the sharing of concrete perceptions, since they might not be capable at that point of discussing anything other than the physical qualities of the environment.

PERCEPTUAL FOCUSING

The arts fully utilize physical objects in psychotherapy. As attention passes from one object to another, therapists have the opportunity to chart the selective course of a person's perceptions. Why does one object hold someone longer than another? Why does a person constantly choose one type of object first and avoid others? Is attention constant in moving from object to object? Consciously performing these actions with real objects in therapy can help a person to interact with the environment in a manner characterized by more care and concentration. The mundane can be elevated through aesthetic perception, and surroundings can begin to take on new significance. During therapy concentration can be focused on absorbing the essence of an object and those qualities which make it unique. Continued observation of an object will deepen an individual's relationship with it and the understanding of its properties. All of these object-oriented exercises can be applied to relationships with other people.

SAFE EXPRESSION

Expressive action with objects may allow for the venting of emotions that would either be too threatening or inappropriate to act out in a situation other than a therapeutic dramatization. One of the great advantages of the arts in therapy is that they allow for the cathartic expression of anger, fear, and painful memories through all of the senses, thus maximizing the effects of expulsion. For the person who cannot directly communicate threatening feelings through language, the nonverbal arts provide an opportunity for their expression in a less intimidating form.

ENACTMENT AND EMOTIONAL CLARIFICATION

The enactment of conflict through dramatic experiences provides a second chance to relive a troubling situation. When self-consciousness has been minimized and the person has become completely absorbed in the dramatized role, penetration to the deepest levels of the pysche is possible. Feelings are aroused spontaneously and in response to the surrounding action. People observing the enactment make every effort to take in the feelings and thoughts of the actor and provide support for further revelation through their engagement. Without this "communion" of feelings, the actor is alone and will be distracted by viewers as opposed to being transformed and elevated by their energy.

The arts are not limited by the time-space restraints of verbal discourse and are ideal for the enactment of dreams and feelings that provoke disassociated mental imagery. Art orders emotion at the deepest levels of consciousness, and it has a scope that can contain the most complex feelings. In addition to being able to express contradictions of emotion, the arts have the power to clarify and bring emotion into focus. Through therapeutic enactments we can try out new roles and learn more about our impact on others within an environment that supports confrontation and the sharing of feelings.

AESTHETIC ORDER AND PERSONALITY BALANCE

A dimension of therapy unique to the arts involves the way in which the perception of aesthetic equilibrium can directly affect the functioning of the whole person. When order is perceived in the environment, there is a corresponding feeling of order within the mind and body of the perceiver. The same applies for feelings of beauty, dissonance, and physical stress. The expressive arts therapist can help in attaining this correspondence of inner feelings and perceptions of the environment through art experiences and forms of meditation that assist in giving order to the varied stimuli which vie for our attention. Feelings of competence in controlling emotion in this manner, together with all successful encounters with art, will in turn build a more complete sense of self-confidence and self-esteem.

SUBLIMATION

Perhaps the best known therapeutic quality of art is the process of sublimation through which the artist channels potentially harmful emotions into socially acceptable expression. The motivation for much great art comes from deeply rooted anger and psychological discomfort, which could otherwise have had a destructive effect on the person. Artists repeatedly discuss how "psychic disease" is often the drive behind their creative urge. Through creating, they cure themselves and grow strong in their ability to deal with stress and emotional upheaval.

TRANSVALUATION

Tis a dangerous moment for any one when the meaning goes out of things and Life stands straight — and punctual — and yet no content comes. Yet such moments are. If we survive then they expand us, if we do not, but that is Death, whose if is everlasting.

— Emily Dickinson

An all-inclusive property of the psychotherapeutic art experience is the alteration or intensification of perceptual reality. Depression and anxiety are for the most part characterized by the absence of life-building forces in the individual. The depressed child does not take delight in the construction and reconstruction of imaginary environments with blocks or sand. Children actively engaged with play find pleasure in process and have little concern with physical permanence. A stone or piece of paper is easily transformed to serve the purposes of imagination. Art offers the emotionally estranged person the power to change the course of the passions from the denial of life to its affirmation. Transvaluation can begin in simple processes that might include a focusing of attention on the rhythms of breath, speech, and walking. This validation of experience is not necessarily built upon illusions of optimism or one-sided positive thinking, nor does it encourage withdrawal from conflict or negation of the will.

Art strives toward an honest and full evaluation of life, and its ability to encompass the polarities of emotion are acknowledged in tragedy. It seems that the ultimate transvaluation of experience involves the transformation of human suffering into a dramatization of the endurance and compassion of the human spirit. "Here, when the danger to his will is greatest, art approaches as a saving sorceress, expert at healing. She alone knows how to turn these nauseous thoughts about the horror or absurdity of existence into notions with which one can live: these are the *sublime* as the artistic taming of the horrible, and the *comic* are the artistic discharge of the nausea of absurdity" (Nietzsche, 1967, p. 60). Nietzsche stresses that the "redeeming vision" of humanity has always emerged from suffering. In the face of tragedy, art continues life with a sense of appreciation for, and an acceptance of, its intensities.

RHYTHM

Poets and philosophers from Confucius to our contemporaries and perhaps many who preceded written history have realized that the person who has rhythm has the world. They see that the perception of the kinetic flow within the self is a continuation of the movements of nature and the universe. As actors and movers, we participate in the divine order of kinesis. Beginning with a process of centering on our individual organism's perpetual movement, we prepare ourselves to connect with other people and extend individual rhythms to the collective. In psychotherapy groups the process is often reversed for those people who need the support of the group and its rhythmic pulsations before feeling their own. The dynamic harmony of rhythm underlies all of the arts in therapy.

COMMUNITY

The verbal exchange in therapy cannot reach the primordial levels of group unity and rhythm that are achieved with relative ease through chant and collective movement. Music, dance, and drama lend themselves naturally to the formation of a collective artistic identity in groups. The common practice of expressive art therapy in groups is an indication of our needs for group inclusion and ritual. Within psychotherapeutic settings even the more individually oriented modes of the plastic arts, poetry, and creative writing are frequently adapted to group activities. Through the enactment and sharing of their art expressions, individuals have the opportunity to receive both the benefits of the private artistic search and the support and validation offered by a group. Engagement in a therapeutic artistic community allows the person to transcend individuality through a celebration of group expression. Group consciousness does not have to imply the absence of individual differences. A sense of the collective can embody the individual and highly differentiated expression of group members. Feelings of inclusion and group identity are often most complete in the knowledge that the individual differences are accepted and encouraged.

ENVIRONMENT

He who is seeking to know himself, should be ever seeking himself in external things, and by so doing will he be best able to find, and explore his inmost light.

— Amos Bronson Alcott,
from his journals of 1834

The healing power of immersion into nature has been stressed by artists like Wordsworth who felt that in rural life "the essential passions of the heart find a better soil in which they can attain maturity." A sense of place orders consciousness. Just as the expressiveness of a particular painting or sound experience has a parallel effect on the inner psyche of the perceiver so, too, the evocativeness of place has a corresponding effect on emotion. Thoreau has given our most illustrious example of the healing power of absorbing oneself in nature. "To him who contemplates a trait of natural beauty no harm nor disappointment can come. . . When I detect a beauty in any of the recesses of nature, I am reminded, by the serene and retired spirit in which it requires to be contemplated, of the inexpressible privacy of a life, — how silent and unambitious it is" (Henry David Thoreau, "The Natural History of Massachusetts," July, 1842).

The physical environment of psychotherapeutic sessions has a definite effect on the range of feelings of participants. A stimulating and pleasing environment will help to motivate participants in artistic expression, whereas an uncomfortable space will create obstacles to expression. My experience with conducting expressive therapy groups in cultural institutions and what might be referred to as supportive art environments has shown that participants are more quickly apt to feel the arousal of artistic impulses in these settings than within a more clinical context. However, even the most oppressive environments lend themselves to transformation through art. Strong negative emotion can provide the fuel for the transfiguration of this energy into powerful artworks. It also goes without saying that the presence of art helps to humanize and soften the harshness of institutional environments.

TOTAL EXPRESSION

Each of the arts has its distinct value in psychotherapy and together, to use a classic axiom from Gestalt psychology, they are greater than the sum of their parts. The visual arts and poetry lend themselves naturally to contemplation of self and nature. They have been more widely used by psychotherapists in the past because of their ability to represent mental imagery concretely. Drawing and poems have a physical permanence that is absent in the more temporal art forms of music, dance, and improvisational drama. However, with the increasing accessibility of audio and visual recording equipment, performing arts experiences can be played back to therapists and clients to be evaluated and discussed. All of these art modes can be approached in a way that either encourages individual self-analysis or group interaction or a combination of both.

In my work, I usually first engage the client through the mode that is most comfortable and least threatening. In a more nondirective context, the client will usually begin to communicate with a familiar art form without suggestion from the therapist. As the client's spontaneity increases, the therapist can encourage what Paul Knill refers to as a "transition" to another mode of expression. This change might be introduced if the client is beginning to grow restless or if the transition has the potential to "amplify" the vein of expression (Knill, 1978). Changing to another form of expression can also serve the purpose of emotional clarification or sharing with others. Yet transition may in certain cases be perceived as avoidance which can be as therapeutically significant as expression itself.

When working with young children in a nondirective play therapy environment, structured forms of intervention may not be needed because the child tends to move freely from one expressive mode to another. "Intermodal transitions" and "amplifications" are common to childhood expression. Although adults regularly express themselves through the various modes of expression, they generally need more structure and support from a therapist in learning to communicate with intermodal spontaneity. The structuring of the therapeutic process as a dramatic enactment generally facilitates all forms of expression in that theatre is the art form that includes all other modes. Role-playing exercises and the enactment of conflictual situations are processes that most closely parallel traditional psychotherapy. However, within the theatrical event there is the potential for communication through the full expressive apparatus of the body and imagination. In the creation of therapeutic theatre, we will discover the complete and natural integration of the arts. J.L. Moreno advocated this integrated theatrical principle, and through his action-oriented psychotherapeutic enactments, he provided a link between modern psychotherapy and its ancient roots. Moreno, a psychiatrist, established the Viennese Theatre of Spontaneity in 1921 and began what was to be a revolutionary force in both theatre and psychotherapy in that he brought the two back to their beginnings. Before he formulated the principles of psychodrama, Moreno's explorations were focused on the complete spectrum of the creative act and its relationship to psychotherapy.

> In the spontaneous–creative enactment emotions, thoughts, processes, sentences, pauses, gestures, and movements, seem first to break formlessly and in anarchistic fashion into an ordered environment and settled consciousness. But in the course of their development it becomes clear that they belong together like the tones of melody; that they are in relation similar to the cells of a new organism. The disorder is only an outer appearance; inwardly there is a consistent driving force, a plastic ability, the urge to assume a definite form: the strategem of the creative principle which allies itself with the cunning of reason in order to realize an imperative intention. . .It was the error of psychoanalysis that it failed to understand the processes going on in artists as specific phenomena of the creative ego — but derived its forms and materials more or less exclusively from the sexual or biological history of his private person (complexes). (Moreno, 1973, p. 43)

Moreno placed value on art expressions that honestly and directly expressed feeling. He laid the groundwork for the expressive therapies in deemphasizing the importance of the technically perfect and finished product in the arts. Spontaneous expression was what mattered to him. He saw significance in unfinished artworks and unconventional statements as long as they followed the flow of the person's feelings. Moreno's concern was the inner adventure of the creative individual, and finished products were valued only to the extent that they facilitated this process. The Theatre of Spontaneity has given the expressive therapies an alternative psychotherapeutic construct, viewing human beings as "actors." At every moment we are actively or passively engaged in the action of creating our lives. Through the supportive environment of therapy, we attempt to become more aware of this reality and the ways in which we can increase the value of life process for ourselves and the people we inter*act* with.

ART AND UNDERSTANDING

I have attempted to write this book as an artist fully engaged in the process of psychotherapy practice and training. The themes that unify my work have been largely adapted from the world of art and the statements of artists. In an attempt to reintegrate the artistic and healing consciousness, I have relied heavily on the contributions of artists to psychological understanding. Psychotherapy must complement its scientific dimensions with the artistry of relating to other human beings and the physical environment. In this respect, I hope that the following pages will provide an artistic alternative to more traditional conceptualizations of psychotherapeutic relationships. We will find within the arts many examples of the artist's sensitivity to the psychodynamics of the interpersonal process. One of the best passages I know is a poem written by Vincent Ferrini.[1] The poem, entitled "Folksong" reveals what I believe to be the essence of the psychotherapeutic relationship for client and therapist alike.

---

[1] From Vincent Ferrini, *Selected Poems,* George F. Butterick (ed.), 1976. Courtesy of University of Connecticut Library Special Collections Department, Storrs, Connecticut.

I pass
by day
   and night
no one has
   seen me

   If you ever
want to find
   me
and know me
   leave behind
yourself
   and enter
the caves
   of other
people

   there you
will find
   me
who is
   yourself

The artist offers an inscrutable spirit of inquiry and a *faith* in the value of a threefold dialogue with nature, others, and the self. These contributions are major gifts to the mental health of the world. The teachings of the arts in relation to emotion tend to have very little to do with orthodox medical practices in the mental health field. I have a definite semantic difficulty with the terms, "therapy" and "psychotherapy" in that they represent a medical tradition that stresses the assessment and treatment of psychopathology. However, I trust that these concepts will eventually evolve into more holistic descriptions of healing relationships.

I believe that our work in the arts is more closely allied with the larger continuities of religious belief and faith. The arts can, in this sense, be viewed as sacramental actions that symbolically represent the mysteries and intensities of inner experience. They are "sensible signs" of the psyche's efforts to become transcendent, and this kinship with religious ritual explains much of their potency.

This book will begin with a description of shamanism as practiced in various regions of the world. The shaman is for us a vital teacher in that this person is able to bring together the various functions of artist, priest, and healer. As we grow critical of the narrowness and separateness of contemporary professions and the negative associations to concepts such as therapy, the shaman demonstrates new possibilities for action.

The truth of the shamanic enactment lies in its continuity through the ages. All of psychotherapy, and even its most traditional forms, is inherently ceremonial. The ceremonial enactment focuses energy. As a result of this focusing there is a transformation of emotion. United with psychotherapy the arts revive lost rituals of healing that lie dormant in all people. Healing ceremonies relating to the "whole of one's being" through total sensory expression, will draw together many sources of energy, and will result in a comprehensive emotional transformation. I like to think of this book as not only a description of the work I have been fortunate to experience in the arts and psychotherapy but also as an archeological study, uncovering the way in which this work relates to ancient continuities of healing ceremony and enactment. I will begin with the shaman and then go on in successive chapters to relate how the arts and psychotherapy can rediscover what Yeat's described as "the rituals of a lost faith".

ACKNOWLEDGMENTS

SPECIAL thanks are due to my fellow faculty members and graduate students at Lesley College with whom I have been exploring and testing the ideas and methods presented in these pages. Our Lesley community consists of people coming together from throughout the United States and many foreign countries to research the psychotherapeutic use of the arts. The sharing and teamwork is at times so complete that it is difficult to determine whether I am describing an idea that is my own, that is an associates or one that originated from the collective that we are together. The international nature of our community has been a significant factor in my growing commitment to the universality of the artistic healing process. We are a group of artists and therapists coming together with diverse backgrounds in the arts, psychiatry, clinical psychology, education, and the various expressive art therapies to learn from each other how we might best contribute to a unified approach to the arts in psychotherapy.

I am indebted to Paul Knill, Norma Canner, Joseph Power, and Peter Rowan for their contributions to deepening my understanding of action and enactment in therapy; to Rudolf Arnheim for his many years of theoretical and psychological guidance; to Truman Nelson and Vincent Ferrini for their friendship and their support of my work as an artist; to Christopher Cook at the Addison Gallery of American Art for giving me the opportunity for five years to create a utopian expressive therapy program within the art museum; and to my wife Karen for sifting and struggling through every particle of this work with me over the years.

CONTENTS

THE ARTS
AND
PSYCHOTHERAPY

I tell you: one must still have chaos in one, to give birth to a dancing star.

— Friedrich Nietzsche,
Thus Spake Zarathustra

Chapter 1

THE ENDURING SHAMAN

T HE ancient predecessor of the expressive arts
therapist can be found in every region of the
world in the person anthropologists call the shaman. In many
ways an early group therapist, the shaman's work is a response to
communal needs. The shaman serves as the intermediary between
people and "forces" that must be engaged in order to influence
the course of community life. Shamanism is characterized by a
belief in the power of human beings to participate in a direct and
personal relationship with the supernatural dynamic of life.

The shaman generally strives to create a psychologically
charged group environment. As the emissary of the group, the
shaman is *propelled* into a condition of altered consciousness
that makes dialogue with "the spirits" possible. The group projects power to the shaman, which can be measured in relation to
the intensity of their collective spontaneity and enthusiasm.
Their chanting, movement, and musical accompaniment takes on
hypnotic dimensions as they transmit energy to the protagonist.
This emotionally charged atmosphere of the shamanic enactment
in turn engages all participants and strengthens their resolve to
achieve transcendence and the neutralization of emotional conflict.

Shamanism was, and still is, most firmly rooted in communities where there is a high degree of uncertainty in daily living. The
shaman expresses and embodies the fears and emotional conflicts
of the community and in this way vents potentially harmful
feelings through ceremonial enactments. These rituals have as their

3

goal the maintenance of social balance and control in relation to the elements of nature. Early societies were keenly aware of the need for their communal life to reflect the harmony and rhythms of nature. The Hopi world view embodies this vision of a dynamic and nonstatic balance as the underlying structure of all life. "The living body of man and the living body of the earth were constructed in the same way. Through each ran an axis, man's axis being the backbone, the vertebral column, which controlled the equilibrium of his movements and his functions. Along this axis were several vibratory centers which echoed the primordial sound of life throughout the universe or sounded a warning if anything went wrong" (Waters, 1969, p. 11).

Within aboriginal communities religious and spiritual life are completely embodied in the rituals of the shaman. Spirituality has a practical and direct link to the everyday lives of people. The community gathers to engage the supernatural collectively in response to specific problems. The shaman is regarded as a spiritual leader, or guide, who is empowered to communicate with transcendent forces. Shamanic practices are always part of a more general cultural belief system that explained the workings of nature. The acceptance of these beliefs by the community is the source of the shaman's sacramental power. Through the use of culturally accepted images, rituals, and other "sensible signs" the group participates in the sacred spheres of life, which are perceived as the origin of psychic wholeness. The expressive art therapists who are reviving the role of the shaman in contemporary society must function in an environment that does not offer a supportive mythology of this kind. The dissonance between the values of the expressive therapies and the technological belief systems of society is the primary distinguishing feature between therapists' work today and the historical continuities of shamanism. Where the shaman's power was invariably created by the collective support of the community, today's expressive therapist usually must work individually to resurrect these primal instincts in groups. Hence, the expressive therapist often feels this work to be of a revolutionary order in that the values of the social system must be realigned in order to accommodate the realities of nature.

Shamanic enactments provided the beginnings of theatre,

religion, and, to a great extent, culture, because group identity and feelings of the transcendent "oneness" of humanity were evoked through these ceremonies. The mythology expressed through ritual and healing experiences gave a consistent order and unity to the perception of the universe. In shamanism were the first psychological theories and the first metaphoric explanations for life. From these early points of origin, the continuation of the fundamental human motive for conceptual certainty can be seen. Shamanism's elaborate myth systems prove that speculative thought and transpersonal ways of perceiving the world were present in early humanity.

The shaman's operational mode is characterized by reliance on poetic and mythic explanations of life. The metaphors used to explain existence are directly tied to the patterns of nature, and they are in harmony with the flux and constant motion of physical matter. Ideas of permanence are conspicuously absent in shamanic belief systems in which the community must repeatedly reestablish a balanced relationship with the forces of nature. This approach to life and time is distinctly cyclical and antithetical to the values of technological culture. It has been maintained that shamanic healing is "predominantly a right hemisphere phenomenon." The individual must take responsibility for the healing process by engaging in an imaginative dialogue with illness, which is perceived as a "teacher" or a voice within the self. The organism must communicate with itself in order to reestablish a functional balance (Villoldo, 1976).

The evolution of ideas and explanations for existence has seen a transformation in our society from mythic theories to formalized psychological principles. According to the evidence of anthropologists, it would seem that the spiritual or mythic constructs of the shaman, together with their healing enactments, have had a far greater curative effect within their communities than the methods of modern psychiatry. Perhaps much of this success has to do with a collective atmosphere of trust and belief that existed in early communities. This contrasts with the fragmentation and disillusionment of contemporary life. It seems that the shaman's and the psychotherapist's effectiveness is determined by the intensity of group support. Early healers also fully appre-

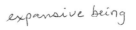
expansive being

ciate the value of the "placebo effect." This faith in the healing process contrasts with contemporary skepticism about psychiatry and mental health methods.

In his study of ecstatic religions, I. M. Lewis (1978) describes psychiatry as a "latent" form of shamanism. He feels that "shamanism is more than psychiatry." Like psychiatry, shamanism aims to maintain a balance in human and environmental relationships, but it surpasses psychiatry in its ability to relate to the transcendent source of life and the dynamic pulse of creative action. If psychiatry is a latent manifestation of shamanism, then the emergence of the expressive therapies is no less than a patent renewal of the shamanic impulse. The psychotherapeutic use of the arts reconnects us to the most arcane and spiritual dimensions of creative activity. Expressive arts therapists are more clearly associated with shamanism than traditional therapists because of the way in which they facilitate group expression as a form of artistic transcendence and celebration. Today's expressive therapist initiates a search for the lost soul of the individual and the collective soul of society just as the ancient shaman went on a journey to other wordly spheres to bring back the soul of a possessed person. As Otto Rank professed, modern psychology has tried to eliminate the idea of "soul." "Psychology is the soul's worst enemy, because in creating its own consolation for death it becomes compelled by the self-knowledge it creates to prove that the soul does not exist, thus it becomes both a scientific 'psychology without a soul' and a kind of overburdening of the inner spiritual self which, with no support from an inherent belief in immortality, goes to pieces in a way the neuroses show so well" (Rank, 1950, p. 31).

Shamanism heals by immersing the person and the group in the unity of collective soul. The role of the shaman will always be necessary, since the attainment of individual and collective psychic integration is an everlasting struggle. Obstacles to psychological balance will continue to be plentiful. The very nature of our universe, which is based on principles of dynamic equilibrium within an environment of perpetual flux, guarantees the inevitable spiral of the establishment and reestablishment of balance. The shaman is a disciplined practitioner of balance who lives close to the precarious edge of total immersion into primary process. Shamanic balance "is a state of acute tension, the kind of tension which exists when two unqualified forces encounter each other. . . It is a position with which the Westerner schooled in Aristotelian tradition, is extremely uncomfortable. . .his [the shaman's] dialectical task is continually to move between the opposites without resolving them" (Meyerhoff, 1976, p. 10).

It is likely that the empirical observer will respond to the more spiritual aspects of this discussion of shamanism by asking for tangible proof of their validity. These contentions are supported by the testimony of artists who have lived with, and documented, the mysterious yet very real power of the creative consciousness, which in its scope of feeling transcends the empirical categories of psychology. The artist, like the shaman, accepts the polarities of experience and their contradictions, whereas the one dimensional empirical perspective increases emotional estrangement because in its pursuit of absolute certainty it negates the ambiguities that characterize feelings.

Today we live in a society that has responded to the previous one-sidedness and closed mindedness of religious belief systems by constructing an equally one-sided denial of spiritual realities within the dogma of empiricism. The psychotherapeutic use of the arts offers an opportunity to integrate scientific knowledge about the psyche with the more imaginative and spiritual hemisphere of the mind, where the power to heal lies.

A CONTINUITY OF METHODS

Modern expressive therapists and the shaman have in common a commitment to the enactment and artistic representation of dreams. The shaman in many cultures receives "power" from personal dreams. Black Elk, the holy man of the Ogalala Sioux, told of how a person cannot receive this power until after the vision has been performed "on earth for the people to see" (Neihardt, 1975). In his 1938 study of shamanism in western North America, Willard Park reports how dreams are commonly the cause of sickness. "Upon awakening, if the dream is recalled, the sleeper addresses a prayer to the sun in order to prevent illness. . . .Very often, however, the dreams are not remembered, and sickness results. Only a shaman can then overcome the evil influences of the dream and bring about recovery "(Park, 1975, p. 39). Park observed that the healing ceremony takes place in the home of the afflicted person, where a group gathers. Everyone participates by singing, which helps to give strength to the shaman in preparation for the journey to meet the supernatural forces that have taken the person's soul.

Numerous observers have documented how a place must be made sacred, and safe, for healing to follow. The performance of the shaman generally takes place within a circle of people. The circular enclosure is common to cultures as separate as the Celts (who referred to the shaman as a druid) and the northwest American Indians. Black Elk spoke of how everything an Indian does is in a circle, and that is because the Power of the world always works in circles, and everything tries to be round. In the old days when we were strong and happy people, all our power came to us from the sacred hoop of the nation, and so long as the hoop was unbroken, the people flourished" (Neihardt, 1975, p. 164).

The circle is similarly a common feature of expressive therapy groups. Dance therapy sessions regularly begin and end with people together in a circular configuration. Group song and chant ideally occurs within circular groupings, since participants are performing for themselves, and therefore, they direct the sound of their voices to each other rather than away from the group. These principles of placement will also enhance group and individual improvisations with musical instruments. Psychodramatic enactments take place within circles where the protagonists receive the energy of observers from all directions. Poems are read and artworks are shared in circles. People describe how the circle furthers comfort, trust, intimacy, balance, and group cohesiveness. Circular imagery is equally common, with the mandala being the best known configuration; it is usually mentioned as a symbol of psychic integration and perceptual harmony. In addition to its impact on our emotions, the circle's order has a direct effect on the nervous system. The circle undoubtedly persists through time in its many different artistic uses because the order and balance of its physical properties has a corresponding effect on the emotions. According to the Gestalt psychologists, "Experienced order in space is always structually identical with a functional order in the distribution of underlying brain processes" (Köhler, 1970, p. 61).

The process-oriented, here-and-now focus of shamanism also parallels contemporary expressive therapy practices. Eskimos are known for abandoning elegant carvings. Their art is transitory, and they perceive the emergence of form from ivory as though it were a song to be released into the air. Sacred art objects used by an Arctic shaman are often hidden in different parts of the village or in ceremonial pouches, since their power would be lost if viewed by others. Kuskokwim Eskimos fashion masks inspired by dream imagery, and after being used only once for ceremonial purposes, they are burned. The Buddhists share a belief that certain mandalas must be destroyed as soon as they are completed. These art experiences emphasize the sacredness of *process*, and they should be of some comfort to us today when our clients insist on ceremoniously destroying their art. In keeping with our culture's reverence for property and products, we often find it difficult to accept what might be an enactment of a birth, death, rebirth ritual by a client with a need to feel some sense of control over this process; so the scenario is acted out symbolically. There are, of course, numerous reasons why clients wish to destroy artworks. Some might be highly therapeutic, and others potentially harmful. We should, however, keep these process-oriented rituals in mind as we assess their value to the client.

Modern observers of shamans in practice are quick to call them "tricksters" when viewing some of their healing techniques. For example, a standard practice in many cultures involves the shaman in sucking out evil spirits from a possessed person through a reed straw. In order to enhance the drama of the event the shaman might chew on some red clay and spit it out at the appropriate moment during the ceremony. Claude Levi-Strauss documents how in tropical America, Australia, and Alaska the extracted source of illness might include a crystal, feather, thorn, or other object that the shaman exposes during the ceremony. The Amazonian Indians believe that disease is caused by physical substances, such as hairlike concentrations that attach themselves to the person and bring about a separation from the environment.

The healing rite involves the shaman in removing these malevolent properties which might include animal hair or feathers. The expulsion of toxic materials from the body provides a tangible direction and focus for healing energies. In light of the documented validity of the placebo effect, these apparent deceptions have strong therapeutic powers. Concrete metaphors for disease are actually regaining status in contemporary medicine through the use of visualization techniques in the treatment of cancer and other physical ailments. By creating an image for the imbalance in the body, the mind can use its ability to redirect and control what have been described as "involuntary" metabolic processes. Research is showing that stress and emotional imbalance significantly influence the development of physical ailments. The notion of psychosomatic disease is being increasingly expanded as a result of these discoveries. In the sphere of emotional disturbance, the use of physical symbolic tools is essential in allowing for the concretization of tension. The mind must be able to conceptualize imbalance so that it can then assume control and effectively manage a return to a functional equilibrium.

Healing rituals that have been described by modern observers as "primitive" and "superstitious" have much to teach us in light of recent trends to investigate the ability of the conscious *will* in controlling physical ailments. We should also keep in mind the numerous gimmicks that characterize contemporary professional practices. For example, the interpretations of drawings by psychotherapists usually have a projective and outlandish quality to them. Drawing analysis is usually done from the point of view of a single psychological theory, which often does not begin to equal the depth and complexity of certain aboriginal world views such as Hopi metaphysics. The American Indian shaman, in approaching a dream or drawing, is apt to see much more than a psychological diagnostician, who is unfamiliar with the dynamics of the creative process and looks at symbolic expression solely from the point of view of a particular theory of psychopathology with its standardized methods of interpretation. Because our own mental health system is characterized by these narrow and highly speculative practices, we should be careful about dismissing aboriginal teachings.

It seems clear that in both shamanism and psychotherapy the personality, experience, techniques, and training of the "healer" have a direct effect on the healing process. Universally, the helping person must be capable of securing the faith and trust of the client. Skillfullness in this work tends to relate to the helper's ability to engage the client's mind positively in the process of healing. The helper serves as a role model for the client in showing that the emotional process can be controlled. In the case of the expressive therapist and the shaman, there is a demonstration of how a person can live with heightened sensitivity and awareness. It seems that a primary objective of the healing process is the transferring of this state of mind to the client.

From shamanism to psychotherapy there is a definite consistency in the major formal structures of the healing experience. In addition to the relationship between the healer and the afflicted person, there is always a place that is a culturally designated site for the healing process to occur. In more spiritually oriented belief systems, the place has sacred qualities; however, in our society the aura of professionalism separates mental health clinics from the surrounding environment. Both the shaman and the psychotherapist function within belief systems that provide not only a theoretical explanation for illness and conflict but also the technical methods with which it is treated. These formalized cultural patterns and rituals to a large degree have a persuasive influence on the client through the very fact of their existence alone.

In all forms of psychotherapy and shamanism, there is an externalization, or symbolic acting out, of the inner feelings and changes that the person is experiencing. The healing relationship thus appears to be a dramatization that not only gives tangible form and clarification to private feelings but which also precipitates insight and emotional adjustment. Jerome Frank has documented that active participation in the healing process is essential and that the person's motivation to improve strongly determines the effectiveness of the therapeutic process. The client who believes in the culture's healing symbols and the socially defined roles of healers is likely to respond favorably to therapy. Frank's studies and his interpretation of the research on psychological placebos indicates that successful therapeutic outcomes depend on the "symbolic power" of healing rituals, relationships, and objects.

He cites numerous experimental studies that show that there is no evidence that one form of psychotherapy produces better results than others. The determining factor seems to be the client's capacity for persuasion and the particular therapist's ability to mobilize healing expectations. Frank discusses the parallels between psychotherapy and shamanism in relation to these issues and validates the power and persuasiveness of the aesthetic dimensions of shamanism. The arts increase the potency of therapeutic enactments and symbols. "They are not only soothing and inspiring aesthetically but they represent tangible reinforcements of the conceptual organization that the ritual endeavors to impose on the patient's inchoate sufferings" (Frank, 1961, p. 53).

The hypnotic and comforting effects of chant and repetitious movement are employed by both the shaman and the expressive therapist. Repetition in the form of ritual is another shared process, which gives order and a sense of predictability to group experience. The power of these activities can depend on the cohesion of the group on one hand and the personal relevance of the ritual on the other. Harry Stack Sullivan's concept of consensual validation applies here to the strength an individual receives from the support of the group. With the Apache and the Navajo, the entire community joins the shaman in songs and dances that build up the person's will to recover. The communal nature of shamanic and expressive therapy sessions again distinguish them from traditional psychotherapy. J. L. Moreno's work in the Theatre of Spontaneity and Psychodrama were among the first developments in contemporary group therapy. This has since been adapted to more conventional verbal psychotherapy. The expressive therapist also works individually with clients, but the large number of people needing this form of therapy in our mental health institutions has been a practical factor in renewing the therapeutic use of communal ritual.

There are precedents in shamanism for the sharing of more private visions and problems. Reichel-Dolmatoff describes how the practice of shamanism within the Tukano tribe in the Amazon region of South America involves individual as well as group sessions. The shaman will often speak alone with a person and explain how interpersonal tensions cause a loss of power and affliction by spirits. The privacy and the confidentiality of these conversations typifies the more secretive aspects of shamanism seen across the world. Many personal experiences are kept in strict secrecy by the shaman for fear that if they are revealed there will be a loss of healing power (Reichel-Dolmatoff, 1975, p. 91, p. 104). In addition to these one-to-one and group forms of therapy, even today's orientation to family therapy can be perceived as a revival of the shamanic practice, whereby the whole family participates in the healing process.

Within both individual and group enactments, shamanism consistently makes use of the ecstatic trance as a form of healing. Procedures vary, with one approach engaging only the shaman in the experience of ecstacy for the purpose of contacting the supernatural spirits to plead for the return of a lost soul. Other manifestations of ecstactic trance include the "patient" or the patient and all participants. Modern hypnotherapy continues these practices but with a more analytic format. Hypnotic trance states are achieved in the expressive therapies through the mesmerization of art experiences and activities that restrict the perceptual field through sensory focusing and meditation. The intensity of psychodramatic enactments can be likened to a trance because participants so completely immerse themselves in their respective roles that they transcend their immediate reality in opening up feeling states beyond the limits of space and time. The individual's demons are confronted in much the same way in these enactments as they are in aboriginal ceremonies. Both provide a means for the release and dramatization of tensions, which can produce peak experiences rather than a continuation that plagues consciousness.

There is some disagreement as to the use of hallucinogens in shamanism. Eliade (1964) felt that a skillful shaman needs only personal resources in achieving ecstacy and does not have to resort to chemical stimulants. McKenna and McKenna conversely maintain that hallucinogens are a natural feature of all forms of shamanism. Reichel-Dolmatoff (1975) describes in great detail the shamanic practices of the Colombian Indians and the central role that narcotic drugs play in their ceremonies. It is likely that, since aboriginal people in the tropical regions of the world live in such close contact with varied forms of plant life, hallucinogens of a vegetable nature would assume a role in healing rituals. Eliade's evidence does show that in most regions of the world narcotic drugs do not play a primary role in shamanic healing, but it does appear that many groups use hallucinogens for spiritual enlightenment. Our culture is distinctive in its extensive drug dependence and its use of chemicals to control behavior and nature as a whole. Where the Colombian shaman introduces drugs to expand consciousness, our psychiatric drug practices generally tranquilize the person and pacify emotion.

Like the expressive therapist, the shaman is fundamentally an open system with effectiveness depending on the person's spontaneity and skillfulness in creating the therapeutic environment. J. L. Moreno embodies the basic principle of shamanic individuality, which is antithetical to organized religions with their standardized ceremonies, when he said that in the past the individual had to adjust to ritual, but now the ritual has to be creatively designed in relation to the individual's and the group's needs. The skill of both the expressive therapist and the shaman depends on the person's ability to create a therapeutic structure or environment that relates to the conflict. The therapeutic activity has to be able to get at the problem and facilitate the process of working it through.

Virtually every behavior of today's expressive arts therapist has its counterpart in the practices of shamanism. The shaman is an expert in the process of role playing and created rites of passage to give symbolic significance to key transitions in life. The passage is often dramatized symbolically in the shaman's movement over an imaginary bridge, which serves as a link between cosmic regions. The bridge is usually narrow, and the crossing is difficult, to symbolize the arduous passages of life. The bridge is a common symbol in expressive therapy enactments and will often be used in dramatizations of birth and rebirth. It also serves as a symbol for feelings of separation and loss. Other shamanic symbols of passage include rainbows, stairs, ladders, vines, cords, and doorlike openings.

The psychodramatic technique of "doubling" appears to have its origin and counterpart in shamanism. The shadow, or mirror image, of a person gives the impression that one can exist in two places at once. From this realization one projects human qualities onto animals and defines the spirits in human terms. The tutelary or helping spirits of the shaman serve in much the same way as the double does in a psychodrama, by acting as an alter ego in supporting protecting, and inspiring the person.

Both shaman and the expressive therapist appreciate the ability of costumes and masks in altering consciousness and transforming the wearer. "In itself, the costume represents a religious microcosm qualitatively different from the surrounding profane space. For one thing, it constitutes an almost complete symbolic system; for another, its consecration has impregnated it with various spiritual forces and especially with spirits! By the mere fact of donning it — or manipulating the objects that deputize for it — the shaman transcends profane space and prepares to enter into contact with the spiritual world" (Eliade, 1964, p. 147).

As with the shaman, clients in expressive therapy sessions tend to identify with different animals as a symbolic source of power and use them to act out their more instinctual drives. Without suggestion from the therapist, clients repeatedly enact the central shamanic "flight" to other worlds by repeating the ancient mythic process of transforming themselves into sacred birds. The journeys taken in therapeutic enactments by adults and children invariably reflect the three tiered cosmic zones of shamanic mythology. Clients reenact both the flight into the upper world of the sky taken by the white shaman and the black shaman's descent into the underworld.

The drums used in both expressive therapy and shamanic enactments are a means of *summoning* spirits or feelings. The drum also furthers the expression of the shaman and is appropriately called the "shaman's horse" (Yakut, Buryat). In the practice of expressive therapy, the drum becomes the "group pulse" and the propulsion of expression. Making musical instruments and other ceremonial objects is a sacred activity for the shaman. The process of selecting wood for a drum, the preparation of an animal skin, and the decoration of the instrument with personal symbols make the process of creation a personally significant ritual. As in the expressive therapies, the person will have a greater appreciation for the sounds of an instrument that has been individually made. Shamanism and art therapy share this *art therapy - making sacred objects!*

power to separate an object from its functional environment through aesthetic perception and thus make it *sacred*. By choosing a specific object, we focus our energies on it and relate to it with emotional intensity. An important dimension of our humanity lies in this ability to perceive and create sacred reality.

The world tree of the shaman, which connects the three cosmic regions of the underworld, earth, and sky, appears regularly in the spontaneous drawings of clients in art therapy. "In a number of archaic traditions the Cosmic Tree expressing the sacrality of the world, its fertility, and initiation, is related to the ideas of creation, fecundity, and initiation, and finally to the idea of absolute reality and immortality. Thus the World Tree becomes the Tree of Life and Immortality as well" (Eliade, 1964, p. 271). As with all psychiatric interpretations, explanations of the World Tree are numerous and differ from culture to culture. Amidst this multiplicity there is the consistency of its physical appearance and its symbolic centrality in both shamanism and expressive therapy.

Verbal psychotherapy and poetry therapy are connected to shamanism in that "the word" plays a key role in aboriginal healing. Abraham Blinderman (1973) reports how the Venidad of Iran believe that healing through the word is more powerful than surgery or medicine. He feels that this view is held by virtually all primitive healers. The shaman must therefore be skilled in the use of language and, according to Eliade, might have three times the vocabulary of other community members.

The expressive therapies have consistently replicated shamanic dramatizations of imaginary battles with evil spirits. Psychodrama most completely engages individuals and groups of people in the process of physically enacting their emotional conflicts. Experience in the other modes of expression consistently shows the need that clients have to enact the inner battles of their feelings. Aggressive instincts may be released and worked through with sound, movement, or visual artworks. Children regularly enact their fears and anger through graphic representations, which allow expression in a form that will not be harmful to themselves and others.

EMPOWERING

The process of becoming a shaman is in many ways similar to the training of expressive therapists. It is commonly believed that the shaman is "empowered" through dream experiences in which spirits communicate directly with the person. Spontaneous vocations also occur during illness and periods of personal psychological crisis. However, Eliade believes that the tendency to attribute the shamanic "calling" to an individual's emotional upheaval is overemphasized. Shamanism is often a hereditary profession, and in many cultures the individual's deliberate "quest" for shamanic power is encouraged. Park observed how the intentional search for "supernatural power" is common in North America. It would seem that in order to ensure the transmission from generation to generation of complex rituals and belief systems, it would be necessary to have an orderly system of training and apprenticeship under the guidance of the community's elder shaman. Eliade describes how "shamanic initiation proper includes not only an ecstatic experience, but. . .a course of theoretical and practical instruction too complicated to be within the grasp of a neurotic. . .if they cured themselves and are able to cure others, it is, among other things, because they know the mechanism, or rather, the *theory* of illness" (Eliade, 1964, p. 31).

Reichel-Dolmatoff lists many qualities that the potential shaman in the Amazon regions of Colombia must possess: an interest in and understanding of tribal myth; a well-developed memory; a singing voice; the self-discipline needed to persevere through long periods of sleeplessness, fasting, and sexual inactivity; skillfulness in interpreting dreams, mythological principles, and whatever expressions a person might offer; and the ability to distinguish the images that appear during a trance state and relate them to the general purpose of the enactment. All of these qualities are developed through years of training and experience over a person's lifetime. In this respect, the shaman's experience supports contemporary attempts to make professional training a lifelong process. With today's psychotherapists, and their shamanic predecessors, the deciding factor in determining ability and effectiveness is the strength of the individual personality. "Above all, a payé's [shaman's] soul should 'illuminate'; it should shine with a strong inner light rendering visible all that is in darkness, all that is hidden from ordinary knowledge and reasoning" (Reichel-Dolmatoff, 1975, p. 77).

The election of the shaman through dream experiences is facilitated by ancestors or tutelary spirits who transmit the energy of empowerment. A lifelong relationship is in this way established between a shaman and these "helping spirits" who assist and guard their charge throughout the shamanizing process. A shaman's power is often determined by the nature of the helping spirits. Bulls, horses, and eagles are signs of strength, whereas dogs and wolves are often less powerful. Power is also determined among certain groups by the quantity of spirits possessed by the shaman. It would appear that animals and birds appear through the world as helping spirits, because people aspire to their physical powers. Aboriginal cultures are also keenly tuned to the unity of nature and thus feel a familial relationship with those animals onto which they project human qualities.

Other attributes of shamanic initiation include the withdrawal of the individual to a state of personal isolation for the purpose of facilitating a relationship with the spirits and initiating contemplative experiences that allow one to symbolically confront death and the resurrection to a new perspective on life. Initial training in Colombian Indian society involves living alone with a shaman and possibly one or two other novices for several months or perhaps a year or more. The initiates pay a fee for the experience. Training is arduous and exhausting due to prolonged fasting and a lack of sleep, together with the tension that is produced by the intensity of the psychological stress caused by exposure to shamanic experiences. The future shaman must become fully engaged in the process of working with spirits and experiencing its intensities before beginning to work with others. Training is a challenge and an opportunity to test one's personal reactions under supervision. It is emphasized that shamanic powers are not *acquired*. The shaman feels that power is infused by spiritual forces. In contrast to the highly structured and ritualistic initiation that certain cultures have their shaman go through, others such as the

Paviotso Indians of the North American West believe that power can be sought out by the person. The Paviotso seek power willfully, and it comes if their ability to concentrate is sufficient for the transformation. "The success of the power-quest is dependent upon the seeker's undeviating adherence to the traditionally recognized form of procedure. If he does not go to the right place. . . failure will attend his efforts. Also, as in unsolicited dreams, the instructions of the spirits must be carefully followed. Consequently, only those who do not abide by these conditions fail in the quest for power" (Park, 1975, p. 28). As with most forms of shamanism, the Paviotso must continue to follow the instructions of the guiding spirits after becoming a shaman; to contradict their direction would involve a loss of power. What we see here is a very disciplined and socially responsive "professional code" that determines which people have the self-discipline and perseverance necessary to become shaman, as well as the commitment needed to maintain the powers once they have been bestowed.

Various observers have reported how shamanic initiation often involves the process of viewing oneself as a skeleton. In shedding the body's flesh and liquids through meditation and trance, the shaman transcends temporal existence and engages transpersonal reality. The mythic cycles of birth and rebirth are experienced directly, and as a result, the shaman gains confidence and skills in passing from one mode of being to another. Initiation visions regularly depict the shaman's descent or ascent to different worlds of experience. "Tree- or pole-climbing rites, myths of ascent or magical flight, ecstatic experiences or levitation, of flight, of mystical journeys to the heavens, and so on – all these elements have a determinative function in shamanic vocations or consecrations" (Eliade, 1964, p. 143). In no uncertain terms, the calling of the shaman is a spiritual process that takes the aspirant beyond the restrictions of mundane time and space to an immersion into the primordial process of life.

Experiences of this kind are not uncommon in today's psychotherapeutic initiations. The perception of one's skeleton can be likened to our confronting the accumulated psychological defenses that we develop through life. The therapist must be able to see through personal armaments and understand their origin in order to avoid projecting personal values and expectations onto others. The clairvoyance of the shaman is as necessary today as it ever was. Ancient training approaches that make of the shaman a seer parallel the intensive focus on the development of observation skills for the psychotherapist. The tradition in psychoanalytic training of personal analysis continues the shamanic initiation of experiencing the process for oneself before beginning to involve other people. Expressive therapy training generally places great emphasis on learning by a person's first becoming engaged in the process. By understanding how an exercise or a ritual *feels*, the person becomes more familiar with its emotional content, less self-conscious, and therefore more capable of being attentive to the needs of other people when taking on the role of the therapist.

Most therapists pursue their work for spiritual and humanistic reasons. Like the shaman, the psychotherapy initiate generally sees through the illusions of society and desires to be in contact with what might be described as the essence of being. People who work with the psyche show an interest in the origins of consciousness, in motivations, in relationships between people, and in the more mysterious and less predictable qualities of life. As with the training of the shaman, skills in these areas are not *acquired* from an external source but are rather drawn out of us and refined through experience. The psychotherapist's calling suggests a way in which life can be lived in close communion with primary process. The choice of a life in art involves similar decisions and insights. The expressive therapist today has typically been called to both a life in art and, at a separate time, to psychotherapeutic or human service work. At some point a third and very powerful calling takes place in the realization that the two can be integrated in the psychotherapeutic use of the arts. The fervor and passion that we bring to this work results from the usually unconscious feeling that we are dealing with "big medicine" and that we experience within us the ancient echoes of shamanism.

Just as the shaman has to study and understand the intricacies of a culture's myths and rituals, today's expressive therapist must spend years in training to become familiar with the complexities of our psychological systems. Training and experimentation are also necessary to develop skills in facilitating psychotherapeutic relationships and enactments. Traditional psychotherapy connects to the continuities of shamanism most directly in its commitment to interpreting and understanding dreams and other expressions of the primary process of feeling. But, all too often the parallels stop there. In the case of the expressive therapies, the similarities with shamanism are inexhaustible because the two maintain the cultural continuity of ritual and enactment through distinctly artistic means, which engage all forms of communication. Within this schema the expressive therapist appears unequivocally as the resurrected shaman.

THE REVIVAL

Otto Rank perceived the psychotherapist as "a new artist-type, such as has not existed since the Greek period and had not been needed since the Christian era began. The type of artist who works in living human material, who seeks to create men not like parents, physically, but spiritually like God" (Rank, 1959, pp. 272-273). If psychotherapy is to fulfill this prophecy, it must fully engage the creative process in its many artistic forms. Although momentum toward the realization of Rank's goal seems to grow steadily, with each year bringing the arts more completely into psychotherapeutic practice, there is much to be done before artistic processes are commonplace and fully accepted within the mental health field. Throughout the history of psychoanalysis and psychotherapy we will find many open doors that have furthered the revival of shamanic consciousness and methods.

In addition to Rank and Moreno, Sigmund Freud contributed greatly to the renewal of the shaman's role within contemporary society. Freud was most influential in the area of dream interpretation. His studies and those of Jung stimulated an interest in the primary process of our experience, and they revitalized the sexual, symbolic, and spiritual continuities of humanity. These primary process dimensions of life had simply gone underground as a result of the combined efforts of the conscious mind and the mechanized social system to dispel them. Freud's discoveries were those of an archeologist of mind and emotion. He, and others, began to pry open the vault door of repression. However, his conceptualization of distinct realms of conscious versus unconscious life have proven to be misleading. Rudolf Arnheim believes that Freud's theories were Victorian constructs that recognized the existence of primal feelings but which tried to separate them from the conscious and morally accountable mind. During Freud's time it was not yet socially possible to integrate primary instincts with the more general life that one must lead in the world of work and emotional repression. Within less mechanized societies there is a more natural flow between conscious thinking and what comes to consciousness through dreams, meditation, and expressive enactments. The spirit worlds of aboriginal thought were the equivalent of the primary process experience that Freud called the unconscious and Jung called the collective unconscious. In reality all of these constructs are an attempt to give form to the mysterious and essentially human realm of emotional life. Freud's *The Interpretation of Dreams* brought us back in touch with primary emotional realities, but his system of dealing with these feelings was restricted by his social milieu and the collective consciousness of his time. Freud could not dance with primary process; he did not engage the hemispheres of expression from whence they came. This cultural task has passed to the expressive therapist.

Within traditional verbal psychotherapy, any form of "acting out" with a client is discouraged. Thus, a client could be sitting in a therapist's office and, while making an attempt to talk about personal problems, might be expressing conflict through the body. The traditionally trained analyst does not deal directly with these messages and thus *does not communicate in the language of the emotions.* Psychiatry is steeped in the Western tradition, whereby the *idea* and the technical manipulation of nature are excessively valued. Through these beliefs, a Cartesian split between mind and body is encouraged. Mind is perceived as the source of change, and the body is but a means of implementation. Traditional psychotherapy has yet to rid itself of Victorian taboos about the *body* and *touch.* By not communicating through the body in psychotherapy, there is a continuation of the belief that sensory modes of communication are less advanced and tied to "the lower" instincts of the species. Messages of this kind will often reinforce the obstacles to living with the full faculty of the senses. In this way we support the forces that precipitated emotional conflict in the first place.

The increasing acceptance of expressive and bodily oriented therapies has been furthered by Wilhelm Reich's studies of how we store tension in the body and restrict expression through bodily "armorments." He described how language in psychotherapy is often used as a defense to avoid getting involved with deeper levels of feeling that are expressed in a person's facial expressions and posture. "The living organism has its own modes of expressing movement which simply cannot be contemplated in words" (Reich, 1973, p. 140). Reich attempted to work with the whole organism and to allow it to "surrender itself" to life experiences without excessive bodily restrictions. "It is the task of orgone therapy to re-establish the full capacity for pulsation" (Reich, 1973, p. 147). In perceiving the constant organismic flow of life process and sensation, Reich rediscovered principles that are well known to the shaman, who perceives the flow of energy in the body as part of the more general "pulsations" of nature. Reich's most complete integration with shamanism came with his discovery that biological pulsations in the body are part of a more universal cosmic energy. The shaman's communion with the "spirits" shows a similar awareness that we are biologically tied to the pulsations of a life source which remains beyond our comprehension.

In light of these psychotherapeutic contributions and the more general climate of our times, a renewal of shamanic expression appears inevitable. Tutelary spirits are as alive today as they have ever been. They have been transformed away from nature and into the machine, which has replaced wild creatures as idealized sources of power, but the direct link to our past remains in the names that we give our tutelary machines — Jaguar, Cougar, Mustang, Barracuda, Thunderbird. . . . These projections go on in spite of a supposed understanding of the "naïve beliefs" of aboriginal societies.

The mechanical and technical values of contemporary culture tend to be stereotypically more masculine than feminine. Today's renewal of the shamanic consciousness through the psychotherapeutic use of the arts is largely a female phenomenon. With the exception of the discipline of psychodrama, women greatly outnumber men in the practice of the arts in therapy. Various aboriginal regions of the world have been known to fluctuate and change patterns with regard to either male or female dominance of the profession (Czaplicka, 1914). Lewis (1978) believes that oppressed women would seek power over men through the practice of black magic or black shamanism. It would appear that today's female expressive therapists are not striving for power over men in their work but rather seem to be drawn to the field by its affective and expressive nature. Women in our society have simply been more open to the emotional spheres of life. This might be due to the socialization process that has encouraged females to seek out helping roles. Some would argue that as the field's stature and pay scales rise, more men will become involved, since men have been conditioned to see themselves in roles of social influence. It is possible too that the high status of the shaman in aboriginal societies accounts for the dominance of male practitioners in certain regions. It is equally possible and certainly more attractive to think of increasing numbers of men becoming involved in today's expressive therapy field, not as a result of the changing status of the profession but rather as a result of changes in our sex role stereotypes. Numerous achievement motivation studies have shown that women and girls respond more to affiliative needs than men and boys. Female achievement is oriented more toward competence in social and affective relationships, whereas males are directed more toward mastery, competition, and control. (Hoffman, 1972, pp. 129-155). These are the values of our society that have been instilled in us over centuries and perhaps through professions like the expressive therapies we can work toward more androgynous sex roles.

No single phenomenon seems to separate the expressive therapist from traditional psychiatry as clearly as the position that each takes in relation to the sense of touch. Expressive therapy relies heavily on the tactile sense, while within classical psychotherapy it is conspicuously absent. The belief that the tendency to touch is more female than masculine might also account for the lack of male expressive therapists. Conventional psychotherapists have strong taboos against touching their patients. The severity of antitouch codes might suggest that they exist not only to respect the autonomous space of the client but also because of the fears and fantasies that therapists have about touching their clients. They thus defend and distance themselves by forbidding all physical contact. Certainly there are inappropriate uses of touch in psychotherapy, but the complete lack of tactile sensation and communication appears to be a form of neo-Victorian restraint. The expressive therapies define themselves by the use of touch and the focusing on the tactile sense in all art modalities. The figure of speech "being in touch" is enacted physically as people explore their tactile needs and styles. The content of therapy often grows from experiences of touching and from sharing how touch is incorporated into one's life.

Since touch, by far the body's "largest" sensory system, plays such a crucial role in the sense perception of the infant, various forms of tactile deprivation, as well as excessive or inappropriate stimulation, are often believed to be the cause of later emotional difficulties. Subsequent conflicts related to touch and the body may be equally harmful, since a person's identity and sense of self grow from feelings of being connected to the body. The person who is not grounded in the body will project this sense of fragmentation into perceptual activity. It can be argued that the personal disassociation of severe emotional confusion relates to an inability to feel complete in one's body. The perception of hallucinatory voices and visions apparently emanating from outside the body validates this principle. Thinking of this kind is also typified by fragmented perceptions of the body with different bodily parts being disconnected from one another. Extreme disturbance results in the feeling that the body is a completely different entity from consciousness. Since the body is the vehicle for the perception of reality, loss of contact with the body will generally result in a loss of touch with the external world. Consciousness thus becomes fully alienated from the environment.

The propensity of the emotionally disturbed person to cling to physical objects and familiar surroundings suggests this lack of confidence in the body as a means of exploring novel situations. Excessive attachment to objects and familiar persons and the repetitious touching of physical materials are often indicative of desperate attempts to maintain some form of bodily presense in the environment. Because of the inadequacies of the body's sensory instincts, exaggerated efforts to make contact with the outside physical world are needed to maintain some form of personal equilibrium. This hard fought for balance is easily threatened by experiences outside of perfunctory patterns, and this accounts for the fear of novelty that the person perceives as a threat to a very precarious sense of self. Diffuse feelings of fear grow from the specific fear of ego destruction. Emotional stability can be measured in terms of the person's ability to distinguish realistic from purely imaginative threats. Since the ability to discriminate real threat from personal projections is very much dependent on the integration of consciousness and the body, therapeutic procedures that do not directly deal with the bodily alienation, which is often at the root of emotional problems, will be incomplete. Thus, it appears that if psychotherapy is to unify consciousness it must engage the body.

Dance therapists have begun to explore the ramifications of touch creatively in psychotherapy. Closely related to the kinesthetic and tactile qualities of the movement therapies is the more all-encompassing *action* orientation of Moreno. Although all of the specific modes of the creative art therapies have made their unique contributions to the shamanic revival, the most complete revitalization of the human continuities of healing rituals has taken place in psychodrama, which in its early stages embraced all of the arts. Moreno's original conceptualization of The Theatre of Spontaneity was dedicated to the enactment of the creative pulsations of our lives in the present, as well as the therapeutic reenactment of past conflicts that live on in us and determine present perceptions. Within this approach Moreno presented a theory that integrates and strengthens the arts in therapy — especially when one views theatre in the classic sense of including all of the arts within a dynamic context which portrays the fullness of life.

Each art form has its place within the unity of drama. Moreno's belief in the centrality of *spontaneity* to health and creativity is a primary tenet of expressive therapy work, which again relates directly to our shamanic past. Moreno's use of the director, the one "most deeply possessed by the idea of the play," closely parallels the role of the shaman. The group context and the participatory audience are also common to both shamanism and psychodrama. Moreno realized that theatre began with the shamanic enactment of conflict, and he strove to bring drama back to this pure source where art and life are one. The very strength of Moreno's methods created problems in that over time his "system" became more and more dogmatic in its technical language and transferable methods. Moreno seems to have been intent, like the psychoanalysts from whom he separated, with cloning his process, perhaps to ensure immortality. However, the idea and the process of psychodramatic enactment, in its more open-ended form, is the primary experience of shamanism, theatre, and the expressive therapies.

Most of the work that has been done in the field of art therapy has been tied to conventional psychotherapeutic forms rather than the shamanic enactment. Art therapy literature generally shows a tendency to be concerned with the introduction of graphic expression and visual imagery to verbal psychotherapy rather than to engage more "art" oriented healing processes. Art, music, and poetry therapy as they are commonly practiced do not use the complete expressive apparatus of the organism. They are more frequently concerned with becoming integrated into classic psychotherapeutic practices. Psychodrama has also moved away from the original Theatre of Spontaneity, where all modes of expression were included in a unifying art event. As the various modes of expressive therapy grow in influence, we must be wary of draining their vitality by continuing our society's pattern of fragmenting the art impulse through the isolation of the different art forms. By separating the parts of the body from one another, we lose their combined strength.

Through the restoration of the multifaceted art experience, we will begin to revive the expressive dexterity of the shaman. Today's increasing stress on professional specialization makes it more and more essential to transcend the narrow outlook of the specialist. We must think and feel holistically about human expression and interpersonal relationships. The broader perspective will show us that psychological "truths" change with the outlook of the historical epoch. What remains intact through time is the continuity of feeling and emotion, the more primary and stable sources of life. The rhythm of the arts continues in stride with these pulsations of human emotion. Wherever there are people, there will be emotional conflicts, doubt, and uncertainty to be transformed by the shaman's song.

Chapter 2

MOTIVES AND NEEDS

I somehow cling to the strange fancy, that, in all people hiddenly reside wondrous, occult properties...which by some happy but very rare accident...may be called forth on earth.

— Herman Melville

THE source of the art experience has eluded scientific investigation and remains a mystery to most psychologists. An artwork is not unlike a river into which many streams and tributaries flow, forming the single current of a particular expression. Many of the river's sources lie underground, while others are readily visible to the observer. Previous investigators have shown a tendency to follow only one of the many streams that flow into the artistic consciousness and overlook the others. Their attention has been focused primarily on the underground, or what is described as the unconscious sources. Theories of art motivation have been heavily one-sided, with the Freudian, psychoanalytic explanation being the best known and most influential. In spite of the fact that there are many different motives for artistic expression, the Freudian viewpoint perceives all art as being precipitated by some form of unconscious conflict that originates in childhood experience. Because of the psychosexual orientation of Freudian theory, it is believed that all artworks will be a projection of an individual's sexual conflicts, and thus, the interpreter views artworks with an eye for psychopathology. Motivational interpretations usually fit snugly into more general psychoanalytic theoretical constructs, which leave little room for alternative explanations. These Freudian psychopathological principles have become so strongly identified with the art therapy field that most people associate the use of the arts in therapy with these practices. Diagnostic approaches to art often proceed to the point where shape, color, texture, and composition have some relationship to sexual conflict. Ironically, art diagnosticians who try to explain creative expression in this way inevitably engage themselves in their own projective tests. Perceptual psychology has clearly described the manner in which personality influences perception and the way we project ourselves into our interpretations of phenomena. As Georgia O'Keefe said, persons who see varied sexual symbols in her art are "talking about themselves, not me."

Because of excessive emphasis on hidden motives, art interpreters have tended to give inadequate attention to the explanations offered by the artist. This is largely due to the psychoanalytic belief that conscious thought tends to defend the person from the more threatening unconscious conflicts that motivate artworks. Sexual conflict, early childhood trauma, parental problems, and instinctual desires are powerful art motives, but they are not the exclusive source of the artistic consciousness. Art transforms these emotional realities into expressions that confirm the human capacity to transcend and control instinctual conflict. The tendency to associate psychopathology with the art experience detracts from a positive emphasis on its healing power. Theories of art motivation that concentrate on psychopathology are a manifestation of the interpreter's inability to experience the spontaneity and emotional energy of artistic expression. In its essence the assertive action of art offers an alternative to passive resignation to psychopathology and personal dysfunction. Yet, art and psychopathology are related within the unity of the creative process. Art's value lies in its ability to transform psychopathology and emotional conflict into personally meaningful action. Psychologically, this process is defined as sublimation. The historical problem of the arts in the mental health field is the tendency of uninformed clinicians to oversimplify the relationship of the arts to psychopathology. They have been inclined to believe that art produced by emotionally troubled people will be psychopathological art rather than to look to the art as an indication of personal strength. As a consequence, art created by clients/patients tends to be uniformly approached with a presumption that it will be a manifestation of whatever is *wrong* with the person.

Throughout this chapter on art motives, the stands that artists have taken on the various psychological issues that will be discussed will be documented. In this way, psychological formulations that have not lost touch with their artistic origins will hopefully be brought out. As we restore art to its place in the healing process, we should be guided by those most qualified to speak on the personal effects of the art experience.

Perhaps no single modern artist manifests classic Freudian themes as vividly as Eugene O'Neill. Because of his explicit revelation of Oedipus and Electra conflicts, his obsession with the polarities that psychoanalysts and classical Greeks describe as *eros* and *thanatos* (love and hate), and his belief in the motivational power of guilt and tension, O'Neill is consistently cited as validating Freudian psychological principles. In *The Great God Brown*, the playwright exclaims his philosophy of life and art in the passage, "Man is born broken. He lives by mending. The grace of God is glue."[1] Mary Tyrone in *Long Day's Journey into Night* articulates O'Neill's belief in psychological determinism and fate. "But I suppose that life has made him like that, and he can't help it. None of us can help the things life has done to us. They're done before you realize it, and once they're done they make you do other things until at last everything comes between you and what you'd like to be, and you've lost your true self forever,"[2] Death is dealt with in *Mourning Becomes Electra*[3] in Ezra Mannon's statement about his Civil War experiences where "death was so common, it didn't mean anything. That freed me to think of life." Here O'Neill deals with the life-death conflict in his customary way of immersing himself so deeply in death that life is more fully appreciated. The same applies to guilt as Orin in

---

[1] From Eugene O'Neill, *Selected Plays of Eugene O'Neill*, 1969. Courtesy of Random House, Inc., New York, New York.
[2] From Eugene O'Neill, *Long Day's Journey into Night*, 1955. Courtesy of Yale University Press, New Haven, Connecticut.
[3] From Eugene O'Neill, *Three Plays*, 1959. Courtesy of Random House, Inc., New York, New York.

Mourning indicates, "The only love I can know is the love of guilt, for guilt which breeds more guilt — until you get so deep at the bottom of hell there is no lower you can sink and you rest there in peace."

In all of O'Neill's plays there is a never ending ambivalence in relation to the polarities of experience that Freud described. Larry, in *The Iceman Cometh*,[4] conveys this consistent theme of insoluble tension: "Life is too much for me! I'll be a weak fool looking with pity at the two sides of everything till the day I die!" And again, the antinomic conflict is resolved through immersion in the reality of the particular emotion, "No one here has to worry about where they're going next, because there is no farther they can go. It's a great comfort to them." In this passage describing the "No Chance Saloon. . .Bedrock Bar, The End of the Line Cafe, The Bottom of the Sea Rathskeller," O'Neill gives an insight into the comfort that many people receive in extreme emotional withdrawal, which serves to equalize and eliminate the never ending presence of psychological tension. Like so many artists and philosophers, O'Neill discovers that acceptance of the reality of the present is the only way to deal with the dualities of experience. Hickey, in *The Iceman,* conveys this message: "after you're rid of the damned guilt that makes you lie to yourselves you're something you're not, and the remorse that nags at you and makes you hide behind lousy pipe dreams about tomorrow, you'll be in a today where there is no yesterday or tomorrow to worry you. You won't give a damn what you are any more." In his plays, O'Neill tried to express personal struggles and what he perceived as the "truths of the emotional past" of humanity. He was often irritated by those who saw Freudian influences in his work. Like Freud, he independently penetrated and attempted to resolve the tragic tension behind human life. He also drew heavily on classical Greek philosophical sources. The difference between the two lies in a duality of resolutions, with Freud representing the medical model of pathological analysis and O'Neill the expressive enactment of art. Rather than submitting to the psychoanalytic belief that his work was fundamentally a response to psycho-

---

[4]From Eugene O'Neill, *The Iceman Cometh,* 1957. Courtesy of Random House, Inc., New York, New York.

pathology, O'Neill maintained that art is rather a transformation of conflict and pain. For him the creative process affirms the need to bring about a rebirth of imagination as opposed to a passive acceptance of enduring conflict. O'Neill's goal was "a theater returned to its highest and sole significant function as a Temple where the religion of a poetical interpretation and symbolic celebration of Life is communicated to human beings, starved in spirit by their soul-stifling daily struggle to exist as masks among the masks of the living."

It is a well-documented fact that the struggles of the characters in O'Neill's plays were those of the playwright himself. Rather than resign himself to the presence of psychological conflicts, he acted upon them creatively. Thus, we see in the work of this particular artist, and others, a model for the use of the arts in therapy. The purpose here in describing Eugene O'Neill's work is to acknowledge through the expressions of a great artist that conflicts of many kinds are part of the essence of art. This is the case with great cultural artworks, as well as the personal expressions of clients in psychotherapy. However, my research into the subject of motivation in the arts has indicated that, in addition to emotional conflict, there are many other primary motives for creative expression.

Interviews with artists, children, and clients in psychotherapy indicate that although there are motives which are unique to a particular medium there are common motivational principles which unify all of the arts. The multiplicity of motives discovered in my research (McNiff, 1977) clearly shows that all of the various motivation theories form a mosaic which, in its entirety, offers a psychological explanation for the need to create art. Interviews and observations in psychotherapy have supported the idea that individual artists not only create art for a variety of reasons but tend to reflect a series of consistent motives in their work. Most of the motives that were discussed were shared by all of the people interviewed. Individual differences were manifested in what might be described as "motivational styles," with certain people placing more emphasis on one motive, or a series of motives, than others.

The motivational forces that lie behind what might be described as the need to create art can be listed categorically for the sake of conceptual clarity. However, in practice, the motives are not separated from one another. They are rather dynamically connected to a holistic process of art. The following description of motives is not meant to be a complete catalog on art motivation. As this research is extended, new ideas inevitably emerge. The categories presented here are intended to give an indication of the many different needs that the art experience responds to, and they will hopefully help the person engaged in the clinical use of the arts in therapy to realize the broad range of treatment possibilities to which the arts can be adapted.

EQUILIBRATION/ORDER   *Balance*

All motivation theories are united in their orientation to the reestablishment of equilibrium. It appears that the organism's basic homeostatic tendencies underlie the various categories of motivation. Gestalt psychologists have shown how perception parallels biological life in its propensity to seek out order and balance in sensory experience. According to the logic of equilibration theory, all forms of art expression are fundamentally concerned with organizing perceptual stimuli and finding a functional balance in behavior. This type of motivation applies strongly to the drive that a person feels to complete an artwork once it has been initiated. There is, in this respect, a need for completion and closure. On the other hand, the tendency of artists to seek out complex, problematic, and unconventional experiences suggests that artistic activity is more than simple tension reduction. As in the case of Eugene O'Neill, the artist will often strive to maintain tension and avoid a static equilibrium. Order and balance is found within change and action. In this respect, creative people undertsand that the natural life process involves incessant kinesis and dynamic tension. Relaxation for the artist generally comes with the realization that one can move in stride with the fluctuations of nature. As Melville says in *Moby Dick,* "There is no steady untracing progress in this life; we do not advance through fixed gradations, and at the last one pause. . . ." When one understands the instability and constant movement of life and learns to move in rhythm with the rise and fall of its pulse, then psychological balance can be experienced. Within the psychotherapeutic context, the power of the arts lies in their ability to organize and express feelings, thoughts, and bodily sensations in relation to the continuous flux of the emotional process.

It is not oversimplifying the nature of emotional disturbance to say that at the root of psychological imbalance lies an inability to enjoy the everyday events that manifest themselves in sensory experience. Psychosis can be perceived as the loss of the ability to relate to the ongoing rhythms of life. During psychosis the life flow is fragmented, and the person experiences a cacophony of sensation and a need for rigid body movements that defend against change. (Health,) on the ohter hand, involves a rhythmic synchrony within the self together with an ability to synchronize with the movements of others and the environment. Through intensifying the natural rhythmic patterns of the body and strengthing the ability of perceptual facilities to engage life within an aesthetic structure, the person can begin to fully participate in the order and balance of nature. The arts offer opportunities for the attainment of psychological equilibrium through dynamic and emotionally charged activities that have as their subject matter the basic elements of life. One has the choice of either letting the pull of emotions and feelings become a burden and a constant irritant or transforming these tensions by the forces of art. The process is like the contact of two dancers. Each person utilizes the energy of the other to create an artwork where different elements of forcefulness relate to one another in an ongoing spiral of tension and equilibrium.

COMPETENCY/MASTERY

The desire to be effective and competent in one's self-expression, as with all art motives, is tied directly to principles of equilibration. In order to feel finished with an artwork, or to achieve a sense of fulfillment, the artist has to be somewhat satisfied with the quality of expression. Quality and competency are not necessarily measured according to traditional artistic standards, but they might be considered in relation to the artist's personal standards of expressive honesty and forcefulness. Within the therapeutic context, quality is generally determined by whatever happens to be in the best interest of the client, as opposed to the art object itself being the sole standard of quality. Artistic expression has quality inasmuch as it facilitates the person's efforts to give value to life.

Competency motivation is particularly strong in childhood and adolescence, where artistic mastery is related to self-esteem and one's ability to feel capable of both acting upon the physical environment and controlling the expressive functions of the body. Success or failure is often considered by the child to be an indication of personal value. This drive for competence continues through adult life as one of the strongest art motives. Self-discipline, the pleasure derived from the mastery of complex problems, and the ongiong passion to maintain a vital and creative relationship with the environment are characteristic of the adult artist. The artist knows that the expressiveness of a particular art work is determined by its structural competence. Even though one might believe that form is forever an extension of feeling, the intensity of an artwork's emotional charge is determined by the person's skillfulness in manipulating the formal structures of the art medium. The ability of formal structures to determine the impact of expression must be seriously considered by the psychotherapist engaged in the use of the arts. It is in this area of expressive therapy that the therapist's personal understanding of the arts, as well as the ability to skillfully facilitate the formal presentation of the client's expression, will directly affect therapeutic outcomes. In the broadest sense, competency can be defined as the capacity to focus and organize sensory experience. When a person is suffering from severe emotional disintegration, the arts can be helpful in gradually establishing perceptual order and clarity. It is the chaos of sensations caused by a weakened ego that has lost its power to control experience which gives rise to the conceptual confusion characterizing emotional distress. As self-confidence develops within a particular art mode, there is a corresponding increase in the person's self-image. Every stage of artistic validation can, in turn, influence the person's more general behavior.

Perhaps one of the greatest contributions of the arts to the emotional well-being of contemporary society is their dramatic demonstration that the motive power behind life does not lie in technical mastery for its own sake. The message of the artist seems to be that the greatest value of life is in the process of living fully in pursuit of the passions and one's own spiritual truth. James Joyce, in a letter written to Ibsen on the occasion of the latter's seventy-third birthday, insightfully describes how the artist views competence. "But we always keep the dearest things to ourselves. I did not tell them what bound me closest to you. I did not say how what I could discern dimly of your life was my pride to see, how your battles inspired me – not the obvious material battles but those that were fought and won behind your forehead, how your willful resolution to wrest the secret from life gave me heart and how, in your absolute indifference to public canons of art, friends and shibboleths, you walked in the light of your inward heroism."

EXPLORATION/RESOLUTION OF UNCERTAINTY/KNOWLEDGE

Psychological researchers (Berlyne, Harlow, Festinger, Kagan, and others) have stressed the cognitive dimensions of motivation, and they have criticized the historical primacy of instinctual theories of motivation. Their research has been in keeping with the way artists view the creative process. Knowing that they are driven by more than unresolved sexual tensions, artists engage novelty for its own sake and generally not for some external reward. The artist characteristically finds fulfillment intrinsically in the process itself. Conceptual conflict, the desire to explore new situations, and the need to resolve epistemological uncertainty are sources of artistic arousal. In addition to our innate curiosity about the environment, we are motivated by what Jerome Kagan calls "cognitive goal states." Art is a very intelligent form of expression, which fully engages the conscious mind in purposeful thought.

The structural expectations of an expressive arts therapy session have a direct effect on a person's motives. Many artists will consciously place themselves in situations where they are expected to produce art, and this will in turn help in the focusing of their creative faculties. The need to create for an anticipated exhibition, performance, or publication has a well-documented influence on motivation. These external and environmental expectations play a primary role in psychotherapy. Clients who create art only within therapy sessions do so because of the *structure* that supports their expression. Often the first motives felt during a therapy session are of this structural nature, and as the person becomes involved in the creative process, more personal needs are aroused. Artists who work independently will use similar forms of structure to incite their art. They will often work in their studios according to an established schedule and, at times, find themselves feeling pressured to follow a timetable or simply work according to a routine. Once in the studio and prepared to work, for whatever external reasons, the artistic consciousness begins to respond to the environment and the task of creation.

As opposed to popularized beliefs that art is an "esoteric" pastime, the artist is, for the most part, immersed in the disciplined use of the conscious mind. Artists tend to work according to rigorous and demanding schedules while striving to improve the quality of life for themselves and others. James Joyce, in refusing to be analyzed by C. G. Jung, once exclaimed, "Why all this fuss and bother about the mystery of the unconscious? What about the mystery of the conscious? What do they know about that?" The artist, in this respect, is preeminently involved in *expanding consciousness and the clarity of conscious thought and expression.* Art is always finding personal ways to bring feelings into the light of conscious thought. This definition applies equally well to psychotherapy; thus we see the inner correspondence of the two processes even as they exist separately from one another. When art and psychotherapy are joined, the scope and depth of each can be expanded, and when working together, they are tied to the continuities of humanity's history of healing.

In an interview that I conducted with the novelist Truman Nelson, he emphasized the conceptual nature of his art motives. "It is a current critical fad to think that life is full of ambiguities and is therefore impossible to define. I reject this because I feel that you should start and not end with the ambiguity. It is the ambiguity that sets me off — the dissonance of two or more disparate factors like a bad chord on the piano. My instincts as an artist drive me to resolve this. By letting this dissonance work on my head — causing me to throw out innumerable lines of resolution — only to find the dissonance is magnified, I find at last a way of bringing it to resolution and clarification" (McNiff, 1978, p. 77). This cognitive effort to resolve ambiguity and to make sense out of one's emotional life is essential to the psychotherapeutic use of the arts. Instinctual theories of art motivation have drawn psychotherapists to the arts and driven others away. Psychological explanations that stress only the emotional eruptions of art mislead more "reality" -oriented therapists, who feel that creative expression might jeopardize their attempts to help clients introduce order and emotional control to their lives.

Art is steeped in reality. It can be a catharsis and more. While expelling demons, it arouses thought to higher levels of integration. Art is a problem-solving activity that is fully engaged with the physicality of the person's environment. In this respect, it is more concrete and tangible than the symbolic abstractions of traditional psychotherapeutic language. Because of their lack of experience in art, many psychotherapists do not understand its cognitive scope and its ability to open up emotional issues within the overall structure and discipline of the particular artistic mode of expression. *In this way art intensifies feeling while simultaneously providing a protective and guiding structure. The arts provide the psychotherapist with the client's metaphors for conceptualizing life. Communication can thus proceed within the context of the client's personal language and symbols rather than arbitrarily being determined by the communication style of the therapist. Each one of us has personal symbol systems and languages that have been shaped by our experience and perceptual inclinations. The task of the psychotherapist is to learn how to relate to and support our different styles of conceptualizing life. When one approaches psychotherapy in this phenomenological manner, rather than assuming that every person conceives of life within standardized spoken language, then the symbolic scope of the arts within psychotherapy can be fully appreciated.*

AESTHETIC PLEASURE/INTENSIFICATION OF LIFE

All of the arts are directed toward the pursuit of some form of sensory relationship with the external world. Art can give value to mundane surroundings and bring us into "touch" with what the poet Charles Olson described as the closer intervals and the multiple layers of meaning that present themselves within the instants of our experience. There is great therapeutic value in becoming more conscious of the momentary qualities of perception, the fleeting changes in light, sound, and bodily sensations, and the search for new and different ways of perceiving. The aesthetic consciousness determines our self-image as individuals and as a society in that we define ourselves through our modes of selectively perceiving and giving value to whatever we do.

The intensification of life by giving sensible form to thoughts and feelings applies to all aspects of the art experience. The work of the poet-physician William Carlos Williams demonstrates the healing power of aesthetic observations that unite the person with the rhythms of nature. Williams is especially applicable to the psychotherapeutic use of the arts because his language and his imagery are simple and direct. His concise perceptions show how any person can conceive of life artistically. Williams worked toward pure perceptual art forms, unrestrained by poetic conventions and their structural constraints on expression. His poems directly describe simple imagery — flowers seen through window glass, reflections on a glass tray, dew on a red wheelbarrow, newly made bed sheets and so forth.

Williams was equally concerned with giving value to the visual imagery of urban environments. Rather than live in a bucolic world of fantasy, he immersed himself in the industrial life of his home environment of Paterson, New Jersey. This drive to give value to apparently distasteful and meaningless experience is a manifestation of the power of the arts to further the transvaluation of perception. Williams could see beauty in broken glass lying amidst cinders and in this way accepted all of life. This aesthetic of acceptance and simplification has ancient roots, and its therapeutic powers have been validated by history. In early China, Chuangtse wrote, "Be expansive, like the points of the compass, boundless without a limit. Embrace all creation, and none shall be more sheltered or helped than another. This is to do without bias."

Spontaneous poems and drawings produced by hospitalized patients have dispelled the unpleasantness and confinement of institutional environments. It seems that the emotional chaos of conflict is somewhat manageable as long as one has recourse to creative action and the power to give value. Over and over again, I have seen patients in locked hospital wards overcome the din of their environment by writing poems extolling the "ringing" of steel doors and the "songs" of their moaning peers. Poets living in poverty have shown the same capacity to transform what for some would be depressing experiences. For example, Charles Olson praises the virtues in leaking faucets, plumbing that doesn't work, the use of paper clips and string to hold up the ball, and flushing by hand.

Olson's advice echoes Thoreau and the transcendentalist belief that in living close to nature's rhythms one will find emotional completeness.[1]

> In the midst of plenty, walk
> as close to
> bare
>   In the face of sweetness. . .
>
> In the land of plenty, have
> nothing to do with it
>   take the way of
> the lowest,
> including
> your legs, go
> contrary, go
>
> sing

The asethetic consciousness, in its ability to heighten and strengthen the value of perception, is concerned with more than the appreciation of beauty as conventionally defined. Beauty in a person's expression might include the skillful portrayal of feelings of pain and tragedy as well as the artistic transfiguration of seemingly unaesthetic objects and events. Expressive therapists working with institutionalized and socially abandoned patients must be able to see the beauty in people that most of society does not easily tolerate because of their seemingly bizarre behavior. Mental patients are generally living in a dehumanized state and, within a relatively short span of time, begin to internalize the

---

[1] From Charles Olson, *Maximus Poems,* 1960. Courtesy of the University of Connecticut, Storrs, Connecticut.

negative impressions of society. They perceive their expressions and their already questionable self-image as having very little positive value. Motivation is the fundamental problem with most institutionalized patients in that their personal sense of power is largely deflated. One also sees patients responding to feelings of inadequacy by creating grandiose and fantasized images of themselves. The expressive arts therapist, more than any other mental health professional, is oriented to relating to the patient's aesthetic consciousness and the corresponding power to give value to perceptions of the self and the environment. Therapeutic sessions heighten experience in the various sensory modes while helping confused or emotionally fragmented patients to organize and control perception in a way that will enable them to appreciate the rhythms of bodily activities as basic as breathing and walking. The order and gratification that is received from artistic activities will have a corresponding effect on the whole personality and will hopefully increase the person's motivation to enter into aesthetic relationships.

COMMUNICATION/RELATIONSHIPS

My research with artists and experience in psychotherapy with children and adults has consistently shown that the most pervasive interpersonal source of art motivation is the drive to communicate and share feelings. This is true for both children and adults. When my son had just turned three years old, he told me that "people make poems to read to each other and pictures to show each other." My research has shown that this simple statement elucidates one of the most fundamental art motives. While many artists and artworks are ostensibly private, most artists direct their creative work toward other people. Artistic action is thus concerned with deepening relationships. This dimension of art has far-reaching implications for psychotherapy as Tolstoy suggested when he said, "It is on this capacity of man to receive another man's expression of feeling, and experience those feelings himself, that the activity of art is based." Artists reach out to others through their work and generally hope to receive an empathetic response. This need is so strong that negative response, especially during periods of self-doubt, can be overwhelming. However, artists have been known to sustain themselves by transforming criticism into a form of fuel for their expression. The person who lives a life of individual creative action must have the strength to sustain artistic energy in the face of the inevitable destructive forces that every artist encounters.

The artist will often direct a work at another person with the goal of starting an artistic dialogue that will vitalize and motivate their expression. Poets and novelists are strongly stimulated by the exchange of letters. Visual artists have found similar excitation by working in groups. Performing artists tend to depend even more on relationships with other artists, and find the group context indispensible to their art. Their expression usually takes the form of response to the creative charge that they receive from another person, and they strive to be equally forceful in their own communication. In describing his work in the theatre, Stanislavski emphasized the need for artistic "communion." He believes that we are always in mental contact with some other person, place, or object. The goal of the artist is to live fully in these relationships and actualize their energy. Stanislavski helps the person to find his true emotional objects and actively engage them in a creative relationship that searches for the living spirit in all forms of life.

These theatrical theories apply directly to psychotherapy and the communion between therapist and client. "If you want to exchange your thoughts and feelings with someone you must offer something you have experienced yourself. . .under ordinary circumstances life provides these. This material grows in us spontaneously and derives from surrounding conditions" (Stanislavski, 1976, p. 193). Actors are encouraged to absorb the feelings and thoughts of other people and purge themselves of personal distractions. The transportation of the actor into a particular role can be likened to the experience of the psychotherapist who must also become immersed in the therapeutic relationship. "Yet without absorbing from others or giving of yourself to others there can be no intercourse on the stage. To give to or receive from an object something, even briefly, constitutes a moment of spiritual intercourse" (Stanislavski, 1976, p. 184). Distraction and excessively self-centered thought will take the person away from the artistic/therapeutic moment and "wherever the object is that maintains a bond of relationship."

Artistic and therapeutic relationships are also motivated by needs to immerse oneself in place and to feel a communion with nature. The person who is estranged from the physical environment will find the arts to be a helpful means of establishing a dialogue with the natural world.

ACHIEVEMENT/SOCIAL RECOGNITION

Motives for achievement and social recognition are closely tied to our needs for communication and relationships. Achievement for the artist is usually distinct from conventional signs of social success. Artists feel achievement in the completion of each successful work. Their sense of success is generally fleeting and tied to the moment. Achievement is not accumulation of material wealth, but rather *a process of ongong relationship* with one's creative energies. The achieving artist is in close communication with the people, places, and objects that serve as sources of inspiration within the context of each moment. As Lao-tse said 2500 years ago, "The sage (artist) does not accumulate but lives for other people and grows richer/ Gives to other people and has greater abundance."

Social recognition for the artist appears to lie in the acceptance and acknowledgment of a personal artistic identity as expressed through creative work. Our more materialistic forms of social recognition are but another manifestation of the need to create a positive sense of self that is accepted by others. As we move away from the tactile recognition received in infancy, we depend more and more on symbolic forms of acceptance. As a personality type, the artist is not content with the stereotypic social identities that are attached to people who fill more conventional and standardized roles in society. Artists are concerned with more than the creation of an individual artwork, or a body of work, since their fundamental objective is the ongoing task of maintaining an artistic identity. Children have similar needs, and people who develop an artistic identity as adults generally received support and recognition for their creative work as children. Within the psychotherapeutic relationship we can give the kind of attention to a person's expression that is lacking in the more general society. A person can receive the recognition that may have been absent in childhood or that might be missing in present life.

Art-oriented psychotherapy is a process that involves the creation of an identity that reflects the dynamic process of our lives. The way in which the artist works with life process and finds gratification in the *act of being* serves as a model for psychotherapy. Rank saw the parallels between art and psychotherapy and described the therapist as a new artist type, or more accurately, as the renewal of the artist/healer archetype. Expressive arts therapists can create the aesthetic/spiritual fulfillment that people like Freud intuitively envisioned but never completely attained in their psychotherapeutic work. As psychotherapy continues to pull away from the restraints of medical science, which has lost touch with its Apollonian origins, it becomes more and more evident that what really matters is the artistic process of people working together in the creation of their lives in the present.

EMOTIONAL RELEASE/SUBLIMATION

To me alone there came a thought of grief
A timely utterance gave that thought relief
And I again am strong
— Wordsworth

As with all aspects of art motivation and the therapeutic use of arts, the value of venting emotions has been well known to artists before psychologists and psychiatrists began to invent concepts such as sublimation. William Blake expressed the same sentiment conveyed in the lines of Wordsworth and raised the issue of what happens when we do not vent anger.

I was angry with my friend.
I told my wrath, my wrath did end.
I was angry with my foe.
I told it not. My wrath did grow.

Cartharsis is not only essential to art but to the psychotherapeutic process as well. Within the therapeutic relationship, an individual is given the opportunity to release feelings of anger and grief that are incapable of being expressed elsewhere. Through the arts the person experiences catharsis while being supported by the structure of the particular modality. The discipline and concentration necessary to produce art makes the venting emotions all the more satisfying because the focus of expression is sharpened and the entire process is controlled by the person. This offers an important alternative to feelings of being overwhelmed by the negative dimensions of our emotions. The expressive sublimation of aggressive and potentially harmful instincts is one of the most valuable and widely acknowledged features of the psychotherapeutic use of the arts. A ten-year-old boy once told me that he makes art to "get things out and express feelings. I think it's better to take it out on paper because otherwise I might hurt someone else's feelings and people won't like me."

FEAR/IMMORTALITY/SPIRITUALITY

George Ripley, the nineteenth century New England transcendentalist and leader of the Brook Farm experiment in communal living felt that art can be valued "not as an end, but as an instrument to help the solution of peoblems that haunt and agitate the soul." The arts provide a vehicle for confronting and working through fears for both children and adults. Children are particularly open in dramatizing their nightmares and personal fears through art. The artistic enactment gives the child the opportunity to control fear by bringing it into the domain of conscious thought and physical manipulation. Monster imagery is common in children's art and in their play. The monster is usually a projection of the many elements in nature that are beyond the control of the child, as well as a representation of those qualities of physically larger adults that arouse the child's fear. Through art and play the child deals with these fears and begins to feel personal power through the realization that fantasies can be controlled and determined by the individual's mind.

Rank believed that the fear of death is the primary art motive and that the artist created with the goal of ensuring immortality and in some form transcending the finality of dying. For Rank the desire to "externalize individuality" is at the root of contemporary artistic activity. He also notes how other cultures and historical epochs have viewed the artist's work as a manifestation of the community's collective immortality.

The awareness of mortality provokes the spiritual dimensions of art. No single phenomenon confronts us with more force, confirming the mystery and tragedy of life, than the realization that all human life was created to die. In light of this reality, art becomes one of our most potent affirmations of life. An artwork that is perceived after an artist's death stimulates spiritual feelings in that the physical artwork is a manifestation of a person's soul that lives on in the minds of others. Perhaps art's greatest spiritual power lies in its ability to confront death as Shakespeare does in his most quoted passage from *Hamlet*.

> . . .To die, to sleep —
> No more — and by a sleep to say we end
> The heartache, and the thousand natural shocks
> That flesh is heir to. 'Tis a consumption
> Devoutly to be wished, To die, to sleep —
> To sleep — perchance to dream; ay, there's the rub,
> For in that sleep of death what dreams may come
> When we have shuffled off this mortal coil,
> Must give us pause. . . .

And Pasternak in *Doctor Zhivago* challenges death with the creative force, "Art has two constant, two unending preoccupations, it is always meditating upon death and it is always thereby creating life."

In dealing with spiritual feelings the artist often takes a political position by expressing things that are not socially accepted. However, psychotherapy, in its more permissive forms, allows for the expression of fears that might be too threatening to both the person and the community if they are revealed outside of the privacy of the therapeutic relationship. Psychotherapy also allows for the testing of threatening feelings to determine how they will effect other people. Fears may be confronted, shared, and ultimately controlled by being expressed and accepted by both the therapist and the client. The client begins to realize that the terrors of life are not so ominous as long as one can act upon them creatively.

VALIDATION

My art motivation research (McNiff, 1977) has clearly indicated that a person's commitment to art is largely determined by the validation, or the lack of validation, received from others. The creative impulse is also reinforced or interrupted by environmental conditions, with certain physical surroundings stimulating art and others serving as obstacles. Hundreds of adults have informed me that they stopped their personal involvement in the arts because their expression was not supported by others. Most artists, on the other hand, have to deal with severe negative criticism and extended periods where validation is conspicuously absent. In order to transcend these conditions, the artist must have the strength and self-confidence necessary to maintain artistic vitality. This is usually done by finding one's own intrinsic gratification from creative action.

The issue of validation is essential to the psychotherapeutic use of the arts. Because so many people in therapy have been conditioned to feel that their creative expression is of little value, the expressive therapist must be capable of counteracting this lack of self-confidence with support. Through expressive art therapy, the client is given the opportunity to renew the artistic consciousness within a trusting environment that responds directly to idiosyncratic needs and expressive problems. Each person is encouraged to rediscover his personal expressive style. Artistic techniques and methods are introduced only to the extent that they support the person's expression and further creative discovery. In order to facilitate the unique expressive needs of individual clients, the expressive art therapist should be knowledgeable of the multiplicity of motives from which artistic activity emanates. Equally significant is an understanding of the various obstacles to artistic expression that present themselves in therapy. The following chapter will concern itself with an analysis of this important subject.

Chapter 3

OBSTACLES TO EXPRESSION

T HE analysis of motivations for art leads naturally to the companion subject of obstacles to
expression. An investigation of barriers to creative activity will
show that a person's ability or inability to express thoughts and
feelings with spontaneity and clarity will reflect the more general
organization of the personality. If we can increase our understanding of the various obstacles to expression and their relationship to
other forms of behavior, we will be that much more capable as
psychotherapists in helping our clients comprehend their expressive strengths while simultaneously transcending their particular
resistances to creative expression. An analysis of inhibitors to
creativity will also approach psychopathology from a vantage
point that views artistic spontaneity as a desirable feature of
human behavior. This orientation will therefore place a high value
on modes of thought, sometimes labeled irrational or imaginary,
which have not been esteemed in more mechanistic psychological
theories that stress the importance of rational and logical thought.

CLOSED VERSUS OPEN-ENDED EXPRESSION

Virtually all obstacles to creativity can be conceptualized in
terms of closed versus open systems of expression. In the case of
emotional disturbance, obstacles to expression that are potentially
present in all people are exaggerated and more apparent. The expressive arts therapist observes these barriers in stereotypic and
repetitious drawings, trite and unimaginative efforts to write
poetry, rigid and mechanical body movement, and unspontaneous

attempts at creative improvisation. Stereotypic and highly controlled statements are indicative of both a lack of self-confidence with the particular mode of expression and a need to defend oneself against the anxiety provoked by being exposed to experiences outside the pattern of daily routines. The repetitive and ritualistic expressions of children and adults in therapy are often a form of self-protection. They indicate needs for predictable experiences with objects and people. In many cases these guarded and stereotypic expressions are all that a client is capable of producing. Rather than rejecting them, the therapist will accept whatever expression is initiated by the client (excluding abusive and aggressive actions that can be dangerous and destructive) and attempt to build a trusting and supportive relationship within which risks can be taken. With encouragement the client will usually begin to extend and differentiate the range of expression from what can be considered "the foundation or expressive base" of the stereotype. In the case of a withdrawn person, this development might involve changing the direction of a repetitious scribble, adding a new color, varying the tempo of a basic rocking movement, adding a new word to a chant, etc.

Vital and fully expressive artistic activity is characterized by openness to whatever is presented. Perception is responsive to chance and accidental events that are treated with seriousness. Rather than limiting oneself to a single point of view, the artist must be capable of seeing the many different possibilities for potential action. Sensory experiences are valued for their ability to arouse and excite the mind to new levels of integration. The creative process functions best when the mind is unencumbered and when the person abandons the distractions presented by the trivial obsessions of everyday life that seem to occupy most of our attention. Spontaneous action and creative incitement can be stimulated by apparently mundane experiences that are perceived with a sense of their aesthetic value. Persons and objects transcend their usual functional or "profane" roles in taking on artistic significance. As opposed to thinking only of the immediate function of an object or person, the creative person thinks in terms of infinite possibilities. When an object or mode of behavior proves itself to be useful, there is little pressure to change and invent alternatives, yet the creative person takes pleasure in seeing things differently and in shattering fixed expectations. Standards of normalicy and peer pressure that have a strong influence on most people, and which are particularly storng during adolescene, do not confine the creative person. Artistic perception is therefore distinguished by its capacity for immersion into novel relationships with people and nature. Discipline and focused attention are also required in all phases of creative thinking because insights have to be refined, sharpened, and conceptually related to one another.

Acute stages of emotional disturbance, on the other hand, involve a fragmentation of perception. Conscious mental controls are limited, and stimuli flood the mind. This chaotic openness is distinguished from the creative process where self-control and perceptual organization work cooperatively with the emotions. Lawrence Kubie emphasizes how emotional disturbance is not a substitute for the creative process (Kubie, 1961). The emotionally troubled person must overcome the obstacles presented by personal conflicts and tensions in order to create art. When the person experiences intense emotional imbalance, uncontrolled feelings dominate the mind, which has either lost or given up its innate tendency to organize perception and to approach life with a functional order. During the creative process the well-integrated conscious mind engages in a dialogue with primary process and does not relinquish its role as a guide in helping the individual to function independently, safely, and responsibly toward others.

The creative process requires the person to let go of certain tendencies to control experience. This openness can be distinguished from the other extreme of emotional stress and insecurity, which rigidly guards and defends the individual against anxiety-provoking experiences. Artists understand how creative action often involves a *letting go* of conscious controls as well as becoming immersed in unpredictable sensory activities. Ernst Kris described this phenomenon in psychoanalytic terms as "regression in the service of the ego." What he meant is that the ego must allow itself to relax controls so that inspiration can come forth from primary process sensations (Kris, 1953). Although Kris' position is largely consistent with my analysis of obstacles to expression, his use of the term "regression" is misleading, since it is tied to the values of Freudian theory. The relaxation of inhibiting ego controls is not necessarily regressive and might rather be perceived as a higher transpersonal state of consciousness than our more mechanical thought processes, which are nevertheless necessary to synthesize and express our insights and feelings.

The person who withdraws from interpersonal relationships and limits the scope of perception to a circumscribed series of actions usually does so because people are not trusted but rather are perceived as a source of stress. Often the client projects onto other people feelings of fear and distrust that are felt toward the self. The highly defended person is also building barriers against feelings of anxiety that are experienced within the isolation of depression. The person who is inhibited by feelings of disconnectedness and who does not feel a sense of belonging with others is typically estranged from the environment and finds it difficult to establish relationships through art.

Another manifestation of the closed system of expressive inhibition is the drive for excessive perfectionism. People who essentially do not trust spontaneous insights and who are constantly unsure of the value of personal expressions will tend to place unrealistic demands on themselves to achieve idealized goals. The perfectionist standard is the state that the person believes must be obtained in order to feel worthwhile. This process amounts to a self-fulfilling prophecy in that the expectations of the person are so inconsistent with reality that they will never be achieved, and the self-image remains inadequate. This kind of perfectionism obstructs the spontaneous expression on which the creative process depends. The perfectionist tends to be obsessed with predictable actions and does not allow for the kind of exploration and incubation that are needed to work creatively. Perfectionism can be an extension of mechanical thinking in the sense that too much emphasis is placed on immediate and controlled results and not enough attention is given to the free play of perceptions and thoughts that spontaneously suggest new and fresh insights. This is not to say that the drive for perfection is contrary to the artistic process. What is needed is a dynamic balance between openness and control. The perfection of the expression, the shaping of it, typically follows "the roughing out" of the idea, which responds more directly to the fluid process of inspiration. Thinking too much about what one is doing, or what one will do, can also interfere with the artistic consciousness. Artists will frequently speak of how there are moments when the work itself takes over and they are instruments of either an unconscious force or a divine mentality that seems to direct their actions.

In supporting creative spontaneity, I do not wish to suggest that occasional expressive restraint is without value. We must learn how to express ourselves with sensitivity to other people and the general social context. Artistically, the haiku poem is a fine example of how limits on the form of an artwork can at times refine and accentuate expressive impact.

Emotional difficulties are precipitated when restraint and control do not serve expression and a more general perceptual intercourse with nature. Excessive restraint and guardedness is usually apparent to bodily posture. Reich referred to these muscular defenses as bodily armor, which wards off outside stimuli while controlling inner feelings. A rigid and unexpressive emotional balance is thus achieved with the body acting defensively toward nature. The defended body tends to close itself off from the perception of itself. One's self-image is therefore limited if one accepts Kierkegaard's formulation that "the self is a relationship to itself." If we cannot completely "belong in" and be comfortable in our bodies, our relationships with others will be adversely affected. The person whose expressive capacity is blocked becomes either more and more withdrawn or dependent on stereotypic forms of communication. "What it had failed to bring about spontaneously from the inside, it would passively and helplessly expect from the outside" (Reich, 1973, p. 101).

Muscular defenses against expression can, over time, develop into permanent bodily postures. This is commonly seen in the rigid facial expressions, physical constrictions, and stiff movements, of institutionalized patients. Muscles hold and accumulate tension and will ultimately join the nervous system in adapting to the body's obstructed flow of energy. In light of these physical impediments to expression, all of the arts in therapy must direct themselves to the body. Émile Jaques-Dalcroze, who at the turn of the century criticized the arts for their fragmentation from one another and for their resulting loss of holistic power, believed that "movement is the basis of all arts, and no artistic culture is possible without a previous study of the forms of movement and a thorough training of our motor tactile faculties" (Jaques-Dalcroze, 1973).

Excessive reliance on largely passive forms of entertainment such as television will severely handicap artistic expression. Rigid educational systems, where children are offered limited opportunities for bodily movement, will have a similar effect. All art forms extend from the organismic pulsations of the body and thus depend on its expressive spontaneity. The consumer orientation of our culture and our contemporary art world, the mechanical movement patterns that we go through both to and from work, and on the job itself, have all conditioned us with broad social obstacles to expression that continuously manifest themselves in expressive therapy sessions.

Our cultural orientation to the separation of the arts from one another has also closed off many expressive possibilities. We are trained to think of ourselves as proficient in a particular art mode, or modes, and thus attach ourselves and our identities to these competencies. Other art modes are then perceived as being unrelated to, and not part of, our expressive behavior. We thus deny ourselves the complete stimulation of all of the senses. I have discovered repeatedly that expressions in different sensory modes stimulate each other. I have learned when I am stuck in one mode of expression, for example, poetry, rather than vainly trying to break through my language barriers, I change to another mode, such as painting, and invariably find that easing the pressure to write poetry results in renewed poetic inspiration.

Psychotherapeutic warm-ups in varied modes of expression tend to open the individual to more spontaneous communication in whatever art form happens to be the best match for the expressive needs of the moment. J. L. Moreno placed great emphasis on the "warm-up" as a technique to be used in overcoming obstacles to expression. He described how the warm-up process helps the person to discover the proper timing for expression and the "most favorable moment of actualization." The whole body, as well as the physical and interpersonal context, can be prepared to facilitate expression. Moreno believed that there were four forms of

4 forms of resistance

resistance to spontaneous expression: personal body actions, the private personality, the bodily actions, ideas, and emotions of other participants, and the audience (Moreno, 1973, p. 49). Other obstacles that limit expressive potential include fear that the quality of previous artworks will not be repeated, excessive rationalization, and the reality that the body, the hand, or language might not be able to express what the mind envisions and the senses feel.

SOCIETY

Today both art and psychotherapy are distinguished by their orientation to helping individuals find their true inner rhythm within a social context that does not provide an artistic forum for collective participation. Society, the community, and the family often prescribe patterns and scripts for living that obstruct, rather than energize, the flow of a person's expressiveness. The pressure to conform to cultural norms can be the most oppressive obstacle to expression. Art and psychotherapy are united in that they exist as a response to the human need to overcome forces that attempt to contain the spirit. By inhibiting individual expression, society sets the stage for art and therapy, which thrive in the process of leaping over barriers to personal fullfillment. Psychotherapeutic uses of the arts differ from the creations of the independent artist in that people come to therapy asking for help from another person, who assists them in finding the meaning that many artists are capable of discovering in isolation.

For me, the work of the playwright Sean O'Casey offers many insights into how art exists as a response to destructive social pressures. Economically destitute throughout his childhood and throughout most of his life, O'Casey used his art as a means of affirming the self and higher ideals of life. His art was a constant response and rebuttal to adversity, and in this respect it serves as a model to the therapist looking to justify the healing power of creative expression. Throughout his childhood O'Casey was sickly and suffered from serious eye problems, which plagued him throughout his life. Poverty and his physical handicaps interfered with formal education. As a child, he did not attend school consistently and was forced to work full time as a young adolescent.

Perhaps O'Casey's literary genius and uniqueness were shaped by this lack of formal instruction, forcing him to fall back on his own inner resources. He described wisdom as "learning by experience that the clang of a closing gate is but the clang of another one opening."

O'Casey overcame obstacles to expression by discovering and amplifying the rhythms of his inner poetic voice. In his play *A Time To Go* the Widda Machree chastises society and affirms O'Casey when she says, "Have yous no music in yous save the din of the marketplace?"[1] In his autobiographical play *Red Roses For Me*[2] he celebrates the role of his mother in supporting his development as an artist: "When it was dark, you always carried the sun in your hand for me; when you suffered with me to starve rather than thrive towards death in an institution, you gave me life to play with as a richer child is given a coloured ball." Again he finds pleasure in the strength and appreciation of life's intensities that social adversity has developed in him when he sings, "Let the timid tiptoe through the way where the paler blossoms grow; my feet shall be where the redder roses grow, though they bear long thorns, sharp and piercing, thick among them."

O'Casey's lifework was dedicated to "the dewy problems that get in th' way of...dancin feet." His monumental six volume autobiography is a crowning example of how the pains and adversities of one's life can be transformed into art. In volume 5, *Rose and Crown*, O'Casey reflects on "the way" to raise his son Breon properly. In this passage[3] O'Casey elucidates the common "way" of art and psychotherapy in helping a person to find purpose in life in a manner that affirms the power of the *will* and its ability to confront obstacles to personal fulfillment.

---

[1] From Sean O'Casey, *Collected Poems,* vol. 4, 1971. Courtesy of MacMillan Press Ltd., London and Basingstoke, England.
[2] Reprinted with permission of MacMillan Publishing Co., Inc. from *Red Roses for Me* by Sean O'Casey. Copyright 1943 by Sean O'Casey, renewed 1971 by Eileen O'Casey, Breon O'Casey, and Shivaun Kenig.
[3] Reprinted with permission of MacMillan Publishing Co., Inc., from *Rose and Crown* by Sean O'Casey. Copyright 1952 by Sean O'Casey. Copyright renewed.

Here they were out to bring the boy up in the way he should go. Which way was that, now? The catholic way, Genevan way, Mahommedan way, or the Buddhist way? These were but a few of the hundred ways carved out under the feet of every stepper-in-life. Eileen chose the catholic way; a way as good or as bad as any of the others. Sean hoped that when the boy grew up he'd take and make his own way. The right way to Sean was the desire to see life, to hear life, to feel life, and to use life; to engender in oneself the insistent and unbreakable patience to remove any obstacle life chanced to place in its own way. The way of the world; the way of the flesh; no one could show Breon the way through these ways; he would have to find a way for himself. Life's way of yesterday wasn't life's way of today; and life's way today couldn't be life's way tomorrow; so neither Sean's way nor Eileens's way, nor Swann's way could ever be Breon's.

DISCOURAGEMENT/SUPPORT

without readers
inky doom

For '63 Olson — Vincent Ferrini

Because art is forever seeking out relationships with the self, others, and nature, the artist tends to hope for, or expect, a response of one kind or another. Art is an interactional process, and in order for the relationship to succeed there must be a mutuality of response. Interviews with adults who are not involved with expressing themselves through art, or who have not done so since childhood, consistently show that their creative work was not supported and valued by other people. In psychotherapy with adults, these problems of negative reinforcement are usually compounded by the person's very low self-esteem and strong defenses, which guard against new and threatening experiences.

Needs for support and validation continuously characterize accomplished artists as well as the average person. Emily Dickinson at one point in her life said how she was not writing as much as she used to because there were few listeners. Georgia O'Keefe believed that she and Steiglitz had such a successful collaboration because they were simply interested in each other's work. Performing artists say that they need an attentive audience because they are striving to bring out their souls to be understood by other people. Artists have also been known to be more prolific when there are outlets for their art that enable them to reach people. Charles Olson, in discussing a magazine that provided a reliable means of publication for him, said that "the thing is because *Origin* exists, I write better, I write more." Although artists have been known to transcend loneliness and isolation through their art, and although they feel connected to an "alive spirit that will never die" (Vincent Ferrini), they must receive nourishment in the form of a response that gives value to their expression.

Artists have shown great ingenuity and strength in finding this support and maintaining their faith in themselves under the most difficult conditions. Their example provides a model for the psychotherapeutic process in that expressive fulfillment is rarely achieved easily. Eugene O'Neill summarizes this point nicely in his perception of life as struggle. In early times this struggle was projected into the heavens and perceived as a conflict with the gods, and today our attention is perhaps overly focused on the conflict with the self. Nevertheless, as O'Neill found, the ultimate form of validation lies in the ability to accept and embrace life in its entirety. "I'm always, always trying to interpret Life in terms of lives, never just lives in terms of character. I'm always acutely conscious of the Force behind — (Fate, God our biological past creating our present, whatever one calls it — Mystery certainly) — and of the one eternal tragedy of Man in his glorious, self-destructive struggle to make the Force express him instead of being, as an animal is, an infinitesimal incident in its expression" (O'Neill, 1925).

In addition to the artist's philosophical and interpersonal struggles, barriers to expression can arise from the technical realities of the artwork itself. Difficulties encountered during the creative process can block the expressive flow, particularly if the person lacks the self-confidence and persistence that may be necessary to persevere. The therapist's professional training should, among other things, include the development of skills in detecting and helping clients overcome obstacles that present themselves within the process of creating art. Each artwork is a microcosm of life and will reflect the thematic ups and downs of a person's existence. Difficulties encountered within the art process of an expressive therapy session can be considered part the totality of a person's life conflict that exists both within and outside therapy. With the help of the therapist, the session becomes a supportive laboratory for experimenting with and strengthening problem-solving and coping skills.

Rather than interfering with the therapeutic process, obstacles to expression are the very subject matter of psychotherapy. In order to dissolve or minimize these barriers, they must first become known and understood. Depending on the client's needs, the expressive therapy process might be concerned with expelling, dramatizing, or confessing inhibiting conflicts. In situations where the conflicts are thoroughly tied to, and part of, the client's personality, they must be accepted and not denied. The expressive therapy process then directs itself to controlling the potentially negative effects of these conflicts and helping the person to find new ways of expanding expression and relationships.

The client's motivation to work toward these objectives through the arts is invariably dependent upon the support and value given to the process by the therapist. *Validation* is one of the most important features of the psychotherapeutic experience. Inappropriate praise, on the other hand, can become an obstacle to expression. Clients see that the therapist's obsequious comments do not coincide with reality. Validating the client in the proper fashion, at the appropriate time, and with regard to the unique needs of each person is a skill of the therapist that can be likened to the behavior of a sensitive teacher. Often words are unnecessary. Approval and support can be given through the eyes and facial expressions, which minimize chatter and intrusive talking by the therapist.

With very withdrawn and nonverbal clients, the therapist might acknowledge and support a person's nonverbal expressions through movements that mirror the client's. Careful observation and attentiveness to a person's work may, in some situations, be a form of validation, whereas for more distrustful clients it may be inhibiting. Like the performing artist, the therapist must work toward a fine sense of timing and must know how and when to intervene with maximum effectiveness. All psychotherapists could perhaps benefit from Stanislavski's theatre training, where the actors are encouraged to become intensely aware of their sensations and ways their behavior either supports or contradicts the interpersonal process of the moment. Like the actor, the therapist must have an intellectual and an intuitive understanding of the roles that are played in psychotherapy and be capable of changing these roles in relation to the needs and the expressions of other people. The art of the therapist is defined by the ability to be consistently oneself within the multiplicity of roles and interpersonal engagements that characterize the psychotherapeutic process. The personal fulfillment that is received from this work depends largely on the ability to find personal validation in validating others.

THE THERAPIST

In order to validate others in their artistic expression, the therapist must have a personal understanding of, and commitment to, the creative process. One must personally *believe* in the power of artistic activity as a healing process, and if this belief is projected to others, it can have a contagious effect. Research on the psychotherapeutic efficacy of persuasion suggests the importance of the attitudes and values of the therapist and the effect that they have on clients in therapy (Frank, 1961). The therapist can become an obstacle to the client's expression if feelings of empathy and support are not conveyed. If the value of creative expression is to be communicated to a client, the therapist must be personally engaged with the artistic process at some level. In order to motivate another, the therapist must first be a model of spontaneous and open expression. With the bodily-oriented expressive therapies of dance and theatre, the therapist is always involved as a participant in the artistic action. The same is usually true for music. In the visual arts and poetry, therapists have often been reluctant to participate artistically because they feel that they will set a standard with their work that might intimidate and/or restrict the client's freedom of expression. I have found in my experience that the potential negative effects of the artistic participation of the therapist can be minimized by sensitive involvement. Except in those situations where the therapist is needed to attend to the needs of more dependent people or clients who have difficulties in controlling their behavior, I have found that the artistic involvement of the therapist is not only appreciated by clients, but it also brings the therapist into more active and complete participation. Cooperative work of this kind reinforces the tendency of artists to motivate and influence one another. Artists depend very much on the stimulation that they receive from other artists, and the same applies to the use of the arts in therapy. The therapist who is highly skilled in the arts must be careful and avoid creating a situation where the stimulation offered exceeds the client's ability to respond. However, experience has shown that very often the reverse is true. Therapists working with the arts are consistently challenged by the expressive intensity, depth, and honesty that characterizes the art of many of their clients. I have found the direct and open expressions of clients to be an inspiration to my art.

In a study involving responses from fifty visual art therapists, I discovered that virtually all of the therapists from time to time involve themselves in artistic activity with clients (McNiff, 1978). Many of the therapists were, in fact, stimulated in their personal art by their work. They described how the relationship with a particular client might affect the therapist's life outside of the clinical setting. In a number of cases the therapist would actually use the personal art experience to resolve conflicts related to their work with clients therapeutically. Other therapists used their professional work as a source of subject matter for their art. All of the respondents felt that it is essential for art therapists to maintain their personal involvement in art, but they described many obstacles and difficulties that they face in attempting to do this. The most consistent problems were attributed to *time* and the emotional drain of their jobs. For some, the demands and responsibilities that they felt toward others were increased by their commitment to attending to the needs of their own families. Graduate students expressed similar problems in being overwhelmed by the demands of professional study. Both students and working professionals decribed the distraction that work can create. When approaching art, they tend to feel fragmented and lack a sense of focus. Expressive therapists find themselves at times overstimulated with subject matter for their art, and the multitude of emotions aroused by their work rarely becomes artistically unified and transformed. This is sometimes due to sheer exhaustion. Modes of art, like poetry, spontaneous drawings and improvisational theatre, dance and music, which can respond immediately to life in the moment, are often useful to expressive art therapists who find it difficult to create art that demands long and sustained attention. Ironically, it would appear that expressive arts therapists have their own expressive problems.

Because so many expressive arts therapists have such serious difficulties with finding time for their art, and since we all seem to agree that personal artistic vitality is essential to our work, we should be encouraged to think of ways of making time within our professional lives for personal expression. If we do not, the chance of burning out and being overwhelmed and "closed off" by the external demands of the job are that much greater. Rather than responding exclusively to the clinical and psychological pressures of our work, we must also make creative expression a professional priority. We must begin to do this within our training programs, where we often exclude the student's art in focusing attention on other pressures we feel relate more directly to the task of becoming a respected mental health professional. As artists, we sometimes feel a certain sense of clinical inferiority and, thus, overcompensate. Graduate students find themselves feeling that they are "neglecting their work" when they make time for personal art. We must begin to correct this problem within our training programs and set an example for the ongoing artistic evolution of the expressive therapist. Our professional associations must also become active in supporting and validating our identities as artists whose professional strength lies in our collective ability to bring an unique dimension of healing to the psychotherapeutic process. If we do not do this, we will lose the power of the artistic consciousness that brought us to this work.

Our effectiveness as expressive arts therapists is directly tied to our personal explorations in the arts. Our ability to support the value, and respond to the intensities, of a client's art will be directly proportionate to the extent that we are feeling these forces within ourselves.

Chapter 4

PREPARATION

THE Hopi Indians perceive existence as a constant process of preparation and *emergence*. Life is either already manifest, or it is in the process of becoming manifest. Emerging forms of expression are "already with us" (Whorf, 1956, p. 59), and our task is to facilitate their manifestation. This philosophy of life relates nicely to the realities of artistic expression in that our inner inspiration will emerge with aesthetic forcefulness only if the person's mind and body are well prepared. James Joyce had a similar understanding of the creative process and described his artistic inspirations as "epiphanies." He used this theological term to describe those moments when life is transfigured and the essential nature of a thing or experience emerges into consciousness and becomes manifest through art. Joyce likened artistic action to the mysterious ritual of the mass. "I am trying in my poems to give people some kind of intellectual pleasure or spiritual enjoyment by converting the bread of everyday life into something that has permanent artistic life of its own." Constantin Stanislavski, whose work in the theatre has very direct implications for the expressive art therapies, based his art on the process of continuous preparation. In order to be in touch with the artistic inspiration that lies inside of us in an unmanifested state, we must abandon mechanical ways of responding to perceptual stimuli. "In our art you must live the part every moment that you are playing it, and every time" (Stanislavski, 1976, p. 18). In both therapy and art the degree of fulfillment that is received from an experience is dependent upon the intensity of concentration and emotion that can be focused upon it.

Preparation and warm-up exercises are needed to help clients transcend obstacles to expression. As with the Hopis, western philosophers have also discovered that "everything is positively somewhere in actuality, and in potency everywhere" (Whitehead, 1929, p. 64). The objective of the therapist is to enable clients to hear their inner voices, see personal imagery, and act out suppressed movements and impulses in a controlled and socially responsive fashion. In discovering personal symbols, metaphors, and expressions, the individual establishes contact with those projections of consciousness which define the self.

Emotionally troubled people tend to complain of loneliness, emptiness, depression, confusion, and a very negative sense of self. Although these emotions can provoke needs to relate to others through art, they more typically interfere with the creative process. Either the person has become so withdrawn that the energy needed to propel artistic imagery is absent or the self-image is so impoverished that the person feels that private expressions are of very little value to others. The purpose of the warm-up experience is to prepare the person, through gradual exposures to the various arts, to think more positively about the capacity for self-expression.

Since therapists are equally involved as actors in the therapeutic drama, they too must prepare themselves through personal rituals, which enable them "to be there" for clients within the creative event of therapy. In the expressive arts therapies, the preparation of therapists and clients takes place at the same time. Even if the therapist is not participating directly in warm-up activities, the observation of clients in action tends to be experienced vicariously. All religious rituals are characterized by a similar process of preparation during which the participants progressively immerse themselves in the "sacred" spheres of action and open themselves for the emergence of the spiritual consciousness. Preparation might also be conceived as helping people to *penetrate* inner worlds that are protected by a veil of illusions. Whether one perceives emergence in terms of *moving in* or *coming out*, the process is essentially the same and unified in its commitment to altering and expanding consciousness. Group rituals and enactments clearly document the process of preparation in that

February
left ovary

individual movements and chants tend to build to a point where group synchrony is achieved and the "participation mystique" generates a spiritual sense of the group's "oneness" and transcendent harmony, which releases each person from the restraints of their individual egos.

How to begin = Group

Most expressive arts therapy warm-ups begin by using action as an emotional stimulus. Relaxation exercises are also introduced to further awareness and control over inner actions and energies. Group experiences seem to use the supportive configuration of the circle consistently as a beginning. A group of people positioned in the form of a circle tends to evoke protectiveness, order, and visual balance. The focusing process of an expressive therapy session might begin with simple movement exercises concentrating on various parts of the body. These movements might then evolve to the use of the whole body in expressing simple concepts such as swinging, stretching, gliding, floating, falling, rising, soaring, turning, etc. The tempo of the motions can be changed by slowing the process down or speeding it up. Attention can be focused on other members of the group by encouraging eye contact and by breaking the group down into pairs to do a series of interactional warm-ups, which might include movement mirroring exercises and, if appropriate, touch activities that help participants to move in synchrony with each other. The exercises will stimulate an awareness of the whole body, and they can be complemented by more contemplative experiences that involve the person in the process of listening to, and controlling, the pace of breath. To facilitate awareness during relaxation, clients are asked to lie still and focus attention on different parts of the body; they start with their toes and work their way up to the tops of their heads. Participants are asked to discover which parts of their bodies are excessively tense and to concentrate on relaxing those muscles. Visualization exercises might be introduced to facilitate this process, involving the client in using imagination to see a tense part of the body as a still lake, a floating cloud, etc. Once relaxed, and while still lying down, the warm-up process can be extended to stimulate imagery and further visualizations by engaging clients in guided fantasies. In therapy sessions where the leader attempts to draw structure from the process of the group, or in the expressions of an individual client, the warm-up activity will inevitably suggest the direction of the therapy experience. For example, in a movement group the therapist will begin to initiate new directions in response to the movements of clients. If a person transforms a movement that the whole group is working with into a new form, the therapist can encourage other group members to begin to experiment with that particular movement, with all subsequent movements growing organically from the group process. As other forceful and expressive movements emerge from the group, they will continue to transform the mainstream of the group process.

Most of these activities apply to expressive art therapy experiences with young children. However, preparatory actions with children do not tend to be as oriented to warming up as to helping the children to control and direct their expression. Although many children manifest the withdrawn, guarded, and rigid behaviors that one sees regularly with adults, the emotionally disturbed child often defends against others through constant random and disruptive action. Relaxation exercises and controlled rhythmic movements are particularly helpful in enabling these children to begin to channel aggression and relate positively to others through their expression.

If the therapeutic session is to evolve into drawing and painting activities, movement experiences can be continued on paper. Clients can overcome their inhibitants to graphic expression by moving expressively with paints, pens, and other instruments as if they were dancing. The therapist encourages them to not be overly concerned with what gestures look like on paper but to focus their attention on the *feel* of the movement. They may be guided in the process of spontaneously making different movements and gestures, which begin to expose them to the ranges of strokes made by the visual artist — pressing, scratching, turning, twisting, rubbing, spinning, slashing, tapping, wiggling, brushing, snapping, floating, etc. The directions of the lines and the speed of the motions can be altered at the suggestion of the therapist to allow the person to experience a wide variety of graphic movements. The movements can be further varied through exaggeration and through the graphic expression of emotions such as joy, anger, frustration, calm, etc. The warm-up activity can become more

warm up

imaginative through guided fantasy experiences, where the line created by the person acts out the felt emotions of the fantasy exercise. The purpose of these exercises is to assist the client in transcending overly controlled and forced expression. If possible, clients familiar with the warm-up process can direct their own movements. Again, the warm-up may determine the structure of the therapeutic session in that the person might develop a picture with the movement, or series of movements, that feels most comfortable or that are the most difficult with which to work. Clients might also wish to develop a picture from an image that the warm-up activity suggested to them.

Art therapists have been known to make consistent use of scribble experiences as a warm-up. Clients are asked to look at their scribbles and draw something that is suggested to them by the line configuration. Analytically oriented therapists have used this exercise as a projective tool and have clients associate freely to their scribbles. All of these warm-ups proceed from basic sensorimotor explorations to more conceptual levels of expression. Problems will be inevitable if a person is expected to function at a relatively high artistic level before the essential spontaneity and expressive skills are developed.

Rhythmic music can serve as a stimulus for creative action. Rhythmic sound patterns have an isomorphic effect on the organism that can fully perceive them. The pulsations of the music are then internalized. As the music swells inside the person, it is difficult not to react. Ethnomusicologists have described how the drumbeat serves as a means of "summoning" the spirits in early cultures. The drum and other percussion instruments play a similar role in expressive arts therapy sessions where they assist in the emergence of the creative process. Repetitious rhythms are particularly useful in warming up in that predictable sounds and movements help the person to relax ego controls and flow with the music. Consistent rhythms also support the emergence of synchronous movement and a sense of group unison. Chanting has a similar effect because the repetition of sound patterns helps to sustain attention while relaxing participants and enabling them to achieve a trancelike state of mind.

Warm-up exercises in all of the arts usually limit perception by focusing attention on particular objects. The object is observed in great detail as surrounding stimuli are deemphasized. Exercises of this kind serve to sharpen figure-ground perception and demonstrate to the person how meaningful contact can be made with different objects in the environment. Similar exercises can be initiated by selectively focusing on sound patterns and movement qualities. Figure-ground perceptions can lend themselves to creative writing warm-ups by having clients write visual descriptions of objects. After observing the physical features of the object, the person can expand the exercise by describing it metaphorically. This might be done by free associating to the object and expressing the various images that enter consciousness.

Clients who find it difficult and threatening to interact with other people can begin to express themselves and enter into relationships through the perception of objects. The perception and manipulation of physical materials serves as a stimulus for expression, since the person tends to find them nonthreatening and responds accordingly. Objects and materials provoke emotional memories and engage the person in a dialogue with physical substances that stimulate associations and feelings. Fabrics and other tactile materials can serve as bridges between people in movement exercises. In situations where clients are not prepared to touch each other, they may be able to interact through an intermediary material that suggests a variety of possibilities for their expression. By focusing attention on the intermediary material, frightened and withdrawn clients are able to interact without having to confront each other directly. The same dynamic applies in one-to-one relationships between a therapist and a client.

Expressive therapy activities help us to draw naturally on emotional resources in our interactions with others. Theatre training exercises as simple as experimenting with different ways of sitting in a chair, walking into or leaving a room, and greeting other people offer a structure for investigating how we can creatively and expressively transform what might appear to be insignificant activities. When we see that the creative process can be allowed to emerge into apparently inconsequential daily actions, we will begin to realize how much of life we take for granted and of how much remains beyond our awareness. The arts demonstrate how to develop sensory attentiveness while accepting the transitory and illusive quality of feelings that "run through your fingers like water." Artists know that the only way to maintain a sense of unity within the flux of sensation is to be thoroughly grounded in your sense of self. The moment we lose this balance, we become handicapped in integrating the multiplicity of stimuli that surround us.

Warm-up activities can help clients to maintain a continuity of concentration while changing their perceptual focus and while interacting with different objects within the environment. The client might be encouraged to study an object carefully in the surrounding space and begin to develop an inner grasp, or feel, for what is perceived externally. When concentration begins to weaken and other objects begin to attract the person's attention, the change of focus from one object to another should be pursued in a way that maintains a continuity of this inner feeling by transferring the concentration of energy to the new object. The person is encouraged to look for the essential qualities of an object. When the transfer to another object is made, the emphasis is on *adaptation* and maintenance of a consistency of inner feeling. Exercises of this kind not only prepare people for expressive activity by bringing them into perceptual communion with the environment but also provide a controlled laboratory for the development of the perceptual skills that are needed if the person is to interact fully with the more general scenario of life. The emotionally troubled person not only has trouble maintaining this perceptual constancy but also tends to fix attention on certain objects and emotions and consequently interrupt the flow of feelings. Psychologists refer to this process as emotional fixation. We find that the arts in psychotherapy offer a unique approach to working directly with these problematic behaviors rather than concerning ourselves exclusively with indirect attempts to analyze their causes verbally.

Activities of this kind can be taken further by having the continuous flow of perceptions evolve into an exchange between people, and not just objects. The interaction might be as simple as having a person give a stone to another and receive it back again, all the while concentrating on the flow of giving and taking and the feelings that are generated. Simulated difficulties and obstacles to expressive continuity may be introduced by having

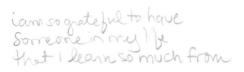
i am so grateful to have
Someone in my life
that I learn so much from

one person resist the exchange of the object and by encouraging the participants to analyze where their resistance appears to originate and how it feels to have the flow of the exchange interrupted. Perceptual focusing exercises can be expanded by encouraging clients to distance themselves from objects with which they have extablished emotional contact. Once this distance and separation have been created, the person is asked to reconnect with the object. This particular activity not only helps the person to understand the dynamics of emotional withdrawal and distancing but provides an opportunity to experiment with the reestablishment of close emotional relationships with objects and people. These exercises might be repeated in different surroundings to explore how environment influences perceptions and feelings. Concentration and adaptability can be tested by introducing unexpected stimuli that might either interrupt the perceptual process or provide new material which expands and enriches the creative relationship.

A person's expressiveness may be furthered by restricting perceptual controls through the introduction of handicapping conditions. For example, Matisse would often try to free up his line drawings by attaching his pencils to long sticks, which forced him to move in new and unexpected manners. Restricting the sense of sound can increase visual acuity and vice versa. The sense of touch might be intensified by having a person move through space without vision and hearing. Exercises of this kind should be introduced with care, since they can be very threatening to certain individuals who maintain a precarious balance with regard to their fear of losing control.

The parallels between these activities and the training of artists reinforce the place of the arts in psychotherapy. The following passage from Stanislavski's description of how he trains actors to prepare for their creative work provides an illustration of how the arts prepare a person to be more perceptually aware of life while also being capable of controlling the process of sensations.

> You know this type of exercise through your drill work. The first necessary step is the relaxation of muscular tension. Then comes: Choose an object — that picture? What does is represent? How big is it? Colours? Take a distant object! Now a small circle, no further

than your own feet! Choose some physical objective! Motivate it, add first one and then other imaginative fictions! Make your action so truthful that you can believe in it! Think up various suppositions and suggest possible circumstances into which you put yourself. Continue this until you have brought all of your 'elements' into play and then choose one of them. It makes no difference which. Take whichever appeals to you at the time. If you succeed in making that one function concretely (no generalities!) it will draw all the others along in its train. (Stanislavski, 1976, pp. 250-251)

The tendency of performing arts groups to work both as a single unit and as smaller groupings within the more comprehensive unity of the artistic company also parallels the process of expressive therapy groups. For example, dancers find a sense of intimacy within pairs that is not characteristic of larger group activities. When working with dyads or triads within the context of a larger group, the dancers create personal relationships with their partners, which they bring back to the large group and its more communal movements. The same dynamic characterizes individual movement in that each person is given the opportunity to differentiate the self within the more general unity of the group. Expressive art therapy groups typically fluctuate between activities that involve the group as a single unit working together and other activities that stress private explorations within smaller groups. The use of small units within the larger group context can be useful in warming participants up to one another. The privacy of the smaller groupings promotes trust and the revelation of personal feelings at much earlier stages than might be possible within the structure of a larger group. The feelings of trust and intimacy that are created by small group sharing will often be projected by clients onto the larger group. In this regard, they will continue to express themselves with all group members in a manner that may have characterized their communication with just one other person within a more private setting. Clients also infuse the larger group with the feelings of their more private dyads and triads by sharing small group experiences with others. The tensions and the excitement about participation within a larger group also provide emotional subject matter for sharing within smaller units. Clients tend to vent and share feelings within private groupings that they might not be quite ready to express within the larger group. Over time there should develop a sense of continuity between small units and the group as a whole. As trust and intimacy develop, feelings that were once shared exclusively within the small units will be expressed with all of the group members working together. The division of a group into smaller units should facilitate the process of exploring the common purpose of the group. Dyads and tyiads allow us to observe and experience the closer intervals of interpersonal process and to exlpore how we personally relate to the group. Breaking down into smaller units should unify and strengthen the group rather than fragment it. In discovering and supporting the diversity of a group and its individual members, we create feelings of unity that have depth and that recognize the existence of opposite and contradictory human emotions within every social context.

Warm-up activities in both individual and group settings and within all of the arts, are similarly concerned with building confidence, trust, and a sense of belonging. In order to become engaged with the objects of a physical environment and with other people, the person must be able to relax ego controls and focus attention on particular sensory configurations. We must feel a unity between ourselves and the objects of perception. These exercises bring the client into relationships with the environment and people while sharpening perceptual faculties. As the person builds confidence and sharpens the focus of perception (often through ritualistic group activities), expression becomes more spontaneous and personal. Although these exercises might be perceived as purely preparatory for a form of therapy that concentrates more on insight, they may also be considered as an essential component of the psychotherapeutic process. With many clients psychotherapy is an ongoing process of preparation for finding fullfillment within the existential context. *The totality of therapy is perceived as a warm-up for life.*

I have found that a vital part of the warm-up process involves the group in developing predictable and relaxing rituals that will be continued from week to week. Many expressive therapists will always begin and end their groups within circular configurations. Psychodrama sessions characteristically begin with a warm-up activity and the selection of a protagonist who then selects other people within the group to play auxiliary roles. There are group leaders and therapists working with individual clients who begin each session by asking the client to express the feelings of the moment; others initiate their sessions with relaxation exercises, and so forth, with each individual therapist using personal preparatory rituals. The consistent time/space dimensions of a therapy session have a similar effect in giving clients a sense of predictability and order, which is necessary if they are to begin to take risks. If one is to engage in powerful and potentially disorienting expressions, there has to be a feeling that there will be a safe and stable place to return for emotional support and nourishment. The purpose of warm-up and preparatory experiences in therapy is to begin to build interpersonal relationships that will offer the validation that is necessary to stimulate the emergence of the person's creative force.

Chapter 5

ORAL AND WRITTEN LANGUAGE

I N this chapter the analysis of the different arts
in psychotherapy will begin with the creative
use of language. This is an appropriate beginning because the expressive use of words relates directly to the historical continuities
of verbal psychotherapy. Since this book has depended upon
verbal language until this point, it might also be helpful to ease
our way into the other art forms through language that does play
an essential role in relating all of the arts to psychotherapy. In
isolating the different art forms into chapters, I do not wish to
stress their "separateness." The arts are discussed in distinct sec-
tions so that their unique properties can be studied. The more we
know about their uniqueness, the more capable we will be to understand their commonalities and the manner in which art modalities relate to one another during a therapy session. When discussing a particular art mode, I will mention how it relates to
other art forms. As with all of the other art modalities, language
has its kinesthetic, aural, visual, and theatrical dimensions. In
each of the arts all of the modalities are unified into a particular
mode of expression. One form can rarely exist without the others.

Over a period of ten years working with adult psychiatric
patients within residential programs, I have observed how they
have used poetry more than any other art mode to express themselves privately. Poems have been written on the person's own
initiative and have been presented to me for comment. I am
speaking here about artworks that have been created outside of

structured expressive therapy sessions. All that a person needs to record serious poetry is a pencil and a scrap of paper, and this simplicity and availability of materials is perhaps one reason for the high frequency of poetic writing within institutional settings. Poetry also tends to be the most solitary of the arts. It can be created within any environment and is easily stored, transported, and shared with other people. Through poetry people are able to dialogue with themselves, analyze and work through problems, and confront and record the process of their thoughts and emotions. All of this is done within the context of an art medium that lends itself to processing immediate insights and spontaneous emotions. Writing poetry can be a form of meditation and personal introspection, and this dimension of the medium lends itself naturally to psychotherapy.

Spontaneous poetry is often written in anger as a form of protest, as an expression of longing or loss, and as an affirmation of the self in the face of stressful situations. A woman in her late thirities, living in a state mental hospital, shared this poem with me and described how it was a response to the "craziness" of the ward environment in which she was living.

J2
locked in seclusion
when you don't feel well
help call
men come over
throw you in room
take your clothes off
and give you medication:
Stelazine
Cogentin
Mellaril
Thorazine
Navane
Fearsol
with a needle
go to sleep
unconscious
like dead
wake up in cell
no bed
just a mattress
no sheets, no pillows

no nothing
it's a shame
this never happened to me
it happened to Beatrice
she was tapping on the window
scratching her face . . .
calling my name: "Mary, Mary, I'm sorry!"
and asked me for a cigarette and
got wise again.

Poems written spontaneously within institutional environments tend to project intense emotional energy. Clients do not always refer to their creative expressions as "poems." For them language serves a purpose in communicating something that must be said. Too much emphasis on the "poetry" of the process might prove to be inhibiting. Rather than be concerned with traditional "laws" of poetic form, the therapist must encourage the person to use whatever formal structure most effectively facilitates expression. Within therapy, form must follow content. However, therapists working with withdrawn or inhibited clients will discover that structuring the process of expression will ironically further free expression. In the case of a person who is tied to stereotypic forms, the introduction of an emotional theme or exercises such as creating a group poem, assembling random words chosen from a newspaper and writing with a voice that is different from your own, can stir up the creative process. Structured exercises thus give the person a sense of what can be expressed through poetry.

Psychotherapists conditioned to think of poetry only in terms of iambic pentameter and other classical conventions should familiarize themselves with the free verse of contemporary writers so that they might more fully appreciate the writings of their clients. Formal structures of poetry, the shape of the verse, the length of the line, punctuation, and the like should be in synchrony with the emotional energy of the client. Structural configurations such as rhyme often interfere with the flow of a person's feeling. Rather than record and express the continuous manifestation of thought from one perception to another, the person often interrupts the emotional process to go fishing for words that "fit." Often this fit is determined by structural conventions and not by the emotional fit of a word and the deeper levels of emotion are not aroused because the poetic process is more concerned with technical formalities than expression. I do not wish to negate the musical and rhythmic value of rhyme in poetic expression, but formal devices of this kind should be used only when they are evoked by the emotional process of the poem. Form should serve to refine and amplify expression rather than predetermine how and what people express. Stereotypic poetry written within psychotherapy is usually caused by the person's trying to write within standard and conventional poetic forms; therefore, it is essential to do whatever we can to facilitate the free and imaginative use of language.

THE READING OF POETRY

Much of the literature on poetry therapy has been influenced by the distinctly medical approach of "prescribing a poem" in response to the particular ailment of the "patient." Emphasis has been placed on the reading of masterworks to people with the goal of making them feel better. The psychological principle of isomorphism has been offered as an explanation of how an emotional state conveyed by a poem will have a corresponding effect on the listener. According to this approach, a hopeful poem will help to build the confidence of a depressed person; the same sort of thing would happen with the other emotions. This poetry therapy strategy does have value as does the entire area of bibliotherapy, where clients are encouraged to read and experience how conflicts similar to their own have troubled other people and see how others have responded to these emotional dilemmas. Literature shows that we are not alone and singularly burdened with personal difficulities. Reading literature in conjunction with psychotherapy can be particularly helpful for adolescents and young people who are struggling with the creation of a personal identity. Characters in literature can be instructive and serve as role models for young people who need this kind of support. Great artworks are inspirational and elevate humanity. As readers and observers we can participate directly in their greatness and thus absorb their life force. Poetry therapists will often read a poem as a stimulus for discussion, or a group might meet to share what they have read between sessions. The poems's ability to clarify and express intense feelings serves as a catalyst for the group and helps them to focus quickly on common feelings.

Poetry therapists are very much concerned with cataloging poems in relation to particular emotional disorders. They would suggest one poem for a mildly depressed person and another for a person who might be suicidal. For example, it might not be recommended that Yeat's great poem, "The Second Coming" be read to a very depressed and confused person who may be overwhelmed by its lines describing the world's falling apart and the drowning of innocence.

A section of Whitman's "Song of Myself" might be a better choice in that it stimulates a sense of hope and gives value to the inner self.

> I believe in you my soul, the other I am must not
> abase itself to you,
> And you must not be abased to the other.
> Loafe with me on the grass, loose the stop from your
> throat,
> Not words, not music or rhyme I want, not custom or
> lecture not even the best,
> Only the lull I like, the hum of your valved voice.

Selections of this kind do not have to be perceived as "censoring" what the client reads but rather as trying to avoid situations where conflicts introduced by the therapist might cause unnecessary and potentially harmful stress. In some cases it might be helpful to introduce conflict intentionally into the therapeutic relationship in order to mobilize the client's emotional resources. These decisions are made on the basis of judgments as to what the person's needs are. Clients themselves might in some instances be responsible for selecting the poetry that will be read to their group. This approach offers much material for discussion because not only can the group respond to the poem itself, but members can share feelings about why a particular poem was chosen. With regard to the selection of poetry by the therapist, cataloging poems according to diagnostic conditions does offer a preliminary resource in determining which readings will be most appropriate for the client. However, this orientation must be tempered by the interests, taste, and cultural background of the client.

DISCOVERING YOUR PERSONAL LANGUAGE

Although from time to time we read poems within therapy groups, the primary thrust of my therapeutic work is toward helping people to express themselves through the creative use of language. Discovering our personal metaphors for life and our true inner voices is one of the most valuable uses of poetry. Through the arts we attempt to respond to the stirrings of the spirit and express their intensity at the appropriate moment. The volatility of art and emotion as experienced in both psychotherapy and life is expressed nicely by Longfellow.

> So when storms of wild emotion
> Strike the ocean
> Of the poet's soul, ere long
> From each cave and rocky fastness,
> In its vastness,
> Floats some fragment of a song. . .

The sharing of our personal imagery and symbols assists others in understanding how we view the world. Even though we might all speak the same language, we each have our personal language systems. Within psychotherapy it is important to become aware of the client's personal language and become effective in both understanding and relating to it. Proponents of "linguistic relativity" believe that our perceptions of "reality" are unconsciously influenced by the language system of our cultural group. Interpretations of life are thus determined by the modes of linguistic thought to which we have access. Rudolf Arnheim (1971) has shown that there are fundamental perceptual modes of thought that are not influenced by language and past experience. The senses themselves are thinking faculties that shape the development of language. Nevertheless, language does expand or restrict our thought within discursive realms. Poetry offers a more personal alternative to society's standardized language systems. Poets are continually questioning, renewing, and expanding the meaning of words. They create new word images and attempt to transform the gestalt, or larger configuration of words, into formal patterns that will forcefully "project" thoughts, feelings, and perceptions.

Charles Olson, who wrote what has become the manifesto of postmodern poetry in his "Projective Verse" (1950) believed that *open* poetic forms would not only change the technical structure of poetry but would transform the consciousness of both the poet and reader. Olson strove to write in a way that relfected the *process* of how one perception "immediately and directly" leads to further perceptions. These innovations, or what may be perceived as a return to natural and innate poetic utterances, are especially significant for psychotherapy in that the goal of the projective poet is to create an expressive unison between the poem and the person's emotional process. As rector of Black Mountain College in the early 1950s, Olson was the leader of one of the most important experiments in integrating art with modern life. The impetus of his writing and theory provides a vital "push" for the use of languages in psychotherapy in that his art was totally oriented toward finding the inner rhythm that one must bring into synchrony with the forces of nature. Through his concerns with process, his attentiveness to the rediscovery of the closer intervals of life within the moment, and his commitment to finding identity in relation to place, Olson admonished people to find "what is native to themselves, even the places, heroes, and gods local to their neighborhoods, is worth all the state of world religions that are being offered on the other hand." His message can also be taken as a manifesto for the arts in therapy.

> the only object is
> a man, carved
> out of himself, so wrought he
> fills his given space, makes
> traceries sufficient to
> other's needs.

A creative approach to language in psychotherapy will support the personal symbols, word usages, dialects, accents, and expressive idiosyncracies that further the emergence of a person's inner feelings as opposed to expecting the client to adapt to the technical language of psychotherapeutic systems, to the personal language of the therapist, and to the more established structural laws of conventional language. The orientation of therapy toward reality demands that the client *relate to* the language patterns of the therapist, but this does not mean that one's personal voice

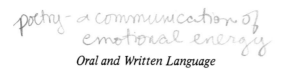
poetry - a communication of emotional energy

must be sacrificed in the process. The linguist, Benjamin Lee Whorf believed that as a major language develops it becomes "increasingly organized around a rationale, it attracts semantically suitable words and loses former members that now are semantically inappropriate. . .It may turn out that the simpler a language becomes overtly, the more it becomes dependent upon cryptotypes and other overt formations, the more it conceals unconscious presuppositions. . ." (Whorf, 1956, pp. 81 and 83). It would thus appear that the standardization and semantic unity of language greatly limits the depth and range of emotions that can be expressed through it. This issue is a vital one for psychotherapists who depend so much on words and who tend to fall into the linguistic camp of a particular psychological "school of thought."

Olson's famed declarations in "Projective Verse" were directly addressed to the tyranny of language and thought that he observed in the standardization of contemporary word usage. His position suggests not only how poetry may be used within therapy but how all of the words spoken in psychotherapy can be conceived as part of a poetic process that facilitates the communication of emotional energy. In order to be truly expressive language must transmit emotion and what Olson refers to as "the kinetics of the thing." Projective verse thus values *open* composition that flows directly from breath and the emotional energy of the feeling expressed.

A typical problem encountered in psychotherapy is the lack of synchrony between a person's conscious thought processes as expressed in language and unconscious sensations, feelings, and rhythms. It therefore becomes difficult to project energy in the manner suggested by Olson. For example, it is common to see a person who is rigidly bound in physical posture and whose verbal expression is similarly restricted, become easily frustrated in trying to act out or describe the imagery of a dream. Perhaps a more serious problem is the rigidity that sets in when a person's inner imagery and unconscious metaphors for life begin to reflect the more general mechanization and impoverishment of their lives. This sensory deprivation is a major problem when working with people who are living within institutional settings. I have found that the degree of sensory contact with the physical world is relfected in the content and expressive style of a person's language. An individual living within a highly mechanized and non-sensory environment tends not only to use mechanistic metaphors, but also to show little rhythm and expressive color, texture, variety, and inventiveness when speaking. Imagery is unimaginative and stereotypic, while the tone of speech is guarded and repetitious. Human beings are metaphorically perceived as machines on an unconscious level, and the concepts of industrial society permeate language — automatic, production. People are *classified* according to function, diagnostic category, etc. At the deeper levels of consciousness, we store images of the human being as a follower of mechanized routines, as a commuter, as an operator, as a consumer or producer, and the like, and these technological specializations disrupt the organic wholeness of sensory experience and imagination. Often we are not even aware that this is happening, but the mechanization of the psyche takes its toll on an unconscious level in that we become estranged from the natural functioning of the organism. The use of mechanical metaphors is not necessarily a distortion of the creative process but can rather be perceived as an artistic transvaluation of our material existence. What tends to be harmful is the condition when the thought process itself becomes mechanized.

Within psychotherapy, I strive to assist clients in becoming aware of the imagery that they might be using unconsciously in their language. If their use of words tends to be impersonal and unimaginative, I try to encourage more open and unconventional modes of expression. People first beginning to express themselves poetically will often lean on the work of other writers to get themselves started. They usually identify with a poet whose world view and style of expression is similar to their own. This is not necessarily a negative process, unless, over time, the person is not able to create a personal style that can be differentiated from those of other poets. When I began to write poetry seriously, my poet-friend Vincent Ferrini warned of how easy and obvious imitation was, and how it is "quickly spotted, by even the casual reader," and he sent me an instructive letter.

. . .hear me
as a living poem

and what are distances for
reporting?

the poem is in your own
veins.

tear it out.

Techniques for getting the person engaged in writing poetry are needed by therapists in most clinical settings. Although certain people will continue to write spontaneously, and out of necessity, others will need help in making contact with the poetic consciousness within them. When one is in touch with this hemisphere of thought, perception is characterized by a state of emotional intensity in which objects and events that would normally pass unnoticed evoke a passionate and imaginative response. Writers and poets consistently describe how a single perception will set them off by releasing a series of emotional memories. Henry James described the source of artistic inspiration as "the precious particle. . .the stray suggestion, the wandering word, the vague echo, at the touch of which the novelist's imagination winces as at the prick of some sharp point." As suggested in the previous chapter on preparation for artistic activity, a narrowing of focus is often needed so that a particular object or sensation can begin to work on the creative imagination and assist artists in hearing the vibrations of their inner voices.

I have found in clinical work with poetry that most of the writing that is done relates to four categories of expression: observation, the dream, the letter, and the story. All four of these poetic uses tend to be in constant intercourse with one another and are not necessarily separate entities. Rather than asking an individual to "write a poem," which invariably raises defenses in the average person and floods consciousness with stereotypic and mechanistic notions of what a poem *is* and how it is *written*, I might ask the client to write a letter to a person who is being discussed in therapy. Within a group context, letters sharing personal feelings can be written to other members of the group. I have consistently found that in the beginning of a therapeutic relationship with both children and adults, it is helpful to ask people to simply describe their dreams, to tell their emotional and personal stories, to share their observations and perceptions, and while they are speaking to me I will record their images. The recording of responses to guided fantasies is a particularly useful technique in helping people discover their poetic potential. We will often consciously avoid using the words "poem" or "poetry" in the early stages of expression because of the barriers they create. Calling a spontaneous utterance "a poem" afterwards seems to have the reverse effect and gives value to expression. We might begin to refer to our work as poetry when the person becomes more confident and understands how to evoke the poetic metaphor from within and how to become aware of poetic thought when it is happening spontaneously. Speaking poetry is also a more developmentally appropriate way to begin, in that our poetic metaphors and personal images are first formulated through spontaneous thought and dialogue. As Vincent Ferrini keeps telling me, "The poem is in the air," and we have to learn to hear it.

Classical psychoanalytic free association techniques are very much related to the poetic consciousness. To stimulate a poem, emotionally laden words, concepts, sounds, visual images and movements can be presented to the person who is then asked to free associate with whatever enters the mind. Through projection and random association, the person transcends the mechanical purposefulness of thought and allows inner symbols and sensations to become manifest in consciousness. As a person's imagery begins to follow certain themes and patterns, the personal metaphor and inner language starts to emerge. The therapist, as observer, can help people to become aware of their personal imagery and work with them in determining how it is either congruent with, or in opposition to, their behavior. Unconsciously, these images are the basis of our dreams, projections, and what the psychoanalysts refer to as the process of transference (the feelings from our past that we project onto other people).

All of the approaches mentioned are intended to help clients get beyond the poetic "mystique" and see how poetry can emerge from them naturally and in response to the events of daily life. Very often the poem will burst forth out of its own inner necessity. Poetry is particularly helpful in communicating with people who are not with us; thus, the poem takes on the function of the letter in that it is used to say something directly to another person. I worked closely with a man in his late forties who was a writer and a graduate of a leading American university and had been hospitalized as a result of a severe depression that ensued after his son, a Vietnam veteran and a paraplegic, apparently took his own life by driving his car off a highway bridge. The son had grown up with his mother and had never known his father until after he returned from Vietnam and shared an apartment with him. They became very close, and the father, who at that point in his life was very lonely, saw the appearance of his son as a gift. The child had been conceived accidently during a brief relationship between the mother and the father who were not married. The surprising arrival of the son and the intensity of the relationship that developed between them made the abrupt death shattering to the father. After many weeks in the hospital, he was for the first time able to release the emotions that he had been holding back in a poem that he described as a free sonnet for his son.

So you're gone; your laughing eyes,
your friendly mouth, your strong and gentle face
soft haloed in copper that sunned to brass,
your voice a bard muted, your wild sweet smell
that came from no bottle, no can, no jar,
all atomized in a microinstant. I ask not Why:
we could not hold you here, your heart too big,
your lovely mind in a manic world, a body broken
senselessly.
But on your *birthday*? A child of twenty-four?
You probably never thought of it, just wanted Out,
decided it was Time. Be FREE my son!
And laugh and sing and RUN again
without obscene appliances. And now I know
you're with me now as never then
while on I still must go.

The discipline, compactness, intensity, and emotional scope of the poem enabled this man to *express* and yet *control* his grief. He transformed the destructive forces of his pain into the life-affirming and constructive energy of the poem. This transformation of pain into a form that supports life contrasts with the tragic incident of a boy who gave his twelfth grade English teacher a poem and two weeks later took his own life. The poem described the pressure to conform and the restrictions on imagination that he confronted in school and ends with these lines:

> And when he lay out alone looking at the sky
>   it was big and blue and all of everything:
> But he wasn't anymore.
> He was square inside and brown.
> And his hands were stiff
> And he was like everyone else.
> And all the things inside him
>   that needed saying, didn't need it anymore.
> It had stopped pushing
> It was crushed
> STIFF
> Like everything else.[1]

Poems of this kind are not necessarily direct suicidal messages. However, the poem can attempt to communicate feelings of pain and desperation. If the poem is related to other indications of suicide in the person's behavior, then extreme caution should be exercised. What appears to matter within the psychotherapeutic relationship is that the person should have the opportunity to express these emotions and receive a response.

There are no simple guidelines as to how a therapist is to respond to the poetry of clients. Our individual ways of responding will be determined by our personalities and therapeutic styles. We must communicate our empathy for the client and our interest in the poem as well as the person. The actual response might be verbal, or with some therapists, it might take the form of a poem that is given to a client. *What seems to be essential is some form of acknowledgement that the poem has been heard.* If there is a need for clarification, this should be communicated to the client so that is is clear *that the therapist is intent upon understanding and receiving the full expressive impact of the poem.*

---

[1] From "Poem to an English Class," *Liberation*, December 1971.

One of the most common problems encountered in sharing poetry is the insecurity that people experience when orally reading their work to other people. Granted, poems have a special effect on people when they are read and experienced visually, but within the psychotherapeutic process, there is a definite power to sharing the poem orally. When I notice that people are having a difficult time reading poems, I will often ask them to read it two or three times until it feels comfortable. Repetitious reading not only helps the person to overcome stage fright but also gives the listeners the opportunity to more completely absorb the poetic imagery. Repetition tends to have a calming effect, and if the poem is a short one, repeated reading can evolve into a chant or mantra. In reading a poem there is a great therapeutic value when the voice and inner emotion are in synchrony with the imagery and words being presented. When this feeling is achieved, the poem has an organic wholeness and flow that is in itself healing.

The poetic exchange within psychotherapy must also be attentive to the significance of *silence*. Life is characterized by periods of silence, pregnant with possibility. These quiet moments provide essential space between experience as well as poems. Clients are often intimidated by periods of silence, which increase their anxiety about sharing poetry. In our therapy groups we try to appreciate silence and the moments in a person's life when it is difficult, or innappropriate, to express oneself through writing. As Longfellow said to the poet Whittier, "Thou too hast heard voices and melodies from beyond the gates, /And speakest only when thy soul is stirred."

One of poetry's most intriguing therapeutic features is its relationship to mythic rather than discursive thought. The mythic consciousness is, of course, more directly tied to the emotions than rational thought. Although it is thoroughly embedded in reality and concrete problem-solving activity, art grows from archaic needs to give value to life through mythic belief systems. Through poetry, clients can clarify and communicate their personal myths and beliefs in a mode of expression that emanates from the mythic consciousness. Both poetry and myth are in close contact with dream imagery. Rather than simply describing what happens in a dream, poetry enables therapists and clients to participate in thought processes close to those of the dream. Like the dream, the poem allows whatever feelings happen to be important to emerge. Within poetry the logical structures of discursive thought are eschewed for a more primal and emotional language.

I worked for many years with a young man whom I first met while he was hospitalized as a result of a series of visions he had while in college. He was a literature and psychology student who took his poems seriously and used to share them with me regularly. As our relationship grew, it became clear that so many of his emotional difficulties and intermittent periods of depression were caused by the lack of continuity between his poetic imagery and the realities of his daily existence. He needed someone to hear, value, and respond to his writing and to accept the personal validity of his visions. Instead, various mental health institutions tended to negate his visions and referred to them as hallucinations. As a result of this lack of acceptance, the barriers between his emotional imagery and the social systems that he lived in were intensified. Neither of the two polarities could accommodate the other. The egocentric world view of the mental institutions in turn influenced them to attribute the difficulty to his inability to adjust himself to the realities of adult life. Expressive arts therapy programs are essential within these institutions to enable them to respond to people who have so much to say in unconventional modes of thought. In this particular case the intensity of the conflict grew, and the young man's emotional responses became all the more desperate, their apparent inappropriateness intensified, because the obstacles to their social acceptance were unyielding. The mechanistic thought processes of the mental hospital could not adjust to his metaphoric mind, and vice versa.

In my relationship with him I tried to accept his writing and use this as a means of understanding and validating the mythological systems that he created to give value to his life. Over time this approach was effective in strengthening and maintaining our relationship. I was able to bring him into contact with other artists who valued his work, and on a number of occasions, I involved him in poetry readings that were supportive of his efforts to express himself through his own unique language. Support and trust played an important role in our work together. When he first shared his visions with me, he said that he had not described them to other people because he knew that they would belittle them and not believe that what he was saying was true. I told him that the truth was what he personally believed and that I would accept his definition of what was true for him. From that point on he continuously shared his work with me. Now that it has been several years since we worked together within a clinical setting, he still maintains contact with me and, like other friends and former clients, sends me copies of his poems. The following is an example of his writing and the intense, sensory and dreamlike quality of his vision.

> ...We are animals, searching passion
> so unconscious are we of the pluck, a
> plumefeather in my cap, a pip and stockings,
> lilies in the pond, a single frog croaking,
> nature resplendent, O' clear liliwana,
> oh doll of the sea. I have searched you,
> you have searched me. In the dusk of our
> life we are but wanderers, searching for our souls,
> the animal within, the phoney without. I look
> for no other, my treasure is here on earth, you
> have brought me solice. Winter grief and fallen
> sticks, dried up dates and yesterday's tears,
> the ache within, the penniless. Tonight I saw
> an angel carrying a basket of bread. Lay down
> upon the earth and love, the sky will rumble.

This young man, like so many artists, needs to feel that his expressions are reaching other people. Within this ongoing dialogue and relationship with others lies the validation of his art, and himself.

Since visual imagery has such a fundamental place in poetry, exercises that engage clients in writing responses to what they see around them can be fruitful. I have discovered that an integrated arts approach is particularly effective, and find it stimulating to have clients write "stories" and "poetry" in response to visual artworks that they have produced. This process seems to work well because the person has, in creating a picture, already focused and invested considerable energy and emotion. The same applies to creative writing experiences in response to expressions in the other arts. In the case of the picture, the person has something tangible and personal to respond to with poetic language. The creation of the picture can be an important first stage in poetic expression in that it tends to open the door to the more difficult to reach poetic forces.

Clients will at times write spontaneously on their pictures. The writing that ensues might be a detailed description of the visual image such as that shown in Figure 1, which was produced by a lifelong state hospital patient in her midfifties. The picture resembles a medieval manuscript, and the writing, though decorative, is largely illegible. She is telling a story about Christ's death and suffering while offering a variety of stream of consciousness images — his disciples, Christmas, King Herod, etc. It appears that the picture of the birth of Christ (the child, Mary Joseph, and a donkey) precipitated a rush of feelings about his later life and death that had to be communicated in order to complete the image. Since all of these feelings could not be communicated within the structure of the picture, language was utilized. Herein seems to lie the power and importance of language in the arts and therapy, in communicating a number of different, though related, thoughts that cannot be expressed through other modes. As in this case, even if the sequence and general use of words does not follow the logic of grammatical structures, each word does have personal meaning and represents an effort on the part of the person to share her imagery and the feelings aroused by her picture. I prefer to look at her art in this way rather than simply attribute the apparent fragmentation of imagery to psychopathology.

Young children regularly write on their pictures in a similar fashion. Their first attempts at written language will often proceed from a need to *name* and *define* what they have created. In my psychotherapeutic work with children, I have consistently found that previously nonverbal children will begin to speak and express themselves verbally when describing their pictures. A six-year-old girl that I worked with in a group therapy context spent months doing stereotypic drawings that involved little more than dividing her paper in quarters with diagonal lines going from one corner

Figure 1.

to the other. She would then randomly color in the four areas. She rarely spoke, and her attempts at speech consisted largely of mumbled words. In a picture drawn in a session the day after her brother (who was also a member of the group) got hit by a car and was hospitalized, she completely broke her past pattern and produced a graphically clear and expressive picture (Fig. 2) in which she first drew her brother. In the lines at the bottom right corner she showed the impact of the accident and with swirling lines represented her brother flying through the air. She clearly said, "This is a picture of Buddy gettin' hit by a car and flyin' through the air." Up until this time she had never spoken in a clearly articulated sentence. The other children in the group, equally distressed by the accident, began to repeat what she said, and they continued in what grew into a collective chant of "Buddy got hit by a car and is flyin' through the air." The chant and the physical enactment of the accident in the picture gave them an outlet for the tension and fear that they were all feeling. The fact that the chant and imagery were created by this previously nonverbal and visually unexpressive child made the process appear magical, and these factors intensified the group's catharsis.

Figure 2.

Children repeatedly use pictures and visual imagery as props for the creation of spontaneous stories. Within these tales they act out and communicate their fears and their perceptions of themselves, and they offer insights into the content and the process of their thinking. A six-year-old boy that I worked with was referred for expressive art therapy because of his continuous sociopathic behavior in the classroom. He would steal things from the teachers and the other children, and when discovered, he would make up extravagant explanations that placed the blame elsewhere. His stories showed this uncanny ability to have an answer and a justification for everything he did. They also showed the deviousness and the complexity of his thought and his dreamlike efforts to avoid "being caught." The pictures and the stories that he created express his confusion, anger, and guilt. He would often tell stories about jails and what happens to people when they are caught. The artworks and the stories seem to suggest the extent to which he had to engage himself in antisocial behavior in order to get attention and a response from other people. His expressions also indicate that he felt a sense of power only when hurting other people. Drawing and storytelling gave him the opportunity to share his feelings and fantasies with another person and *act out* his conflicts in a way that *will receive a response* and will only "hurt people" within an imaginary and symbolic context.

The story that he told in relation to Figure 3 offers an insight into how he projects feelings of being indestructible. I believe that he was actually very vulnerable and created fantasies of impregnable shelters for the purpose of protecting himself. For me, the picture also suggests that violence and the deceit of one's actions will ultimately turn back on oneself.

Figure 3.

Robbers are in their shelter being bombed by a plane. The bombs are sucked into a special duct where air blows them back out again toward the plane like a boomerang. One of the robbers is in the control room operating this machine together with a conveyor-belt that stolen diamonds are passed out on and they go into a sack with a hook on it (right bottom) that is picked up by a helicopter that deflects bullets. The helicopter holds the sack on its hook and drops them into another opening (left bottom) where they fall beneath a hot top road where nobody will find them because there are no pipes that need repair.

Figure 4 and its accompanying story continue the themes of personal omnipotence and the need for protection. They express anger (the mad face) and the fact that all people seem to be intruders into his personal world and threatening in one form or another. Even the policeman can be harmful in that his gun might go off accidently. The fear of accidents also gives a sense of his precarious balance and self-control. Note how his story changes to accommodate whatever new thought enters his mind. This coincides with the more general pattern of his behavior.

Figure 4.

Dreaming that I was robbing a bank and I got thousands of dollars. It is a make believe picture. This is a bank boat. It's a house-bank boat. Ships pull into it and they cash checks. I didn't get caught. I got away with the money and bought a giant oil tanker as my house. It takes up the whole ocean – no, I use the oil tanker to pump oil into the oil-burner in my house. See where I broke the window. It's cracked. You can't have people around to tell the police so I threw them into the tanker. They go down a slide into the bottom of the boat. They liked it in the boat. I treated them to good things and they came to be robbers. (PAUSE) See the net going up to the building that grabs the people. They stole the boat from the U.S. Army so they have cannons on top. Every ship should have protection. I made a mad face on the person in the net. A guy put a plug in the chimney so the smoke wouldn't get in his way. (PAUSE) I'm going to be a policeman and a fireman. I don't think it's nice to carry guns. A policeman has to. You can accidently shoot someone.

This story is more confused and considerably more ambivalent. However, the fear of getting caught is maintained together with his tendency to try to win other people over to his personal point of view.

Figure 5 continues the theme of fearing accidents and mistakes. The picture started out as a house with a burglar alarm and later became the boy in a rocket. Nothing appears to have stability in his world of uncertain and threatening transformations. The response to my question at the end of the story shows how he ingeniously has an answer to everything and continuously accomodates himself to a threatening circumstance and slips away.

Boy sitting in a rocket and someone pressed the blast off button by mistake. The boy was up in space and he pressed the wrong button when he was trying to make it land and the bombs began to fall out and landed on top of the White Mountains. Then the rocket crashed into the sun and began to burn up.

(Why is the boy smiling?)
Because he thought he had landed.

Diagnostically, this child's stories and pictures demonstrate how artistic enactments with children will vividly project the content of inner feelings and thoughts that are too threatening, or too diffuse and hidden, to be shared through discussions which do not allow for fantasized dramatizations. From a therapeutic perspective within the action orientation of expressive art therapy, this boy was able to clarify his feelings and confront his behavior

Figure 5.

and its effect on other people on a level that was not excessively
threatening.

Another six-year-old boy expressed similar fears of being hurt
in his pictures and stories, but his imagery is clearly defined in
terms of the evil force being projected onto something outside of
himself. His play and fantasy were immersed in monster dramatizations. These monsters were perhaps extensions of the self and
representations of fearful feelings that most children have about
their ability to do harm. The monster was possibly also representa-
tive of the threatening qualities of adults. In this particular case,
the child was extremely frightened by adults. He was referred to
expressive art therapy because he was totally nonverbal in school.
He was in a regular first grade classroom in a public school, and
the teachers became alarmed when after two months of school
he would continuously involve himself in private fantasy play, all
the while making strange noises, which we later discovered were
"monster sounds." The teachers noted that he was developmentally behind all of the other children in virtually all school activities with the exception of art. His drawings were quite sophisticated for a child of his age. This discrepancy between the intelli-

gence and sensitivity of his art and his inability to pursue other school activities led the teachers to believe that his academic difficulties were due to emotional problems. They felt that a one-to-one therapeutic relationship might draw upon his strengths in the visual arts to stimulate development in other spheres of his behavior.

One of the first pictures that he drew, Figure 6, was of a large shark swimming after him. In response to my questions, he began to talk about the picture in a barely audible whisper. He said that "the boy was at the beach with his mother and father, and he swam out too far, and the shark came after him, and got him, and ate him, and his mother and father were sad." This picture and the accompanying story seem at one level to be directed towards dramatizing how his parents would feel if anything happened to him. He had to feel that they cared about him; however, the picture and story were primarily created to confront his fears of being devoured by forces beyond his control, as well as the potential within himself to do harm.

Figure 6.

Figure 7 was described as "a ball on the water that got away from a boy because he threw it too far, and it went out into the ocean." These first two pictures were part of a series of early pictures within our relationship that dealt with "going out too far" and being carried away by the ocean where evil forces attack him. As a defense against being overwhelmed, this child severely retreated from all contact with other people and hid within himself. It seemed that other people were a kind of symbolic ocean to him in which he did not want to be immersed. He lived in an oceanside community, and thus, the sea was an important part of his imagery. Sharks were conspicuous in his art because at the time all of the children in the school were drawing and acting out monster imagery precipitated by the film *Jaws*. In a later picture he drew a shark with an open mouth swimming up to a ball. "The shark is going to bite the ball and pop it. Someone threw it out too far."

Figure 7.

After drawing and talking about a number of monster fears, he began to take a more *inward* course in his creations. Interestingly enough, his monster pictures and stories were discontinued after he was able to draw a picture of me as a monster, thus confirming my belief that this theme emerged from his fear of adults. He began to tell a series of stories about rocks and digging holes in which to put them. The rocks are, of course, passive objects that do not respond and thus possibly do not threaten him. He was also from a poor family, and he told me that he played with rocks all the time because there was nothing else with which to interact. He revealed his more private fantasies in a series of pictures and stories that always began with the drawing of a mound in the middle of the page. The mound would then be filled in with a network of inner passageways. He was sharing his more introspective imagery, which involved secure and multifaceted enclosures. He was beginning to give indications of the richness and complexity of his fantasy life, which up until this point was not revealed to adults.

In response to his drawing of Figure 8 he told how "this is a mountain with orange trees and tunnels that people use to get to the top to have a sun–tan. It's a fun mountain. Some kids come up and play. They throw rocks! They bury rocks. They put rocks on a pile. They make a hole. Then they put rocks inside it. Then they fill it up. Then they go down the mountain. (PAUSE) They play with rocks because it's the only thing they can do. I wash them off at home and put them in a bowl with fish."

Symbolically, his later stories and pictures show an emergence from the inner sanctum of the tunnels. He continued to draw the mound at the bottom center of the pictures, but it became less and less significant and gradually disappeared. The later pictures were initiated by drawing planes, and these ultimately developed into weapons of war and violence. He began to aggressively *act out* inner fears and tensions in a series of battle drawings and stories. He would accompany his drawings with battle sounds and the whole process was a lively dramatic enactment. Six months had passed in our work together, and he was noticeably more articulate and responsive to the total classroom environment. He was transferred into a much smaller special room where there were only five other children. His teacher worked with him in supporting his verbalizations by making tape recordings of his voice and played them back to him, which he greatly enjoyed.

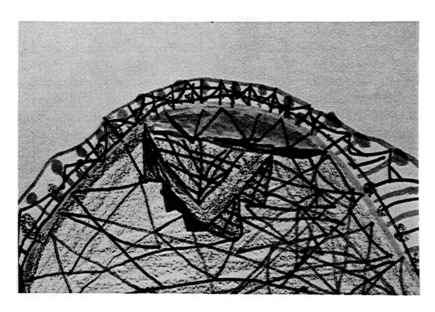

Figure 8.

Figure 9 provides an example of his expressive battle art. Note the small mound at the bottom of the page. This was the last of the mound pictures. "This is a pool of burning blood. These are bombs at the bottom. The good guys are coming down in parachutes, and they are going to fall into the bombs and into the blood that the bad guys put there. The guy in the middle is carrying the guns and they can't get to them to fight back. (PAUSE) I would like to be a dead guy. (PAUSE) These two guys are getting murdered. *Look* at this — the men are falling and getting bombed up. They both got bombed up at the same time. They all got murdered...but the good guys that got killed got operated on by doctors in the army, and they got better, and they came back and got the bad guys...." His teacher walked into the room and he said spontaneously to her, "Guess what team got killed, the good guys or the bad guys?".

At this point in our relationship his language and verbal expression had developed markedly from our first sessions when he would only make soft, whispering, and very terse statements in response to questions. His stories had become completely self-initiated, more complex, and forceful. In the following session he

Figure 9.

extended the scope of his battle art into space with Figure 10. "The rocket bombed up into the sky and saw guys shooting people, and some guys smashed into him, and he got on fire, and then the world bombed up. Then the police and fire engine went on fire. Then the rocket and everything fell." In this picture and story, he acted out the inferno of total devastation where even the keepers of the social order (police and fire engines) were destroyed.

The story and picture that he shared with me in our last session continued the battle enactments but were much more focused on protected and "safe" places. He described Figure 11 as "an airport with a place on top of the building where they watch the men. That plane is the bad guy (right) and that one is the good guy (left). That's the stuff to put out the fire on the good guy's plane (lines connecting plane to bottom left). They're shooting from inside the building because it's safe in there."

Figure 10.

Figure 11.

As our year together progressed (we met once a week), he not only became much more spontaneous and creative in his dramatic enactments, but his stories were so imaginative that they attracted the attention of other children who began to respect him for his artistic and storytelling skills. The last story and enactment seems to be saying that he is bringing the battle under control. He has let the chaos of fear be expressed, and he has begun to feel quite confident in his ability to direct the process. The battle enactments are much more than just war pictures. They dramatize mythic confrontations between good and evil, life and death, all the while allowing the child to express, and vent, personal feelings that he has about these conflicts. Within his pictures the child enacts the myth cycle of the hero through a process of separation, penetration, and return. He separated himself from the ongoing flow of daily activity in school through his art, and ultimately he penetrated to the chaotic source of fear and death in his battle pictures. In completing each picture and story he brought about a return to the school environment.

Children's war dramatizations are an important form of expressive release. Through their art they confront the reality of wars both outside and inside themselves, and in their families, while coming to grips with the harm and devastation that can result. Acting these fears out was the essence of the therapy for this child. Through drawing, storytelling, and visual dramatization he would relax his rigid defense of "retreat" into himself, and he began to enact his feelings with other people. The characters in the battles are always men in whose abilities to do good or evil he harbored ambivalent feelings. He showed the same ambivalence towards his monsters, which were both objects of fear and affection. The men in his battle pictures are both the "bad guys" and the keepers of social *order*. All of the art presented here can be viewed as an enactment of the mythic forces that both support and destroy life.

In summary, what I have tried to stress in these exerpts from my work with this child is the way in which our conversations and the imagery of his language and stories were stimulated by his highly theatrical process of making pictures. He became so engaged in these visual–motor enactments that he experienced a compulsion to tell me about them. The drawings gave him a very much needed sense of control and perceptual focus that he did not have when speaking to adults without intermediary objects. They allowed him to make his inner language tangible and evident to both himself and others. The drawings provoked the verbal discussion of visual metaphors, and his growing ability to articulate feelings in turn expanded the imagery of his art, together with his confidence in pursuing the continuous enactment of inner struggles and fears.

SHARING POETIC IMAGERY

Over the course of my experience in various forms of group and individual therapy, what I remember most vividly are those moments which have left emotional memories because of the intensity of the manner in which I *felt* the particular therapeutic process. These memories are always tied to strong and clear sensory images. The same is true with memories of past life experiences that I bring into the therapeutic event. I have found that specific words and the imagery that we attach to them tend to summarize and abstract the essentials from my past. A single word or image will often provoke a tremendous outpouring of emotion. My work with poetry in therapy is oriented toward the discovery of our essential imagery and our metaphors for explaining and giving value to life. Interestingly enough, we might have our greatest personal insights into the nature of our imagery when responding to the poem of another person. In sharing our responses to a particular poem, we will often discuss which of the image's affect us most. This attentiveness to a poem's subject matter not only supports the author, but it can provide the motivation for poetic expression on the part of the listener, who might find that the poem provokes an emotional response and fresh insights. Other people can also help us to appreciate our writing more. They provide varied interpretative viewpoints, which can raise emotional issues that expand our awareness of the different levels of meaning in a poem.

In a poetry therapy training group that I was conducting, a young man created a free association poem with the group. His words were written down by a group member who read the poem back to the other people. The poem contained a series of images describing an old man climbing a mountain and contrasted the analytic, careful, and strenuous ascent of the old man with the adventuring of a young man who was also going up the mountain in a carefree fashion. He discussed how his imagery was stimulated by the tarot card of the fool and the hermit. The poem was intended to express how we are at times very self-conscious of our perceptions of life, while at other times we are completely immersed in the process of what we are doing. He said how "one side of me looks at everything, the other is just *there.*"

In response to the poem, another group member shared how the imagery reminded her of the last two stanzas of Yeats' poem "Lapis Lazuli." In the poem, three old Chinamen, carved in lapis lazuli, climb toward a halfway house on a mountain. The poet imagines that once they reach their destination they sit and look down at the tragedy in the world. Yet, their wrinkled eyes have a sparkling vitality that seems to vindicate life.

The reading of Yeats' poem further intensified the group's involvement in the feelings expressed by the young man. He felt a similar intensification and described how the lapis is his favorite stone. He described how even though he does not have one himself, his two most important relationships were with people who wore lapis rings. The scope of his poem was taken further for all of the group members through the reading of "Lapis Lazuli," and he now has yet another interpersonal association with image of the lapis stone. This brief interpersonal exchange is an example of the ongoing process of sharing imagery in therapy, and it demonstrates the role that words play in transmitting feelings between people.

Within the same group another interesting interpersonal process grew out of a specific image. One of the group members had just returned from a vacation on a Greek island. Her memories of the visual imagery of the island permeated the poems that she was writing in the group until one of the group members referred to her as "a Greek island" in his poem. The metaphor was intended to be complimentary, but she perceived the comment to mean that she was separate and cut off from the other people in the group. She was in part still mentally in Greece because of her reluctance to separate herself from very pleasurable and personally meaningful memories. However, this was something that she was feeling much more intensely than other people, who were not upset with her difficulties in being totally there with them, in the moment. She was intrigued to hear that the metaphor was intended to refer to her attractive qualities and that she was perceived as the kind of person one would like to be with, just as a Greek island tends to attract people. The group as a whole went on to share their interpretations of the Greek island metaphor as it related to her. In response to this session and the introduction of the "island" image, she went on to write a series of very powerful identity poems, which confronted feelings of separateness, loneliness, and estrangement from loved ones.

> The grapes are ripe.
> The table is set, she presumed,
> But nobody comes to the island.
>
> The ferry is there
> But nobody comes to the island.

The metaphor of the island triggered something very deep within her, and at the close of the poetry group she said she was not at all finished with it. This is an example of how the poem of one person can pick up on the imagery that another is working on and transmit it back, transformed. This woman was provoked into new insights about herself, and the experience completely reversed the manner in which the island imagery had been pulling her away from the group. The interchange around the image of the island drew her deeply into the group process, perhaps because the group was able to help her to achieve a powerful integration of the imagery of the islands with her past life and her ongoing concerns. As a poet she was also motivated by the opportunity to work with the imagery of her trip on a deep psychological level.

These group interactions show how sharing poetic imagery within a therapeutic context can expand and enlarge upon the feelings being expressed. In responding to one another's expressions, people suggest extended possibilities for self-analysis and creative exploration. The tangible manifestations of the arts document an interpersonal process, which takes place in all forms of psychotherapy where the exchange of feelings and observations amplifies, clarifies, and augments the way in which we interact with the world. The arts also help people to become more aware of areas of conflict that can provide subject matter for psychotherapeutic analysis. Poetry is especially capable of assisting people in bringing conflict into focus. We repeatedly confront our insecurities, lack of trust, poor self-confidence, and weak self–esteem when we are in the position of reading our poetry to others. Defenses about the personal value of our expressions are manifested through excessive explanations about why we did what we did, through repeated disclaimers of the poem's importance, through the inhibited, stammering presentation of the poem, or through the lack of personal expression within the poem itself. People are often reluctant to share spontaneously written poems and are more apt to read only poems that have been carefully worked over. This tends to be done not so much because the person wants to hide personal feelings that might be manifested within a spontaneous and freely associated poem, but because they want the poem to be technically perfect. In the beginning of a therapy group, people often feel that their self-image is tied to the artistic proficiency of their poems. This does not appear to be as much of a problem within one-to-one therapeutic sessions, where intimacy might be experienced sooner. Participants must come to an understanding that the hierarchy of value in therapy is oriented toward honest and immediate expression. This does not necessarily exclude concerns with artistic competence, but technical issues should not interfere with the process of sharing the emotions of the moment.

When creating art within a therapeutic context, I try to direct myself toward the creation of spontaneous expressions, which serve the purpose of the group and myself as a group member. The value of a peom can be considered in relation to its commitment and energy within the present moment. If the poem is one that I ultimately save and include with my ongoing collection of poems, that is fine, but if not, it has served its purpose within the psychotherapeutic experience. Spontaneous poems also suggest new imagery that can be expanded in more extended writing outside the group. It is often valuable to bring the finished poem back to read to the group so that they can appreciate its complete evolution. Serious poets have benefited from poetry therapy groups of this kind, which stimulate their work and help them to become less self-conscious about their writing. In our groups we try to further creative expression by getting beyond restricted ways of bringing a poem into existence. In addition to writing poems down, we record more sound explorations with audiotape and videotape and later play these recordings back for the purpose of sharing and observing our capacities for spontaneous expression.

The sharing of poetry will at times precipitate conflict between group members or between the therapist and client in that the expression of different interpretations and values can provoke people into confronting primary interpersonal issues having to do with relationships, expectations, leadership, control, etc. In therapy groups, I have repeatedly encountered the type of situation where people, when asked what they value most about their poems, answer, "Oh, nothing; nothing in particular," or, "It was just an exercise and really doesn't mean anything to me." These negations of one's work can at times produce conflict when other group members begin to grow tired of repeated disclaimers. For example, in a poetry group that I led, a man referred to his poem as "nothing important" and a woman responded by saying, "I knew you were going to do that." This interchange created a tense atmosphere, and we tried to deal with it by determining precisely what the two people were attempting to convey in their respective statements. The woman said that she was confronting him not only because she was growing irritated but because she wanted to initiate a sharing of feelings. She believed that he was defending himself with his disclaimers and thus separating himself from other group members. She also spoke of how her desire to communicate with him through confrontation was tempered by a fear of hurting his feelings and alienating other group members. During this exchange, the man whom she engaged spoke about how it felt to be confronted, and he shared his perception of what he did to stimulate her response. We questioned whether or not disclaimers of this kind were part of a more general pattern of negating what he does in order to provoke a response. As we discussed the situation, the man and woman grew progressively embedded in their respective viewpoints, and a group member suggested that they "switch roles" and try to explain the problem from the other person's vantage point. The role reversal resolved the problem in our group, but it could have been taken even further into a full dramatic enactment involving all of the members, since the conflict was a universal one that each of us had confronted at various points in our lives.

This experience, together with other case materials presented here, demonstrate the fundamental unity between creating and discussing art and the total psychotherapeutic process. As each of the other arts are presented in the following chapters, spoken language will continue to play an integral part in all of the expressive therapies. We will see that all aspects of psychotherapeutic expression are part of a dramatic enactment wherein language usually plays an essential role. A creative approach to language suggests new possibilities for verbal communication in psychotherapy, and the application of the poetic process to healing restores the spoken word to one of its most ancient functions.

Chapter 6

MOVEMENT, DANCE, AND THE BODY

*To have a soul separate from the body is to have a body
separate from other bodies.*

— Norman O. Brown, *Love's Body*

OVEMENT is at the root of all artistic activity.
In addition to dance, it is in the art of theatre
where both classical and experimental companies work most
seriously with the body as a vehicle of expression. Some schools
of music education and therapy also encourage the "eurhythmic"
integration of movement and sound. The visual arts and poetry
have traditionally been more cut off from their movement sources.
The term "visual art" is itself misleading in that the graphic and
plastic arts are as tactile and kinesthetic as they are visual. Jackson
Pollock's revolutionary *action* paintings and the expressionist
movement dramatized how art objects are extensions of kinesis
and inner movement. In poetry, Charles Olson's emphasis on
process and *breath*, together with his long dance poem, "Apollonius
of Tyana," restored bodily action to poetic expression. Nietzsche
described how his most inspirational writing was closely associated
with rigorous physical expression, "My most creative moments
were always accompanied by unusual muscular activity. The body
is inspired: let us waive the questions of the 'soul.' I might often
have been seen dancing in those days."

All of the arts in therapy must repossess the body if they are
to actualize their healing powers fully. The denial of the body by
conventional psychotherapeutic practices and mental health insti-

110

tutions is but symptomatic of the lack of mind/body integration within the society at large and within the lives of thoses who deliver mental health services. Physically active children and adults, bursting with a need to act out their tensions, are treated within programs that *manage* their behavior and provide emotional outlets only within the restrictions of *controlled discursive speech.* There are times when I must run for miles or dance intensely for extended periods of time in order to discharge and purge myself of emotional conflict. This type of physical exertion takes my body to a point where emotional conflict is transcended and all there is is an ongoing process of maintaining motion and a sense of balance within myself and the physical environment. At other times, a less intense, more rhythmic, flowing and gentle process of movement helps me to focus attention on my sense of balance and motion in the world. Because of my own needs for physical activity and bodily expression, I am all the more sensitive to the restrictions that institutional routines, schedules, and values place on children and adults. What tends to happen in my work, and with the average person in society, is that the movement patterns of the job and other fixed expectations for action within life take over, and I begin to move like a robot within a highly conditioned, unconscious frame of reference. I not only lose touch with my own movement but with that of the people and the objects around me.

Traditional psychotherapies have stressed the importance of unconscious imagery and thought, whereas I feel that equal attention must be given to unconscious movement and kinesthetic conflict. Most of us go through life unaware of our most essential mode of expression and survival, kinesis. Everyone of us is in constant relation to, and interaction with, ourselves, others, and the physical environment through movement. With the exception of dancers, physicists, and other people who focus their lives on the phenomena of kinesthesia, we are largely *unconscious* of this fundamental dimension of life. Because of the advances being made in the understanding of how the body stores tension, how the muscles have emotional memories that restrict the functioning of the whole organism, how the body and muscles block the flow of creative and spontaneous thought in all modes of expression, and how all thought is dependent upon muscular sensation, the new era in psychotherapeutic practice will be the era of the reuniting of the body and mind.

The split between body and mind has been furthered by our philosophical, religious, and economic traditions. In both the East and West, religion and philosophy have separated the spirit from the body. In the quest for transcendence, the body was seen as an obstacle that tied the person to a fixed position in space, thus limiting the flight of consciousness. As a result, mystical traditions would try *to liberate the spirit from the body.* In the Christian tradition, the fundamental association to the body is the symbol of the crucifixion. With the body suffering and nailed to the cross, transcendence can be achieved only through the spirit. The great early Christian philosophers, St. Augustine, Thomas Aquinas, and Pierre Abélard, discouraged any sensual expressions that might even suggest the Dionysian dance. Even the medieval poet, Petrarch, condemned dancing and wrote, "From dancing we get nothing but a libidinous and empty spectacle, hateful to honest eyes and unworthy of a man; take lust away, and you will have removed the dance also." The industrial work place, with its emphasis on mechanical repetition at the lower levels of production and a high degree of abstract thought at the top, has further alienated the body in modern life. Because of the restrictions on movement exploration imposed by the work place, the contemporary mind has continued the historical denial of the body and its potential for highly differentiated, varied and unconventional kinetic expression. Even our cultural commitment to athletics tends to lay more emphasis on mercantile and competitive values than the aesthetic appreciation of the body's movement. Because of the way in which these problems and the *repression* of unconscious movement impulses affect therapists as well as clients, this area has consistently been one of the more threatening and *foreign* forms of human expression to the traditionally trained mental health professional.

I believe that emotional conflict originates in feelings of separation between consciousness and the body. If this is true, then traditional psychotherapy more often than not can be a continuing source of conflict. All forms of personality *splits* and emotional fragmentations grow from the disunity of body and mind. We fear the body – its mortality, its potential for disease and pain, its unattractiveness, etc. – and thus constantly estrange ourselves from it. The Gospel according to St. John offers an answer to this dilemma in professing that "only love can drive out fear." So, it appears that we must begin to embrace and appreciate our bodies, their movements, weaknesses, strengths, and idiosyncratic qualities if we are to establish an underlying unity and balance for behavior. If we continue to live in a condition that encourages a disunity between mind and body, our expression and consciousness will be a projection of this imbalance. It is difficult, if not impossible, to give feelings of concern and love to other people when we are not feeling them toward ourselves. Psychological integration, love, or whatever one wishes to call this phenomenon must start with the individual person's physical existence in time and space and the remarriage of consciousness and physical sensation.

We must also revise our thinking toward physical space. Our culture has taught an attitude of opposition toward the physical environment where space is something to be mastered and conquered rather than embraced as the larger body that we inhibit. We encourage instincts of separation and competition between people, social classes, and countries and place restrictions of the unifying power that evolves from feelings of respect toward everything that lives. Actually, we are all very much a part of each other because our identities are established through relationships. Also, the capacity to perceive life is formed through interactions with others. Our psychological theories of identity and reality place too much emphasis on the individual as a separate entity. Reality is a process of constant change in which we are forever creating ourselves in relation to other people and the environment. Just as we place a cultural stress on eliminating boundaries to open communication between people throughout the world, we must also do so in relation to the closer intervals of interaction within ourselves. It is impossible to have one without the other. Physical boundaries within the individual person, between the individual and the environment, and between people will continuously influence the content of feelings, thought, and behavior within interpersonal relationships.

Whenever I walk through mental health institutions, I am overwhelmed with the realization that what is needed today is a massive realignment of the mental health field. In the numerous psychiatric hospitals that I have visited, people are always sitting, rocking in chairs, smoking, walking back and forth, sitting, and sitting. In schools for emotionally troubled children, the classrooms tend to be traditionally designed with desks and chairs where the children are required to *sit* for the greater part of the day. The pattern that I have observed is that children tend to resist aggressively the constriction of their movements, and this behavior is viewed negatively, whereas most adult psychiatric patients accommodate themselves to the movement expectations of the institutional environment. The hospitalized patient loses touch with the uniqueness of the body and its expressive potential as the muscles, posture, gait, and style of moving adapt to the movement patterns that are perceived within the institution. The present orientation to treatment in our mental institutions should be abandoned for an approach that engages clients in an ongoing process of action within varied and stimulating settings. Within shcools for children, we must be more creative in channeling aggressive feelings into gratifying physical activity. Ironically, the greatest strength of many emotionally disturbed children is their capacity for forceful bodily actions, with which our treatment programs are often incapable of dealing.

My experience with severely disturbed and emotionally withdrawn children and adults has taught me that they discover their bodies while simultaneously beginning to explore their ability to make *contact* with physical materials and other people. Insight and self-understanding evolve from action. Self-understanding at the very earliest stages of development is never purely egocentric; it must develop from experiences with people and the environment. My work with body movement and dance is oriented toward *interaction and relationship*. The concerns of contemporary dance in exploring the immediacies of *time and space* are particularly adaptable to dance therapy, where the temporal and spatial perceptions of clients are often confused and in a general state of disorganization. Movement experiences focused on the process of actively relating to, and interacting with, physical materials and other people can help clients to transcend their isolation and physical boundaries.

Dance and music therapists are united in their mutual concerns with the therapeutic dimensions of rhythm. The beat and tempo of the dance is synchronous with the rhythms of nature and the internal pulse of the body. The research of William Condon in viewing slow motion films of interpersonal interactions has revealed that there is a gestural synchrony between people as they communicate with each other. Condon's analysis of the closer intervals of movement interactions shows that there is an ongoing coordination and mutual rhythm that is maintained between people in the most elementary of conversations (Condon and Ogston, 1966). His research has been of enormous importance to dance therapists in that he suggests that human communication can be likened to a rhythmic dance. He also puts before us the possibility that bodily synchrony is as significant in our interactions as the content of our verbalizations. Emotional difficulties, as Condon demonstrates in films of emotionally troubled people, tend to interrupt the physical rhythm of interpersonal action. Disturbed clients additionally tend to exhibit a lack of rhythm within the movements of the different parts of their own bodies. For example, one arm will move out of synchrony with the other, or both arms will not be coordinated with the movements of other bodily parts.

Poetry, philosophy, and religion have through time understood that through rhythmic movement we become united with the rhythms of the universe. The dancing gods of ancient Greece and India, Dionysus and Shiva, reflect a world view where the highest manifestation of the spirit is achieved through participation in the movements of nature in which we are all part of a cosmic dance. Life is perceived as *divine kinesis*, and the fundamental unity of humankind rests in the ability to move in rhythm with these forces. Through the dance, we transcend the boundaries to full participation in life, and we enter the "participation mystique" where self and non-self are experienced as one. The ecstacy of the dance is transcendent and takes us beyond excessive concerns with the body as an entity, separate from the rest of nature. This is not a denial of the body but a sense of our physical connectedness with all there is. We have in our society, and certainly within the mental health field, lost touch with the importance of maintaining rhythm as the most fundamental form of communication with the natural world.

Dance therapists have tried to restore this sense of balance and belonging through rhythmic movement experiences. Clients are given the freedom to find their own unique movement rhythms — often beginning with an exploration of the movements of daily life. Severely disturbed or withdrawn clients will need a more structured and supportive environment to help them to participate in rhythmic exercises. Dance therapists repeatedly use the circular configuration as a means of establishing contact, building trust, and creating a group rhythm. Marian Chace, whose work at St. Elizabeth's Hospital in Washington, D.C. had a strong influence on the dance therapy field, based her dance therapy practice on principles of rhythm and always worked with the circle as a means of bringing people together. "All classes, whatever the degree of illness of the patients in that particular ward, are conducted in a circular formation. Hands can be held around a circle and a group unity is achieved with patients who are too confused to remain attentive without the support of the group" (Chace, in Chaiklin, 1975, p. 53). In beginning to work together, clients will generally start by developing a feel for their personal movement, and then after establishing eye contact with other people, they will progressively accommodate their movements to one another until a group rhythm is achieved.

As mentioned in the earlier chapter on preparation, the therapist can further individual exploration and group unison by structuring activity around common movements such as swinging, swaying, and reaching with separate body parts and the whole body. I will often start group sessions with "rocking" and breathing experiences. Within psychiatric environments "rocking" motions are quite common, and I like to first build on familiar and pleasing sensations. The rhythm of rocking is comforting and brings a sense of relaxation that can be likened to fundamental prenatal rhythms. According to Ashley Montagu, "The mother. . . who rocks and pats her baby may in some measure recreate the stimuli of her breathing and pulse rhythms, rhythms that were significant to it before birth, and thus give the baby reassurance of the familiar environment that it so much needs" (Montagu, 1971, p. 135).

After the group begins to move together with a certain degree of spontaneity and comfort, changes in movement can be suggested by the movements of individual clients who begin to add a new dimension to the group movement. The therapist might observe these significant individual movements and bring them to the attention of the group. The principle of following and imitating movements of another is very widely used in one-to-one dance therapy sessions, especially when the client is withdrawn and unresponsive. The therapist might first establish contact by imitating or "mirroring" the person's movement. This approach helps clients to become aware of their movement and gradually to feel a sense of synchrony and togetherness with the therapist. As the relationship grows and the client becomes more confident, personal movements are differentiated from those of the therapist. Over time, the client might also be encouraged to mirror the movements of the therapist. This will help to develop feelings of mutuality within the relationship and give the client an opportunity to internalize the expression and feeling of another person.

Movement improvisation with higher functioning groups of clients tends to support the theory of Carl Rogers — that when left to establish its own direction, a group will proceed to a state of functional equilibrium. In my work I stress the importance of improvisational movement, alone and with other people. There is continuous excitement and creative gratification in the way in which group formations naturally develop from individual movement explorations. We might start our dance with simple walking motions, and then as contact and interaction with other people and objects in the environment grows, the flow of movement changes in response to the various stimuli. This approach clearly approximates the change and flow of energy in everyday life. The action of dance mirrors the transitory realities of life's motion, and within the improvisational framework, we become engaged in the ongoing process of losing and gaining balance, control, and gratification. The orientation of Steve Paxton, Merce Cunningham, amd other contemporary dancers to the movements of daily life has brought dance and therapy to the point where there are few

teaches
being present

major separations between the two. In our dance therapy work, we help participants to become more aware of the body's movement configurations by taking everyday activities such as reaching, lifting and walking and enacting them in *slow motion*. We might also help people to concentrate on their bodily gestures by having them *stop and hold* movements. Commonplace activities can be transformed artistically not only through aesthetic concentration but also through exercises that *exaggerate* their fundamental rhythms and patterns. We are also very attentive to accidental and chance movements, with the therapist helping clients by pointing out interesting new expressions that they might be making. Videotape has been very useful in enabling clients to observe and become more aware of their movement. The ability to stop the tape and frame significant movements during playback is another very helpful, and at times exciting, way of stopping the action of the dance for the purpose of observation.

As with the other arts in therapy, my work in dance is based on principles of relationship, interaction, expression, enactment, and balance. In all forms of movement and dance, our bodies are in constant contact and relationship with physical space, and usually, with other people. A primary goal of dance therapy activity is to become more aware of these ongoing interactions, and through increased awareness, we will hopefully develop an ability to control and extend the scope of our body's movements and rhythms. The forces of gravity keep us in an ongoing relationship with the floor or ground. Balance is thus a constant concern of the dance. As we further our sensitivity to the essential qualities of our movement, touch also becomes a more fully appreciated sense. Through the dance we are given the opportunity to explore the more general place of "touch" within our lives. According to Montagu, "The skin, like a cloak, covers us all over, the oldest and most sensitive of our organs, our first medium of communication, and our most efficient of protectors" (Montagu, 1971, p. 1).

With many clients the process of establishing movement relationships within time and space must begin with the essentials of motion. Clients who have withdrawn to virtually motionless, "catatonic" states of consciousness might find it very threatening to leave the security of their chairs to stand or walk across an empty space. Movement experiences might begin for them from their chairs and progressively build to more complete bodily action. I encountered a situation similar to this when working with a five-year-old child who had just entered kindergarten. He was so threatened by the school environment that he did not speak and would stand alone in a corner of the classroom, sucking his thumb. Whenever the teachers tried to engage him in some form of activity, he would begin to cry. When I first met with the teachers, we noticed that he tended to look toward the art activity area within the classroom, and I began to take him there to explore the space.

In the first stages of our work together, I tried to encourage him to move with, and relate to, physical materials. In our first two sessions he spent virtually all of his time (forty-five minutes) stirring various bottles of paint. He took great pleasure in the rhythmic motions and was also stimulated by the movement configurations and kinesthetic swirling designs that he made with the paint. We were at a stage in our work together where it was much more appropriate for him to be relating to objects that he could control and that did not threaten him. The repetitious stirring motion had an effect similar to the repeated motions of a trance dance as focusing on a continuous motion enabled him to forget his fears and inhibitions. (The teachers later informed me that he subsequently developed an interest in water play and took great delight in repetitious pouring motions.) The paint and the brushes were *props* for his movement explorations. As he began to tire of the stirring movement in later sessions, there were longer and longer *lag times,* which were important because *out of inactivity came a significant transition* in his movement. He took the brushes out of the jars and began to paint randomly on the paper while standing at the easel. His art evolved to a form of action painting resembling a dance in which he changed the brush from hand to hand, used two hands, and developed a wide variety of imaginative gestures in expressing himself. In focusing his attention on the brushes and the paint, he developed a sense of direction for his energy. Out of this concentration came a kinesthetic power that propelled him through an increasingly broad range of movements. He was so fascinated by the texture and flow of the paint that he literally forgot himself and began to incorporate its fluidity into his movements. The time spent at the easel allowed him to separate himself gradually from his pattern of immobility and withdrawal, and he gradually began to integrate himself into the more general movement flow of the classroom. From the painting we became involved with more aggressive and forceful movement activities in the carpentry area, all the while keeping our attention focused on moving *with objects*. He greatly enjoyed the carpentry and began to make complicated wooden structures exploring principles of balance. From the sculpting and arranging of wooden materials, we progressed to constructing physical environments, which then provided a space in which he could begin to move with his whole body and with other people. He began to act out fantasies as he moved within the space, which changed within one session from a house, to a ship on the ocean, to a spaceship, etc. The developmental orientation of this child's expression shows how dance and movement often evolve *in response* to the physical environment and grow from activities such as stirring paint, which might have no apparent relationship to the art of dance. This child in effect constructed an environment for his movement, and as the physical space became more suggestive, he progressed from exploratory and manipulative movements to dramatic enactments. His enactments of feelings, tensions, fantasies, and mythological principles were often pursued through movement alone and without the use of words.

Over the course of our work together, his movement within the classroom with other children grew progressively independent and expressive. By the midpoint of the school year, he was participating in all aspects of the school experience. He grew increasingly confident in his ability to move in space, and when engaged in communal dance experiences, he was one of the most energetic and expressive of the children. Although the focus of our relationship was on the severe problems that he had in moving within the classroom, this particular case demonstrates how with young children the different art forms tend to flow into one another without any design or plan.

I will often accompany the children's movement with drums or other percussion instruments, trying to pick up the beat and rhythms of their movement as it changes, rather than determining the form of their movement through the structure of sound. When working with a group of children, I work together with them in providing musical accompaniment to their dance. The group might make music together while a child dances alone, or one or two children may join me in creating sounds while the group dances.

Most dance therapists work regularly with recorded music, which induces different emotional states. As with the principle of isomorphism in poetry, the rhythm of the music will usually have a corresponding effect on the person's consciousness and movement. Perhaps because of my therapeutic and aesthetic orientation to working with whatever emerges from within us and with our interactions with the physical environment I prefer to work with the sounds we make with our bodies, our voices, and physical materials and musical instruments that we explore. I find that our sense of creative fulfillment is more complete when both movement and sound emerge from our explorations. My years of work and cooperation with the dance therapist Norma Canner, who together with Barbara Mettler is a leading proponent of *pure movement*, has had a definite impact on my attitudes toward the use of dance in therapy. Rather than repeating the socialized movement patterns that emerge in response to familiar sounds, we have investigated the reversal of that process in placing the emphasis on movement and introduce sounds as they relate to and intensify the force of the movement.

This approach is particularly effective within psychiatric institutions where patients tend to respond to recorded music by falling into social dance patterns, which are repeated over and over again and which are not expressive of their unique movement potential. In my work with a woman in her late fifties who has lived within mental institutions for most of her adult life, I noticed that whenever recorded music was played she would respond with standard social dance movements, but in her more general behavior on the wards of the hospital, her movement was highly imaginative and expressive. When working with her alone or when she would take her turn in the center of a circle dance, I would encourage her to begin a dance with the repetitious, yet varied, tapping of a foot that I observed her moving, with the expressive gesturing of the fingers of one hand, with head movements, or with a hand moving in front of her. A simple structure of this kind gave her something to relate to, to bounce off, and enlarge upon with a successive flow of movements. As she began to move, we would pick up her rhythm with drums, piano, or whatever other sound sources were available. The accompaniment and musical *response* created an artistic interaction between the entire group, further motivating her to dance and to continue the basic theme of her first gestures. Ultimately the *energy* and attention that she received from the group stimulated sustained and highly imaginative movements, with a remarkable sense of timing and relatedness to one another. She was masterful at picking up a long stick or other object and not only moved with it as a prop but would use it as a musical instrument during her dance. As the dance progressed she drew other group members into her circle until we reached a point where the whole group was involved. This particular woman not only danced for herself but was very concerned with both the response she received from the group, as well as her ability to serve as a catalyst for the more general group process.

In addition to beginning our dances from stillness and the sounds of breath and the body moving, where even the simplest gestures become the focus of aesthetic attention, we will often start with simple musical patterns motivating movement. As a six-year-old boy told me at the start of a session when I was using a hand drum, "The drum makes me tingle and want to move." As the dance begins, the sounds become synchronous with the movements of the dancers, and there is a continuous give and take between the two. The contact and interaction between sound and movement is parallel to the relationships that we encourage between dancers. We focus a great deal of attention on moving together in pairs that break down from, and ultimately rejoin, an all-encompassing group process. Within the pairs we strive to accommodate ourselves to the motion of another person as well as to influence that person with our movement and energy. Within these experiences we are both acting upon and responding, forceful and pliant, giving and taking — and completely focusing on our relationship to another person. In this way we work on

Dance —

the *actual behavior of relating and interacting* and pattern ourselves to be more effective in the ongoing interpersonal relationships of daily life. *Through the dance we experiment with our capacity to work cooperatively with another person,* and we explore the actual points of physical and expressive *balance between us.* Working together in this way, people discover what Steve Paxton calls the "easiest pathways available to their mutually moving masses" and achieve "the ideal of active, reflexive, harmonic, spontaneous, mutual forms."

I must again emphasize how this quality of mutual interaction also characterizes the relationship between sound and movement. Dancers like Paul Taylor have spoken often of how music "can be aggravating, a terrible whip, that. . .puts all kinds of harnesses on the dancer and choreographer." Yet, Taylor and others say that music is essential, that it provides stimulus, structure, and discipline, that one can either establish a relationship with it or move in opposition to its rhythms, and that it is one more element of life "to be coped with."

One of the greatest problems presented by recorded music in therapy is that it does not respond to the immediacy of individual and group emotion. For example, a movement group using recorded music might undergo a striking and emotionally significant change of direction while the music just goes on its own merry way and thus causes an impediment and distraction to group process. Recorded music can also exercise too much control over the group's movement. Yet, a familiar melody might have a deep emotional effect on a person by stimulating important associations and significant feelings from the past. The melody may also be comforting and could relax inhibitions to movement. Recorded music might also be necessary in one-to-one sessions or group experiences where the therapist must be directly involved in the individual's or group's movement. I do not want to give the impression that I am against the use of recorded music in dance therapy, but I do feel that the movement process can become overly dependent on mechanical aids, which have so transformed our lives and expression within their relatively brief existence that we lose touch with what dance has been for so many thousands of years.

When focusing on the pure perception of the formal qualities of movement within time and space, we deal with movement concepts such as continuity and discontinuity, tension and relaxation, changes in direction, and repetition. This perceptual awareness approach helps the person to develop more control over, and appreciation for, personal movement. In addition to working with imaginative and highly expressive gestures, these concepts can be explored through the commonplace movements of daily activity. While maintaining a sensitivity to the dance elements of our natural movement faculties, I also introduce more classical, dramatic forms of dance into psychotherapeutic sessions so that we may enact our feelings through movement.

Dramatic dance allows the dance therapist to relate to the broad spectrum of psychotherapeutic issues. Dance as emotional enactment continues an ancient continuity of art where the *content* of feelings, fears, and conflicts is made tangible and expelled through the body. Within an integrated arts context, attentiveness to the dramatic elements of dance can increase the significance of gestures and movements that are made in conjunction with other modes of expression, as we unconsciously and consciously act out inner feelings through our bodies.

Within our dance therapy sessions, we are equally concerned with dance and movement as a means of developing perceptual awareness and with the use of the body to act out feelings and conflicts. We often discover that the expressive release achieved by a dramatic enactment is more complete and primal when we do not use words and communicate feelings only through the body.

MOVEMENT OBSERVATION

Dance therapists have made important contributions to psychotherapy through the adaptation of the movement notation and observation techniques of Laban to the psychodiagnostic process. In beginning to look and think analytically about movement expression, dance therapists are offering new insights to the mental health field, which has historically been ill-equipped in understanding the messages of the body. The movements of the body are especially valuable sources of diagnostic information in that they are tangible and objectively manifest behaviors that contrast with the highly speculative, projective, and symbolic sources of traditional diagnosis. The basic presupposition behind the use of movement as a diagnostic indicator is that a person's outer movements, or lack of movement, will be a direct extension of inner feelings and the more general personality structure.

Laban's system of evaluating and describing movement is concerned with two major components: the "shape" of bodily movements within physical space, and the movement's "effort," which might be described as the rhythm, or energy, behind the body's expression. Dance and movement therapists have either adopted the standard "effort-shape" movement notation system or they have adapted it to their own categories for assessment. In analyzing movement categorically, we determine the style of a person's expression as well as the body's interaction with space and other people — are the person's actions closed/bound or open/flowing; is there interaction with other people; is the whole body being used; are the various body parts in synchrony with one another; does one influence other people through movement or primarily respond to the movements of others? Additional qualities of movement might be determined by looking in terms of the polarities of spontaneity and restraint, fluidity and mechanical expression, social responsiveness and egocentrism, continuity and change, precision and randomness, unity and fragmentation, strength and weakness, variation and repetition, imagination and stereotypes, focus and diffusion, firmness and limpness, energy and passivity, heavyness and lightness, etc. I am also very much concerned with a person's degree of awareness about the nature of the body's movement.

Principles of movement analysis are equally applicable to the assessment of group dynamics. Just as a choreographer analyzes the movements of groups of dancers so, too, therapists and participants can observe group movement sessions with an eye for interactional patterns, the placement of people in space, leadership, group synchrony and cooperation versus isolation and separateness, the degree of group identity, as well as individual differentiation, spontaneity and expressiveness, etc. All of these characteristics of group personality can be evaluated from the point of view of movement, as well as from the perspective of what the group verbally says about itself.

Because of the personal association to words and the reality that certain semantic categories will tend to overlap, there is a strong rationale for developing concepts for evaluation that are replicable and constant and that allow us to speak a universal language in movement observation. Critics of standardization on the other hand feel that no one system of diagnosis will ever begin to categorize the infinite varieties of human expression. Laban believed that there are four primary motion factors relating to the use of *space* (the quantitative measurement of the body's angles and patterns when moving), *weight* (the measurement of the strength and force of an action), *time* (the temporal span of a movement), and *flow* (the assessment of the continuity, pauses, and interruptions of a movement). In addition to these four categories, I am very much concerned with gestalt of a person's movement and the ways the categories of action either cohere or remain separate from one another. The assessment of transitions is especially significant, and in working with all of the arts in therapy, we are not only assessing the continuities of movement but we are equally concerned with the manner in which an expression is transferred from one sensory mode to another. All of the principles for the evaluation of movement can be adapted to the other senses because movement is a universal source for all of the arts. We observe principles such as the synchrony between the different sensory modes of expression just as we might assess the expressive integration of different body parts in the dance. For example, we might compare the effort or forcefulness of a visual symbol to the person's more general body movement, the precision and/or spontaneity of voice improvisations to body movements, the sensitivity and delicacy of expression in poetic verse to body movement, etc.

This approach to the assessment of the "effort and shape" of total sensory expression has been enormously significant in our therapeutic use of the arts. First, we discover that the evaluation of movement characteristics is as necessary in the other arts as it is in dance. For example, in the visual arts traditional psychiatric diagnostic systems tend to be unusually speculative and very one-sided in terms of seeking out psychopathology in a person's arts. Art diagnosis is usually constructed on the basis of a particular theoretical system for explaining symbolic expression. Assessments are thus focused on the projection of unconscious conflicts into the art object and rarely concern themselves with the strengths and weaknesses of tangible behavior. The traditional diagnostician overlooks *the process* of creating an artwork, which must be understood in order to fully appreciate a person's expression. The scope of art diagnosis can be greatly expanded with movement observations of effort, shape, time, flow, interaction, transition, etc. The perspectives of dance and music therapy toward time and space can be useful to art and poetry therapists in helping them to be more observant and appreciative of the closer intervals of behavior in the present. In art therapy there is sometimes too much emphasis on the symbol itself and its relation to the person's past, while the process of creation is overlooked. The very strength of art therapy, which is the creation of an art object with a fixed and continuous identity within the flux of time and space, can become a detriment.

In assessing the consistency or inconsistency of expression in different sensory modes, I regularly observe situations where a person's creative writing or drawing might be free and expanisve, while the general body movement is tight and bound. This condition is most frequent with clients whose behavior would be described as catatonic, withdrawn, and highly immobile. Whether this state is due to depression, shock, fear, or anger, the general movement characteristics are similarly stiff and labored. I have repeatedly observed how the person who is completely withdrawn in their speech and movement will express emotions through the visual arts or poetry, and in many cases as speech and movement are restored to their normal levels the poetry and art will lose their intensity. This is perhaps due to the fact that the person must in some way transform experience symbolically, if only through private and sometimes unexpressed fantasy. I have also observed clients whose ongoing behavior patterns are characterized by large discrepancies in the expressive quality of the different modes of expression. Although people who might be categorized as severely emotionally disturbed often show pronounced incon-

sistencies between the different modes of expression, this characteristic tends to be present in the behavior of many people in
society in that expressive fragmentation is a malaise of our age.
Also, in order to function in society, certain behavioral qualities
are in greater demand than others. For example, a woman that
I worked with was highly expressive and intelligent in her poetry
and paintings but severely bound and restricted in her speech
and general body movement and consequently found herself
to be quite dysfunctional in society. A common goal of total
expressive arts therapy programs is the integration of movement
and the style of expression from one communication modality
to another. Expression will be more complete and gratifying
because the person is living in a manner that actualizes the potential of the organism as a total unit in transforming experience. The
model is somewhat *classical* in its orientation to living with the
full use of the perceptual faculties, yet it is not beyond the reach
of the average person. One does not have to have *talent* in all
areas of expression but needs only confidence, which can be
developed within a supportive and trusting environment.

Another positive feature of evaluative procedures that orient
themselves to the assessment of observable movement is the way
in which these techniques lend themselves to self-analysis by the
client. In this respect the recent introduction of portable videotape equipment to psychotherapy has greatly advanced the practice of movement assessment by both clients and therapists. The
evaluation of their observable behavior generally makes more
sense to clients than the analysis of highly speculative psychological complexes, which tend to be very "foreign" to the average
person. In analyzing one's personal behavior, the diagnostic process becomes more egalitarian and mutual and draws the client
into the therapeutic relationship. The videotape recording of
expressive therapy sessions also provides tangible documentation
of both development and regression over time. Clients often see
great contradictions in their behavior through the use of videotape. A young man in his early twenties was very agitated in the
first expressive therapy sessions that he attended and enacted a
series of intensely emotional and forceful dances characterized
by aggressive, yet well coordinated leaps, turns, and vocal expres-

sions. The dance was very dramatic and finely executed from an artistic perspective. A few months later when he was preparing to leave the hospital, he had gained weight and was very slow moving as a result of the medications that he had been taking. His forceful bodily expressions were gone, and his potentially violent and aggressive behavior, which originally brought him to the hospital, had been transformed into a subdued and placid appearance. When we played back his dance of three months before, he was amazed and said that he could never do that at the present time. He left the hospital and returned again within a few months and continues to live at either of these two expressive extremes. If we had the opportunity to pursue a long-term expressive therapy program with this young man, our goal would be to help him establish a functional equilibrium within his life that does not entail the complete denial and repression of his primal feelings, which must be given regular expressive outlets.

Another more successful use of videotape recording in cooperation with movement therapy can be demonstrated by my relationship with a young man in his early thirties whom I worked with over a period of four years. We were able to save tapes of his bodily expression spanning the complete sequence of therapy sessions. I worked with this man in an experimental expressive therapy program conducted within an art museum where we met on a weekly basis. The large, sunlit galleries provided a magnificent environment for our dance and movement therapy work. In his first session with us, this man was completely nonverbal, and he would move by shuffling his feet across the floor like a robot. His posture was stiff, and he rarely would bend the trunk of his body as he moved. His body movement was sharply vertical and his passage through space was characterized by straight linear patterns. He would not move his head and his eyes would always be focused straight ahead. Changes in direction would be achieved by altering the angle of his movement.

When he first viewed videotapes of himself he would watch carefully, and his first expressions of emotion were in the form of smiles and eye movements in response to the tapes. We observed that over time he first began to move his body with some degree of spontaneity while viewing the tapes. When he began to speak with us, he described how he was constantly experiencing an intense burning sensation within his stomach and chest area that caused him incessant suffering and made it very difficult for him to move. He began to show an interest in the operation of the videotape, and we demonstrated to him how it was operated. After the third month of his participation in the program his movement was continuously rigid and *bound into himself.* At this point he expressed an interest in running the videotape machine, and we began to involve him in the recording of our sessions. The running of the videotape portapak *demanded* fairly sophisticated muscular coordination, as well as the integration of the visual, motor, aural, and tactile senses. The rather cumbersome portapak was strapped over the shoulder, the hands had to press the appropriate recording buttons, as well as manipulate the camera with its different light and focus adjustments. When operating the camera he had to follow the flow of movement within the group with his eyes and *body,* framing the action with the camera, and all the while coordinating the various movement described.

As he became more familiar with the videotape, he began experimenting with the process of "in-camera editing" and he would begin to record various thematic aspects of the group's movements, for example, hand, foot and facial expressions or a particular person whom he would follow through a group movement experience. He described to us how he forgot himself when he was behind the camera and completely fused his body with it. He said, "The pain goes away when I am shooting videotape. I am so busy concentrating and being challenged that I forget my pains and how afraid I am to move."

Toward the end of our first year of work together, this young man became quite skillful and continuously interested in using videotape equipment. The portapak involved him in a form of combined art and movement therapy. He described how the more he used the videotape, the more he forgot about his pains. The rigid and bound quality of his movement began to change gradually to a more fluid and easygoing style of moving. We felt that his intense concentration on the recording of dance movements helped him to internalize their rhythms. His verbal expressions began to develop in a parallel relationship to the visual quality of his videotapes. We discovered this man to be very intelligent, articulate, and artistically gifted person. Over time his sense of rhythm became apparent, and he began to move with a noticeably smooth and flowing sytle. He became increasingly interested in dance, and during the third and fourth years of our work together he spent less time videotaping and more time in dance and drama groups. After his second year with us the pains were gone altogether, and he began to attend the therapy sessions as a volunteer. He helped us in videotaping as well as assisting less functional clients. For me this case documents the importance of an integrated and holistic approach to the arts in therapy. From a dance therapy perspective, my experience with this man shows how the dance of life must be expanded to engage whatever objects interest a person and serve to motivate and expand movement potential.

Probably no single feature of artistic and general human expression is as consistently missing in training psychotherapists as the language of the body. The same tends to be true in the training of music, poetry, and visual art therapists. Increased sensitivity to, and understanding of, expressive movement will begin to bring into consciousness the extensive range of present and past movement experiences and memories that comprise our vast and largely untapped kinesthetic unconscious. As we begin to grow in our awareness of the expressive potential of our senses of movement and touch, we will see how they can agument the power and scope of psychotherapy, as well as our lives as a whole. The artistic consciousness is a matter of *emphasis*. What was simply an unconscious walk through space can be transformed into a dance of passage. The fundamental inspiration of the arts in therapy, both positively and negatively, is the realization that *we create our lives*. This artistic conception is contrary to traditional psychological theories of determinism. Although the environment does have a strong impact on the shaping of consciousness, there is a complementary power in each of us to shape and change the environment. In the words of Nietzsche's prophet, Zarathustra, "Valuing is creating; hear it, ye creating ones! Valuating itself is the treasure and jewel of the valued things. Through valuation only is there value; and without valuation the nut of existence would be hollow. Hear it, ye creating ones!"

Chapter 7

SOUND AND MUSIC

Most. . .lead lives of quiet desperation.

— H. D. Thoreau

WITH the possible exception of gesture and movement, sound is the sense modality that is most directly connected to the expression of emotion. Making and listening to musical sounds can be cathartic as well as gently stimulating and calming. The therapeutic qualities of music are well known to the western world where our ancient mythologies recognize the ability of music to assuage the soul. Within early Greek society, the Dionysian cult used music as a primal form of expressive transcendence and ecstasy. The later, more contemplative and rational worship of Apollo valued a more orderly approach to music and accorded this art form a place equal to that of medicine as a healing art. But, it is the Greek myth of Orpheus that provides the most vivid revelation of the spiritual and healing powers of music. The descent of Orpheus into the underworld where he calmed the wild beasts with the music of his lyre is a reenactment of the universal shamanic journey into the lower regions of life in search of a lost soul. The pacification of the dark forces that he encountered is symbolic of music's ability to calm the turbulence of inner feelings. Each of us experiences a similar descent into mysterious underworlds when we confront our primal emotions. Orpheus, son of Apollo, when playing his lyre and singing, was able to bring tears to the eyes of the Furies and soften the hearts of Pluto and Persephone, lords of the underworld. Evil activities were put to a stop by the music as the shades listened to the poet's song. Music thus summons life from the dead, calms the most aggressive of beasts, and motivates malevolent forces to act benignly toward others. What we might call the Orpheus syndrome, as well as the ecstatic Dionysian tradition, deserves a place alongside the Oedipus and Electra complexes in psychology's efforts to develop a science of behavior, which takes into account the historical continuities of human expression. This integration of artistic and spiritual realities into psychology will ultimately occur as the study of behavior evolves from its earlier, and very exclusive, focus on parental conflicts and other forms of "psychopathology." The gods that the Greeks hoped to propitiate through music are perhaps an extension of a desire to please parents, but they also represent the human longing to make contact with the personal inner spirit that exists within each of us, and collectively within humanity.

Music is referred to as the language of the soul, and as an art form it is consistently associated with spiritual phenomena. The spirituality of music is perhaps largely due to its "invisible" nature in that sound vibrations closely approximate the physiology of feelings. Music is "in the air" as are the sounds of nature, but the human element transforms these sounds to express the pathos and joy of the spirit.

ENVIRONMENTAL SOUND AND MUSIC

The use of sound in psychotherapy can include an increased sensitivity to the aesthetic qualities of the sounds of the everyday world. Through concentration alone, what was once either not heard or perceived as "noise" can be transformed into music. Whether street sounds or a squeaking door are perceived as music or noise depends on the mood and interests of the moment. Associations to pure sounds are apt to precipitate different kinds of feelings than those which are stimulated by verbal discussion. This capability, or power of the arts to expand the scope of the emotional process in psychotherapy, is one of the strongest justifications for their inclusion in all clinical programs. The analysis of the person's perceptual response to the sound configurations of the environment can also be helpful in the assessment of feelings

music or noise

and personality. The content of the associations to sounds as well as the ability, or inability, to organize auditory perceptions will reflect on the nature of thought, feeling, and emotional organization at that particular moment.

In listening to the sounds of the external environment, personal taste will often determine what a person finds to be either pleasing or distracting. One person might enjoy the mechanical sounds of the city and find the silence of the country to be depressing, whereas with another the situation might be reversed. Within psychotherapy we explore these sound preferences with clients to help them become more aware of their surroundings together with the effects of sound on feelings. We also focus attention on the intervals of silence in our experience and the sounds of the body breathing and moving through space. After becoming more attuned to the sounds of the environment, we can interact with and relate to the auditory milieu by adding new sounds or simply walking about to change the perceptual perspective.

Poets and novelists offer wonderful descriptions of nature's symphonies, showing that artistic perception is primarily a matter of sensitivity and emphasis. In *Rose and Crown*, the fifth volume of his autobiography, Sean O'Casey demonstrates how artistic perception can transfigure life by emphasizing the aural, visual, and kinesthetic dimensions of daily experiences. What for one person might be perceived as a bothersome thunderstorm was witnessed as a great dramatic event by O'Casey.

> Throughout the night they had stood there, in the open doorway, watching the rain, the lightning, and listening to God's concertina, the thunder, in full play. The square in front of them was lit from end to end with vivid, rapid-following flashes of lightning, so vivid, so frequent, that it seemed there were many mingling and whipping through each other, like a weave and warp of furious streaks of bluish light, knitting themselves together throughout the sky at the same moment; flashing the great Customs House before them in a sea of flickering light; farther off to the right, the thick and thinner masts of the ships moored to the dockside, sticking up and wavering in the bluish glow, like conductor's batons guiding the rhythms of the storm. Only for a few brief seconds, and at long intervals, did a sudden darkness ease their eyes, to give way again to the flash and the flow of the fervid lightning: so expansive as if light were enveloping darkness, and filling the firmament with luminant aggression. And through it all the rain falling, falling, diminishing at times

to a heavy shower, then rushing down again with vehement speed, slashing itself even into the portal where the two of them stood: watching God having a little play-about in the streets of Dublin.[1]

Musical exploration should start with tuning ourselves into the sounds of the physical environment and the sounds of our bodies as they move. Rather than first exposing clients to recorded music or pieces played on an instrument for them, I try to begin with an awareness of the aural characteristics of their surroundings. By first exploring the environment's sound qualities, we will be better prepared to interact with this auditory space when making our own sounds.

RECORDED MUSIC

As with dance, my psychotherapeutic and artistic orientation encourages "pure and natural sound." Other than occasionally listening to recorded music in therapy groups or from time to time encouraging a performance for the group by a musically inclined client, my work with sound and music is oriented toward exploration and the improvisational expression of the feelings of the moment through sound. I have, however, conducted group psychotherapy sessions where every week we listened to recorded music and shared our responses. Music is a rich source of personal associations, and it stimulates the recall of emotional memories. Recordings are also very useful in facilitating guided fantasy experiences. They can be selected by the therapist to precipitate certain feelings, and the sequence of the music can be arranged to first bring about relaxation and the removal of defenses. This might be followed by more intense stimulation, which can be either steadily maintained or it may build to a climax. The music could end with an emotional catharsis, which is followed by discussion and sharing, or closure might be encouraged more gradually through the music itself. Clients will at times select the music for the group with the goal of increasing the sharing and interactional process. When listening to music, which might extend from either one minute to fifteen or twenty minutes, depending on the attention span of the group, I encourge clients to become

---

[1] Reprinted with permission of MacMillan Publishing Co., Inc., from *Rose and Crown* by Sean O'Casey. Copyright 1952 by Sean O'Casey. Copyright renewed.

aware of the visual, kinesthetic, and tactile images that the sounds stimulate. In one group of adult hospitalized psychiatric patients, we were listening to a rather abstract Rachmaninoff recording and ten of the twelve people in the group associated running water to a particular segment of the piece. This experience not only consensually validated the ability of group members to relate to music that they might have previously found intimidating, but the consistency of their imagery allowed them to become deeply involved in the sharing of associations to moving water. One person spoke of her childhood living near a large river in a Massachusetts mill town; another spoke of a cabin in the woods that she had visited a few months before she was hospitalized; a young man shared his feelings about the soothing and healing powers of running water and the mythology of Lourdes and the sacramental powers of baptism through which the soul is symbolically cleansed and born again through immersion in water. In response to this discussion about water and healing, a man in the group who had lived in the hospital for many years spoke of how all of the patients would formerly receive hydrotherapy treatments in large shower rooms where jets of water shot out at them. They compared this kind of involuntary, aggressive, and coercive form of treatment to the way they have privately relaxed in, and near, water. The associations of the two people who did not experience memories of water while listening to the music were, however, similar to those of other group members in that they were evocative of comforting experiences. After discussing our responses for twenty minutes, we listened to the piece again and found that our appreciation of the music was intensified all the more through the sharing process. We also discovered in this group that the development of our abilities to discriminate sound qualities and associate emotions to them had a direct effect on our capacities to listen to one another within group discussions.

IMPROVISATION AND SOUND DIALOGUES

Although many music therapists will frequently give "music lessons" to clients to help them structure and organize their behavior and gain a sense of fulfillment through either instrumental or vocal mastery, I have never approached music therapy in this way. As with artists, expressive therapists will pursue their work with distinct styles and differences, and this multiplicity of methods in my opinion is desirable. Rather than attempting to "clone" our methodologies, we must encourge therapists to find a way of working in which they are most effective and responsive to the needs of others. My experience in training and clinical work has indicated that there will be significant differences in the way in which individual therapists integrate the arts into the psychotherapeutic process. After a childhood full of traditionally structured music lessons, I have discovered that I do not learn in this way, unless the artistic goal is simply mechanical mastery. My style of learning is through exploratory discovery processes that are related to my interests of the moment. In addition to furthering the development of technique, personal interest plays a crucial role in learning because, simply stated, we tend to remember those things in which we are interested. From a psychotherapeutic perspective, I am concerned with activities that are attentive to the expression of the feelings of the moment. My work with sound is therefore oriented toward *sensory awareness and listening skills, interpersonal and environmental interaction or dialogue, and the musical enactment of feelings and conflicts.* Sound dialogue

Sound dialogues may take place between therapists and clients, between individual group members, or between subgroupings within a larger group setting. Withdrawn and unresponsive clients can be engaged in a sound dialogue by the therapist's imitation, or "echoing," of their expressions. This process, similar to mirror movements in dance, shows people that they are being heard and acknowledged by another person. The principles and goals of sound imitations are closely related to dance therapy, and in my work they are characterized by a "eurhythmic" approach, which holds that music and movement are inseparable. It is generally true that sound expressions made with objects and instruments are more tangible manifestations of this integration than vocal improvisations, where the movement is primarily within the body. However, when observing the bodily expressions of a person while singing or making improvisational voice sounds, one will note that the whole body tends to move in synchrony with the sound patterns, giving them a visual form of expression.

Because they do not rely totally on the inner resources of the person, sounds made with objects and instruments tend to be less threatening at first than vocal improvisations. However, whether or not this is true from person to person depends upon the personality and expressive style of each client.

Physical environments are usually full of possible sources for music. As a warm-up activity we might explore the surrounding space with hands, feet, sticks, or stiff bristle brushes to determine its percussive potential. Wonderful individual and group sounds can be created by shaking and moving with unlikely musical materials such as newspaper, cloth, aluminum foil, and Mylar®. Plucking and stringlike sounds can be produced with combs and rubber bands, and wind sounds can be made by blowing into metal containers, small paper boxes, and tubes. Making musical instruments out of found materials is an interesting process in itself, but the person also tends to become very much involved with, and very sensitive to, the sounds that are made by a personally constructed instrument. It is often not only developmentally appropriate but also less threatening to initiate musical expression by investigating the sound sources within the environment before introducing instruments. Vocal improvisations can develop from sound play and dialogues with physical materials. As a person's own sounds begin to fill the space, it becomes less threatening to use the voice as an instrument. Within this context, music results from spontaneous sound interactions that begin to relate to one another or play against each other. The structure of the environment is important, and a certain amount of acoustical privacy is necessary. Within most therapeutic situations, sounds must be controlled by the flow of the therapy session. Consequently, it is usually essential for the music making to be the only source of activity within a given space. Music is in this sense different from the other arts in that a physical space cannot be simply roped off and isolated. Sound not only passes from one activity area to another on an open ward, classroom, or studio but will in some cases pass through walls and other physical barriers.

As sound dialogues proceed within a group or one-to-one context, there is typically a back and fourth, stimulus and response, give and take process that might allow clients unable to converse verbally to interact with others. One person may initiate a series of fast tapping sounds that another might repeat vocally or respond to with a series of personal sounds which were stimulated by the other's expression, after which the person who first initiated the sound expression dialogue can reply, and so forth. In a group context one person might create a sound improvisation, and other individual group members will respond when they feel that they have something to offer. Group improvisations of this kind are usually conducted in circles to facilitate the communication and reception of sound. A typical session might proceed from the differentiation of the sound sources and personalities in the group to the creation of a repetitive group rhythm. Groups tend to proceed naturally to this kind of musical equilibrium. Group sound improvisations support theories that stress how groupings of people have an innate drive toward unity. Within group improvisations, I strive toward an integration of tendencies for group cohesion and the necessity to differentiate the unique identities of individual group members.

A group rhythm promotes feelings of oneness, and it unifies people on a physiological as well as psychological level. The synchrony of sound vibrations draws people together in a manner that provides aesthetic and sensual gratification to each member of the group. With more withdrawn and fearful clients, it is important to be patient and let the rhythm continue, since they might need more time to join in a group expression. The rhythm might also reach them on an unconscious level and draw them into the group activity. Once they are engaged, I have found that rhythmic sound will energize the most passive people. The basic variations and combinations of rhythmic sounds are as old as humanity itself, and (I believe rhythm reaches to the deepest feelings of our psyches, where its pulsations bring about a sense of participation *chanting* in a primordial order.) This might at times occur through hypnotic trance states, which are achieved through focusing on repetitive rhythms. The rhythmic trance is all-encompassing, and it eliminates feelings of perceptual fragmentation through the complete participation of consciousness. A man that I worked with in a training session shared the following statement about his first drumming experience: "I felt like a shaman and enjoyed seeing people dance to a rhythm to which I contributed. There was an initial difficulty letting go, but I learned that I can express myself in a way that contributes to constructive frenzy."

Rhythmic expression is one of the most widely discussed properties of the arts in therapy. Rhythmical sounds and movements not only have a psychological effect on groups and individuals but also have an impact on the body's physiological operations. These aspects of music are reminiscent of the spiritual powers of Orpheus' lyre. Different musical instruments and rhythms have distinct psychological effects. The seductive and celestial sounds that Orpheus played on his lyre are characteristic of the auditory spell created by instruments of that type. The drum, on the other hand, reaches into the pelvic regions of the body with its penetrating vibrations, and just as early cultures used the drum to summon the spirits, so, too, the drum draws out the emotions and physical expressions in therapy groups. Drum rhythms stimulate action and outward movement, and they are associated with the inner pulsations of the body and the earth. String and wind instruments tend to have a more calming effect when they are used to create melodic sounds. They also facilitate contemplation, and where the drum is reminiscent of the rumbling of the under regions of earth and sea, string and wind instruments are often connected with the sounds of the upper regions of wind and sky. No instrument functions within a narrow and stereotypic range. Drumbeats can be very calming, whereas string and wind instruments can be used to make jarring and cataclysmic sounds, depending on the mood and expressive style of the musician. However, it is important to understand the basic emotions that can be evoked through the different instruments in order to adapt their use of the varying needs of the therapeutic situation.

With a group of six-year-old children, I worked on a weekly basis over the course of a year in creating musical improvisations. All of the three children had difficulty in working within groups, in listening, in controlling their impulses, in being sensitive to adults and their peers, and in expressing themselves clearly and appropriately. Within our group musical dialogues we were able to work directly with all of these behavior problems. After first exploring the sound materials in our environment, I gradually introduced a variety of percussion, wind, and string instruments. The children would typically experiment with the different instruments as we began our group sessions. This process resembled the tuning up period of a band or orchestra. After relating to the instruments, and each other, in this way, the children would settle into working with an instrument that suited them on that particular day. Each instrument has an unique personality, and we try to encourage a choice that will match the feelings of the children. As we began to play together and search for a common rhythm, the children's playing would at times become continuously chaotic, at which point I would intervene and attempt to create a supportive and orderly structure. If the sounds were random and quite loud, I might ask them to play as softly as they could, and out of this transition some form of cohesion would usually develop. I find that musical disarray of this type is generally due to confusion and a lack of self-confidence. I usually try to deal with the problem of sensitizing participants to sound, to their capacity to create sound relationships, and to enjoy the process. Another suggested structure for introducing order and cooperation might involve asking one child to begin a rhythm, which the others add to on a one-by-one basis. When we did this with the group of children, the activity produced a sense of excitement in that variations and new sounds grew out of a constant theme in which each of the children was immersed. Exercises of this kind involved the children in listening closely to one another as they worked in a organized and rhythmic fashion. They also developed a sense of timing and an aesthetic sensitivity as to the most appropriate and effective way of expressing themselves in a given situation. Within the structure of a group musical improvisation, there was a *negative value* placed on impulsive and egocentric expressions. The children themselves determined that sounds of this kind destroyed the group musical process. We then tried to extend this aesthetic sensibility that the children had with regard to their music to their more general social interactions, where they often perceived interruptions and impulsive actions *positively*.

In addition to letting their improvisations develop naturally, I would at certain points conduct the music by encouraging them to speed up their playing, slow the process down and gradually come to a stop and a period of silence, begin again by moving progressively from soft and gentle sounds to more intense and loud sounds, experiment with varied rhythms involving intervals of silence, and so forth. The children enjoyed the feelings of order that accompanied their working together in unison, and they liked having their sounds conducted by another person. They would take turns conducting and received tremendous gratification in controlling the group musical process. We also engaged in improvisational dialogues, where one child would direct sounds to another person, who would listen and then transmit what was received, in a transformed state, to another person, and so on. A group dialogue of this kind has qualities of ongoing continuity together with variations, which tend to result in the creating of interesting musical compositions.

SOUND ENACTMENTS AND THERAPEUTIC OPERA

Musical improvisations with this group of children invariably evolved into the expression of feelings through sound enactments, or what I refer to as therapeutic operas. As the children became comfortable in expressing themselves with musical instruments and their voices, they began to act out personal conflicts and dramas spontaneously. They would also enact their dreams through sounds that expressed the flow and emotional process of the dream experience. In expressing a family conflict, one child represented each member of the family with a different instrument and vocal sound and expressed his feelings toward them and the way he perceived them acting toward him with his musical improvisation. At one point he engaged the conga drum and xylophone in a fierce argument, which he went on to resolve musically. Another child used voice improvisations to tell the other children musically how she was feeling that day, and she went on to act out with her voice the various things of which she was afraid. Group activities of this kind are often extended by having the individual whose emotions we are focusing on engage other people in the sound enactment. Group members will act out parts in the person's emotional drama, which we refer to as a therapeutic opera when we are working primarily with music and sound. The script, or flow of action, is suggested by the person whose conflict we are dealing with, and as a group we work cooperatively to create a therapeutic enactment through sound. In my psychotherapeutic work, these sound explorations are incorporated into an ongoing dramatic structure that might at times focus more on body movement and mime, as well as the other art modalities. Sound is used in relation to the particular needs of the group. We do not always deal exclusively with the script of one person's life in our enactments. With a group of adults, we once acted out how the various people in the group felt about each other through sound. This operatic process allowed for the expression of a dimension of feeling that had not emerged from our verbal discussions.

An integration of voice, instrumental sounds, and body movement allows for a primal and very direct expression of the emotions. The power and forcefulness of these modes of expression can at the same time create difficulties. Unless it is carefully controlled, the process of making sounds conveying feelings about a person or a group can become very threatening and damaging if the sounds reach people on a level where they do not have adequate defenses and the ability to control their emotions. More often than not it is the person who is making the sounds who can easily lose control. For example, I was once conducting a sound improvisation session with a group of severely disturbed eight- and nine-year-olds in an art museum where a number of the galleries had been set aside for the purpose of conducting expressive therapy sessions in cooperation with local mental health centers. One of the boys in the group was consistently interrupting the group process with angry gestures. I thought at the time that it might be helpful to give him the space to act out his feelings fully rather than have him continuously interfere with the group activities in order to receive attention. I spoke to him and the group about how we might resolve this problem by letting him musically express his anger and thus get it out of his system. After randomly banging on a series of objects with long sticks, he let loose a number of primal screams and began to lose control. The screams were shockingly loud. Fortunately, the museum staff were supportive of our work, but nevertheless, the kind of sound that he was making was not appropriate within the museum setting. The screams not only frightened the other children but threw me and the other therapist working with me off balance. Unexpected and uncontrolled expressions of that kind tend to be as threatening to therapists as to the clients in that they jeopardize our personal feelings of order and control. In order to stop the child's scream- ing, I had to pick him up and hold him, all the while speaking to him in a gentle voice. After we had restored feelings of control within the group, I realized that primal expressions of this kind might be perfectly appropriate in a private, one-to-one session in a soundproof room, where the purpose of the therapeutic process is to help the child express primal rage within a setting where it will be acknowledged and supported. With this particular case, not only was the environment incapable of supporting this kind of expression but it was questionable whether or not the child was capable of "purging" himself of his angry feelings. His rage was so all-encompassing that he completely lost control whenever he began to express it directly. The child's anger seemed endless, and one, two, three, or four screams were not only futile in vent- ing his feelings, but they only served to stir up more conflictual emotion. From this mistake I learned that emotionally disturbed children need help in *controlling* the expression of their feelings. Anger and aggressive conflicts must be channeled through expres- sive modalities that will not overwhelm the child. In listening to this particular child's screaming, I encountered the depth and power of his pain, over which he had a very precarious control. This particular experience also taught me how primal sound ex- pression has an unique ability to disrupt social situations. The same is not true for painting and poetry, where primal rage can be expressed within more highly controlled and private structures.

In leading sound enactments and operatic musical dramas, what is needed is an ability on the part of the therapist to provide a safe and orderly environment over which control is maintained. At the same time, the therapeutic space should also encourage spontaneous and free expression. Rather than arbitrarily establish limits, the therapist should explore boundaries with each client. As harmful as primal vocal expression might be for a person who is immersed in the chaos of anger and rage, it might on the other hand be a positive therapeutic objective for the inhibited and tightly controlled person who is afraid and severely blocked in relation to expressing fundamental feelings. Each case is different, and the skill of the therapist lies in being able to relate to, and adapt, artistic expression to the needs of individual clients.

LISTENING

The process of listening is highly valued in psychotherapy for both clients and therapists. Listening skills are essential not only to hear the expressions of other people but also to tune into the rhythms and inner messages that come from within the self. As with the visual observation of gestures and movements, the listening process is not simply directed toward the content of what a person says. The more subtle features of sound expression, the texture, pitch, color, and tone of speech, convey perhaps more emotion than the actual words used. As with musical expression, a person's style of speech is a projection of personality. Sound improvisations with voice and instruments will often parallel speech patterns. A person whose speech is highly controlled, mechanical, and unexpressive of feeling will typically follow a similar course within sound improvisations. The same applies to individuals whose speech is compulsively guarded and repetitious, as well as those who exhibit a spontaneous tendency to explore sounds and not be overly concerned with the ultimate outcome.

Listening skills are essential for all therapists, especially those who work creatively with sound. The primary responsibility of the therapist is the observation of action for the purpose of making appropriate interventions and interpretations. The development of an ability to listen to the self and to others is also a fundamental goal for most clients in psychotherapy. Within our therapeutic musical dialogues, we will often work within dyads for the purpose of encouraging individual clients to participate in an ongoing process of sharing verbally with each other what they heard being expressed in their respective sound improvisations. Intellectually sophisticated clients can in this way sustain a process of sharing observations with each other. This sharing process, directed toward understanding the subtleties of sound expressions, also characterizes one-to-one psychotherapeutic sessions.

As with visual and tactile perception, auditory acuity can be developed by analyzing the structural qualities of sound expression. Figure-ground relationships are discussed by sharing which sounds stand out and attract attention within auditory expressions. Clients might also discuss similarities and differences between sounds, patterns, groupings, time intervals, rhythms, etc. Emotional qualities can be discussed in sharing the feelings that are associated with particular sounds and the attractions that are felt to certain sounds more than others. Exercises of this kind are extremely important with severely disturbed, withdrawn, or institutionalized clients who tend to need structured and highly focused activities in order to become more aware and discriminating in their perception of sound. With perceptually disabled clients these activities can become the primary focus of the therapeutic process. With more socially sophisticated and expressive clients, auditory perception exercises serve an important purpose in preparing people to become aware of the messages conveyed through sound in psychotherapy.

With musical expression, an attentiveness to and understanding of what we hear is integrally related to the perception of movements that make sound. This integration of sense modalities applies to other art modes where, with the possible exception of the visual arts, sound perception and listening play an essential role. In speaking, listening is integrated with vision and the muscular movements of the body in virtually all forms of communication through language. Therefore, the analysis of how we perceive and respond to sounds, both emotionally and intellectually, can make us more aware of how we are using our other senses. The process of analyzing sound and listening in psychotherapy invariably focuses on how we project our feelings and past experiences into what we hear. In my work with clients, we discuss the commonalities of our auditory perceptions, together with the differences. This process not only helps us to become more aware of our listening patterns and styles but tends to expand the scope of auditory perception as we become more aware of what we hear and do not hear. We also explore our respective attention spans as well as our ability to concentrate emotional energy on the listening process. As with all of the sensory modalities, we discover that the quality of our hearing is determined by the degree to which we can focus our perceptual faculties on the listening process. I must also mention how the perceptual development exercises that I have discussed here with reference to sound are easily adapted to the other sense modalities. In addition to working with our perceptual acuity and ability to discriminate between different sensory experiences, we explore memory faculties within the various sensory modalities and experiment with the transfer of perceptual configurations from one sensory modality to another.

With the therapeutic use of musical and movement expression, the perception of aesthetic relationships and meaning is an extension of personal *emphasis and effort.* Within the temporal realities of our lives, there is an ongoing flow of sound and movement with which we interact and through which we determine what will be perceived. Psychotherapy helps us to be more aware of this process and become increasingly effective in responding to the stimuli of the environment. My philosophical approach to sound in therapy is such that I believe that all musical expression is integrated with, and helps us to become more appreciative of, the sound qualities and rhythms of daily life.

MEDIA

One of the most valuable ways of becoming more aware of our sound expressions and the auditory stimuli of the environment is through the use of audiotape and videotape. In all of our music therapy experiences, various forms of taping and playback are essential in the recall and analysis of sound. Since psychotherapy, like all of the performing arts, occurs in passing time, the development of portable media equipment has enabled therapists to establish a degree of permanence in their sessions, which has added a new dimension to the analysis of behavior and relationships. With the increased availability of portable equipment since the mid-1960s, videotape has rapidly grown in use within the mental health field. The popularity and clinical significance of videotape is due to its ability to record expression and interpersonal interactions in all sensory modalities. Within the art world, videotape use has grown in a similar fashion, and I believe that the expressive arts therapist is in a unique position to integrate the strengths of the respective artistic and clinical approaches.

In my expressive therapy work, videotape has an essential place. It is often helpful to focus exclusively on sound interactions without competing visual and kinesthetic stimuli, and I find that videotape can be easily adapted to this use by eliminating the picture on the monitor screen. Since we are not restricted to working with pure sound in using videotape, I tend to prefer it to audiotape equipment because of the range of contributions that it makes to expressive art therapy sessions. In addition to its ability to record integrated arts experiences where all sensory expressions have equal value, videotape has proven itself invaluable within music therapy sessions. Perhaps most essentially it helps us within group experiences to determine who is creating the sounds that are heard. From a eurhythmic point of view, we have discovered in most cases that the perception of movement together with sound during playback increases the involvement of clients in the analysis of their expressions. Videotape has an invaluable ability to bring clients closer to their musical movements by providing close-up shots of hands playing instruments and mouths creating song. Within group improvisations, videotape records the group process and shows the role of each person, and each instrument, in creating a mosaic of sound.

The use of videotape with music therapy activities as well as with the other arts inevitably draws clients into a more general psychotherapeutic process of personal analysis. Through videotape they are able to confront and evaluate their own behavior without having to rely on the interpretations and observations of others. The *immediacy* of video playback also has a powerful effect on the therapeutic process, in that clients can either have the equipment arranged so that they are viewing and listening while they are expressing themselves, or the playback can immediately follow their expressive activity. I generally have the playback process follow artistic activity. Among other things, I have found that playback is a very helpful motivating agent. In the cases of a few clients that I have worked with over a period of six years, I have discovered that they still do not tire of seeing and hearing themselves on videotape. Extended exposure to videotape has, in most cases, deepened the person's understanding of and appreciation for the medium. Clients have over time become more discriminating in their analysis of the playback. In working with disruptive children, I have found that the anticipation of playback helps to motivate them to exercise more control over their behavior. I discovered with these children that a videotape focusing on group activities was not nearly as effective in gaining their attention as individual portraits of each child. They not only needed to focus exclusively on themselves, but they preferred the sense of order that they received from observing a series of portraits. It seemed that the orderly progression of the playback helped to introduce order into the group.

Over and over again, we have observed how a technically organized playback experience supports tendencies for order and balance in a group, whereas the fragmented and poorly structured playback tends to precipitate perceptual and emotional fragmentation. The poorly organized videotape simply does not hold the attention of the viewers. This reality has strongly influenced our determinations as to which members of the group will produce the tape that will be used for playback. For viewing purposes, we will generally use those tapes which have been shot by people who are adept in the use of videotape. With these clients who are exploring the videotape equipment, we will usually have a private playback and might, in some cases, show their tapes to the entire group.

We have also discovered that artistically stimulating videotapes will increase the responsiveness of group members. In our work we perceive the use of media equipment as an artistic process that is integrated into the totality of the expressive art therapy event. We encourage in-camera editing and the selective recording of group experiences rather than the traditional videotherapy practice of placing the camera in a stationary position and recording the entire session. The videotape not only helps to objectify the therapeutic process, but it is also a projection of the personality of the person who is using the equipment. The videotape equipment moves with the group, it changes focus and spatial perspective, and *by interacting with us* in this way, it becomes less threatening and obtrusive than the stationary camera. For the purpose of receiving the best possible sound reception, we will, whenever possible, have another person accompany the camera with a microphone.

The well-organized and edited videotape tends to intensify the therapeutic significance of the playback process. Clearly framed close-up shots increase the significance of the expression that is being recorded. Video portraits invariably bring clients into closer communication with each other because the playback process dramatizes and amplifies the individual's expression. We have found that sound amplification has enabled groups to hear from people whose vocal or instrumental expression was barely audible under normal conditions. The succinctly edited videotape provides an important alternative to either viewing the entirety of a long "verbatim" tape or searching through the tape for particularly significant interactions. We have discovered that it is more appropriate to engage in a "selecting process" while creating the tape, and this has been to the great advantage of our clients, particularly those who have great needs for order and stimulation within the therapeutic process. We will at times record verbatim tapes of particularly significant interactions. The value of the verbatim presentation lies in its ability to present the ongoing process, or flow, of expression and interaction. However, we must maintain a constant sensitivity to time, since even a well-edited tape running for ten minutes will appear to contain an infinite number of interactional qualities for analysis.

We use a variety of playback techniques to further the perception of the tape. Within music therapy sessions, as with dance therapy experiences, we might stop the action on the monitor so that participants can see still pictures of their musical movements. In playing back instrumental and vocal improvisations, we will often compare the first showing of the videotape with both sound and visual documentation to a second running of the tape with sound alone. In our sound enactments and therapeutic operas, the use of videotape is much more effective than audiotape alone, since the communication through sound is thoroughly integrated with body movement and gesture. The video playback gives participants the opportunity to live the experience for a second time from a more analytic perspective. By focusing in on significant expressions and interactions, clients are stimulated to share their feelings about the particular incident.

There are, however, times when videotape recording and playback interfere with or dilute the therapeutic process. Recording media of any kind might be inappropriate with certain private and very personal psychotherapeutic situations. In this respect, media hardware can present obstacles to total immersion in the interpersonal process. We have discovered, though, that videotape can work itself into most psychotherapeutic sessions in a nonintrusive fashion as long as the people operating the equipment are members of the group and are personally involved in the emotional process. The deciding factor seems to be the importance of convincing people that the videotaping of sessions has therapeutic value and that the use of media is sensitive to their emotions. There are also instances when we will not play back a videotape to a group because the reliving of a particular powerful experience will either distract feelings or reduce the power of the group's catharsis. The use of media cannot become routine and must be introduced, like all of the other arts in therapy, only when it can be of value to the psychotherapeutic process.

Chapter 8

VISUAL IMAGERY

*Any object, intensely regarded, may be a gate of access
to the incorruptible eon of the gods.*

—James Joyce[1]

T HE visual arts have been closely associated with
the mental health field throughout the twentieth
century. The relationship of art to psychiatry has been chiefly
determined by both the correlation of visual imagery with dream
experiences and the generally accepted belief that pictures produced by emotionally troubled people will provide tangible evidence as to the nature of the person's inner conflict. More than
any of the other art modalities, visual expression has been tied
to diagnostic practices, which have grown considerably in their
use and influence. Diagnostic art manuals are plentiful in the
mental health field, with approaches that vary from the standardized analysis of drawings of human figures, to houses, trees and
persons, families, etc. Virtually all of the traditional psychiatric
techniques utilizing the visual arts have been restricted to drawing
and painting. Closely related to these systems of art diagnosis
are the projective techniques such as the Rorschach and Thematic Apperception Tests, which engage clients in the projective
analysis of visual configurations. Rorschach inkblots are used
because of their ambiguous forms, which are considered to be
effective in facilitating the process of projecting personal and

_____

[1]From James Joyce, *Ulysses,* 1934. Courtesy of Random House, Inc., New York,
New York.

nonstereotypic interpretations, while the photographs used in the Thematic Apperception Test are chosen because of their ability to stimulate an emotional response.

In addition to the standardized drawing tests developed by clinical psychologists, there has been a history of psychiatric investigation into the supposed psychopathological imagery of spontaneous artworks produced by patients as well as the creative expressions of artists. Systems of interpretation have been developed in which certain colors, forms, textures, and subject matter represent various forms of psychopathology. These approaches to interpretation are concerned with both the psychopathology of form and content. When reviewing these practices, one will observe that they are extensions of a particular theory of psychopathology, which, for the most part, is of the Freudian psychosexual nature. These practices of art interpretation have been developed by nonartists who have adapted visual artworks to psychodiagnostic testing for the purpose of supporting their psychological theories.

From a therapeutic perspective, art's healing powers were not fully understood until experienced artists began to engage themselves in clinical work. After the publication of Hans Prinzhorn's striking book, *Artistry of the Mentally Ill* (1922), leading artists such as Dubuffet became keenly interested in the creative work of mental patients. Prinzhorn's book featured a collection of remarkable paintings and drawings produced by mental patients throughout Europe. The book was not a therapeutic study, but it did suggest the healing powers of art by describing how patients would consistently create their art spontaneously with whatever materials they could find. Prinzhorn also focused on the tendency of patient-artists to take pleasure in universal human tendencies toward order, geometric design, and ornamentation. Although Prinzhorn's research had a strong effect on the artistic movements of European expressionism and other artistic developments seeking to restore the naïve and primitive methods of natural visual expression, it was the practice of psychoanalysis and the growing interest in dream imagery that provided the strongest stimulus for the development of the profession of art therapy. As a result of this relationship with psychoanalysis, the visual arts have been

history

more closely associated with traditional psychotherapeutic practices than the other expressive art therapies.

The work of early art therapists like Margaret Naumburg in the 1940s involved the introduction of drawing and painting into psychoanalysis. The art process was perceived as an opportunity to manifest unconscious imagery. The therapist would involve the client in the procedure of verbally free associating to, and interpreting, the imagery of pictures. Although this approach closely paralleled diagnostic uses of art because psychologically, they both attributed the emergence of visual imagery to unconscious conflict, the therapeutic orientation placed its emphasis on the client's, rather than the therapist's, interpretation. When the therapist offered an interpretation, it was not presented as scientific fact but rather as a personal response, which might be of interest as well as helpful to the client.

The great strength of the visual arts in therapy can be attributed to the physical permanence of art objects. The *process* of creating art is a fleeting manifestation within time and space, as with the performing arts, but the final *product* has a lasting power that transcends temporal realities. The practical, manual, and material qualities of creating within the visual arts have a manipulative and technical appeal that can be distinguished from the other arts. In addition to its value in revealing personal symbols, the visual art object can provide a lasting manifestation of order and balance. After arranging a physical environment, picture, sculpture, or photograph into an orderly and aesthetic configuration, the person can continuously interact with the artwork as a means of internalizing its visual qualities. This psychological principle accounts for the use of mandalas, as well as views from nature, for the purpose of meditation.

As with the other arts, my orientation to the visual arts in psychotherapy is primarily focused on their ability to further the process of establishing relationships with the self, others, and nature. I am concerned with the role of vision and visual expression within interpersonal communication and the way in which what we see has an isomorphic effect on what we feel, and vice versa. The experiments of the Gestalt psychologists in the area of visual perception have been applied to the visual arts by Rudolf

Arnheim, who has demonstrated how the perception of order, disorder, beauty, and other feelings in an art object has a parallel effect on consciousness. Arnheim has also shown how we can expand the scope of visual awareness by becoming more attentive to what we see and do not see. Vision is, in this respect, one of the means by which we interact with and relate to the world, and by increasing our visual awareness, we extend and intensify our relationship to life.

Emotional crisis and stress characteristically interfere with, and fragment the perceptual process, and one of the goals of each of the arts in therapy is to restore a sense of order within the sensory modalities. Other psychotherapeutic uses of the visual arts include: the introduction of visual communication into relationships, especially in those situations where other modes of communication are not available to the person; spontaneous association to visual artworks as a means of furthering the expression of personal feelings that are difficult to share verbally; the use of the *process* of creating art as a direct expression and catharsis in venting conflictual feelings; the use of artworks as intermediary or "transitional" objects of communication between people when verbal discussion might be too threatening; the development of skills, personal competencies, and feelings of accomplishment, which can increase the person's self-esteem; and the encouragement of tangible development within a person's artistic expression as a means of furthering a more general integration of personality.

I have repeatedly observed how all of these features of the art therapy process will manifest themselves in individual cases. A woman in her late thirties was referred to art therapy within a hospital setting in an effort to draw her out of the catatonic stupor in which she was immersed. She would not speak, and her eye contact with other people was minimal. Her movements were extremely stiff, and unless she was asked to move, she would remain motionless in the same chair all day. In our first session she was reluctant to explore the art materials in the studio, and toward the end of the session, she produced a small biomorphic shape on the page. In the next session she made a composition with a number of these shapes (Fig. 12). In our ensuing sessions she began painstakingly to build geometric and floral patterns that had mandala-like characteristics. Throughout the time that we worked together, she continued to create complex and highly ornate pictures in which she would elaborate upon a shape of a figure placed in the center of the page.

Figure 12.

As she became more comfortable with the art therapy process, her pictures were more expressive of inner feelings. Instead of creating her designs around geometric or biomorphic shapes, she later began her pictures by drawing human figures. Figure 13 graphically illustrates how she used her art to express feelings that could not be communicated through language at that time. On the picture she wrote "Nobody, August ?, 1970." In a later session when she was speaking again, she described how this picture relates how she felt bound to herself within her silence. All of her tension was pushing inward, since she was, until this point, unable to vent her tension. While drawing, she heavily shaded the elbows to emphasize how they were pressing into her. The tension-filled facial expression resembled her own face when she would sit silently in the hospital.

Figures 12 through 19 courtesy of J. M. Snyder, Addison Gallery of American Art.

Figure 13.

After this picture she began to depict bizarre and devilish figures (Fig. 14). One of her most frightening (Fig. 15) was constructed in her typical style of ornamental design, but as she proceeded with the drawing, she placed a small person in the creature's mouth. After completing the picture, she became agitated and scribbled over it with her pencil. Her decorative use of line, form, and color was strikingly similar to many of the drawings included in Prinzhorn's 1922 book. I believe that this similarity is a manifestation of an universal artistic consciousness as opposed to being an indication of schizophrenic thought.

As we continued to work together, she took her art seriously and began to create drawings outside the studio as well as continuing her involvement in our therapeutic sessions. She was highly motivated to express herself visually, and she gradually began to speak when looking at her pictures. Her imagery changed from expressing fearful and angry themes during the period when she created Figure 16. The picture is of a crying woman, and like many of her other drawings with either two mouths or two sets of eyes, it can be reversed and hung in two different ways.

As her speech and body movement became more spontaneous,

she increasingly used color in her pictures, and her imagery became less frightening and more pleasant. Figure 17 was the last of her human figure drawings, and within the picture she is becoming more and more interested in the use of color, paint textures, and the overall composition of forms. Figure 18 followed her figure drawings and was produced when her art became completely immersed in carefully executed ornamental designs. When creating this picture, she was very much committed to art and enjoyed the process of working in the art therapy studio. I believe that her pictures were at this time helping her to establish control and closure in relation to the more torturous imagery that had been expressed in earlier sessions. It seemed that once she had purged herself of her chaotic and fearful feelings, she was able to appreciate the beauty of pure aesthetic configurations.

After a period of three months of expressive art therapy sessions, during which we used this woman's interest in drawing to reenergize her speech and body movement, she had completely emerged from her emotional withdrawal. Her progress through this period was inconsistent in that after working together for six weeks, when she appeared to be highly motivated to begin speaking and acting in her normal fashion, the picture that she was working on evolved into a very threatening monster image, which she violently ripped up. She began to rip up all of her previous work, and for a week after this incident she was extremely withdrawn.

Toward the end of our work together as she was preparing to leave the hospital, she found it more and more difficult to continue her art. Her visual imagery became much less intense as her language and bodily gestures were able to express feelings. She left the hopsital for a visit, and when she returned to the art studio, all she was capable of drawing was a stereotypic Christmas scene, lightly drawn in pencil and poorly placed on the page (Fig. 19). It seems that, while she was completely withdrawn in terms of language and physical gestures, she still felt a need to express feelings and transform experience symbolically. She was able to do this through drawings and paintings because they were not as threatening as verbal expression. When her language was restored, it appears that her art was no longer needed.

Figure 14.

Figure 15.

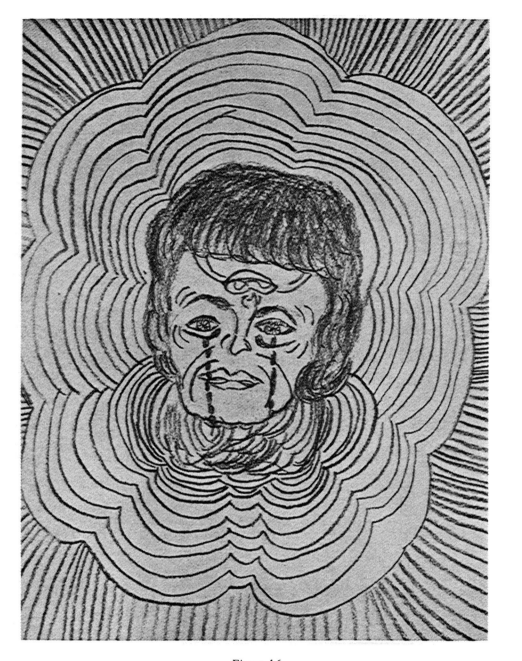

Figure 16.

Figure 17.

Figure 18.

Figure 19.

Three years after she left the hospital, this woman returned to meet with me. She described how angry she was when first admitted and how she had withdrawn because she was afraid of hurting herself and other people. Her catatonic condition was therefore an internalization of her anger and fear. It was also a form of defense, keeping her from acting on her feelings. She then went on to describe how *angry* her early pictures were and how they allowed her to release feelings in a way that would not harm anyone. She was thus able to relate to herself and her emotions through art. Her drawings and paintings became a form of *visual enactment* through which she could dramatize and free herself of anger and fear. This is not to imply that expressive art therapy permanently frees a person from conflict and tension. As with all of us, this woman's fear and anger will always be part of her. What we can accomplish in therapy is the development of a pattern for dealing with these conflicts as they occur. Although I do not wish to exaggerate or sensationalize the healing powers of the arts, I have discovered over the years that artistic enactment does have a definite *magical* power in resolving conflict. Art's enchantment is difficult to comprehend in psychological terms because it originates from a different hemisphere of the mind.

In this particular case, the woman's art served as a bridge between herself and other people while her drawing enactments were, from a personal perspective, somewhat like a magical spell through which she confronted and expelled her demons. Her art was thus able to serve many different therapeutic functions. In addition to her communicating to me through her pictures, we began to show them to other people in the hospital who expressed a similar interest in her development. Her involvement in art helped to rebuild her self-image and sense of personal value. She first spoke to me only in relation to her pictures and the process of creating them. As she mastered drawing techniques, she seemed to enjoy the attention that she received from other people and the warmth they extended to her in acknowledging her art. The drawings thus not only acted as a means by which she could express her emotions to herself and to other people, but they gave others an opportunity to relate to her.

Her visual imagery reflected inner feelings, while the pictures gave tangible and external form to the emotions. I have had experiences with other withdrawn and severely troubled psychiatric patients where a similar developmental pattern and self-emergence took place, but these emphasized artistically representing objects and people from the external environment. For many (withdrawn clients) this outward orientation is desirable in that artistic activity enables them to begin to *interact with and relate to* the outside world. A thirty-five-year-old man became involved in expressive art therapy after living in a state hospital back ward for twenty years, where his withdrawal and behavioral regression gave people the impression that he was severely mentally retarded. His records, on the other hand, indicated that he had been an "A" student and a gifted athlete but that he was also a very shy child up until his first psychiatric admission at age fifteen for serious emotional disturbances of an *wow!* unknown origin. Electroshock therapy and the general conditions of institutional living increased his withdrawal, and for twenty years he rarely spoke. He would mumble, "I don't know," in response to questions that were addressed to him. He was referred to expressive art therapy with the hope that he would become involved in some form of expressive and goal-oriented activity. At the time of his referral, he would spend his days pacing or lying in a fetal position on the hospital ward. He had over the years successfully conformed to the expectations of institutional life. He was completely dependent and never troublesome, just extremely withdrawn.

In our first session he resisted art activity, and toward the end of the session, he quickly made a line drawing of a human figure (Fig. 20). In our subsequent sessions he continued to repeat this same figure in drawings that would take no more than a few seconds. After much coaxing from me in latter sessions, he began to move away from his reliance on this stereotypic figure and showed an interest in drawing picutres of objects in the studio (Figs. 21 and 22). The structure of drawing from nature intrigued him, and he progressed over the following months to creating pictures from looking at other art objects (Fig. 23) and to making drawings and paintings of other people working in the studio environment (Figs. 24 and 25). We discovered that he had an innate graphic ability, and I continued to encourage his representational drawings. He began to introduce color to his pictures at my suggestion and went on to do much larger artworks. His subject matter became more complex as he drew pictures of interiors and landscapes (Figs. 26 and 27). Throughout my work with this man, much coaching and one-to-one contact was necessary. I would speak to him constantly for the purpose of supporting expressions that he initiated and with the goal of encouraging further development. We would listen to music while working, and he would occasionally stop for a moment and walk about the room humming. We had extensive tactile contact and in the beginning of our work, I would try to reinforce and relate to his work through touch as well as language.

Within the latter part of our first year of working together, he began to utter words in stream of consciousness speech. Some of his statements were quite dramatic. He once said to me, "I have been dead for a long time," and he went on to say, "Dr. Crush got me in Waltham. . .Waltham shocks." While talking about "getting shocked," he would hold his fingers to his temples where the electroshock electrodes were placed. He began to speak to me about his father, who had died of a heart attack shortly after he was first admitted to the mental hospital at age fifteen. With clear and intelligent handwriting, he would write the names of the people in his family, childhood friends, street names, and other neighborhood sites. He would regularly look at me, ask me who I was, and then refer to me as his father (I was ten years younger than he). Time for this man had stopped when he was first hospitalized, and he constantly referred to the year as 1953 and gave his age as seventeen, thus denying the twenty years that had passed since he was first admitted to the hospital. He did not want to accept the death of his father. At other times he would refer to himself as an infant, and he would curl up his body on the floor.

His artistic development drew significant attention within the hospital, where staff and other patients were stunned when they saw him producing sophisticated drawings. The entire process seemed miraculous to me. When he started to change in our art therapy groups, I immediately met with his mother who had been visiting with him at least one day a week over the period of his twenty years of hospitalization. She was surprised and spoke of how he always stood in a corner, paced, and never spoke when he was with her.

Figure 20.   Figure 21.

Figure 22.   Figure 23.

Figures 20 through 23 courtesy of J. M. Synder, Addison Gallery of American Art.

Figure 24.

Figure 25.

Figures 24 and 25 courtesy of J. M. Synder, Addison Gallery of American Art.

Figure 26.

Figure 27.

Figures 26 and 27 courtesy of J. M. Synder, Addison Gallery of American Art.

I continued to work closely with him on a daily basis over the four years that I was employed at the hospital. During this time I observed how his tangible growth within the visual arts gave an indication of the intelligence, aesthetic sensitivity, and human *potential* that could possibly be extended into his total being. This case more than any other in my experience taught me how the totality of a person's life must be considered in psychotherapy.

As we continued in our art therapy work, I observed his excellent physical coordination, and I began to engage him in movement activities. I noted that if I met him after breakfast every morning and did a series of physical exercises he became much more alert and motivated. After a year of this morning exercise, his body became quite trim and fit. He had a fine baritone voice that we began to develop. I would sing statements to him, and he would sing them back to me playfully. These games not only revitalized his voice but also increased his spontaneity when speaking. He had not spoken for so long that he was intrigued with the vibrations of his vocal chords, and he would feel them with his fingers while singing. After our second year of working together, he took a job in the hospital laundry and our focus changed to social responsibility, his physical appearance, self-initiated action. We were able to have him taken off a locked ward for the first time in over twenty years, and I met regularly with his mother and brother during their weekly visits. He began to speak with her and kissed her regularly showing genuine affection. Being a devoutly religious woman, she was convinced that this was a miracle.

We continued with his art, and I tried to extend his creative expression into the other art modalities. In addition to reading literature, we would read the newspaper in the morning. It took more than a year for him to stop reading the date on the newspaper as 1953. As he continued to expand the range of his expression and his social interactions with other people, I went one day to eat lunch with him and observed his rather barbarous eating habits. With the financial support of his mother, I began to expose him to the "art of dining" at a number of different restaurants. The going was at times very difficult, but his prevailing interest in eating turned out to be a strong motivation for developing social skills. As his behavior outside the hospital continued to improve, I began to take him to visit with his mother at home on a regular basis. All of this progress was not without incidents. He walked away from a summer camp that we brought him to and was returned to the hospital by the state police, who had found him walking along a major highway. Much to our surprise, the police said that he was very cooperative and clearly gave them his name. Instead of giving the hospital as his address, he gave them the street number of the house that he grew up in as a child. This incident and a number of similar events took place during a period when he was not quite sure whether or not he wanted to give up his defense of withdrawal into himself completely. I also think that he was trying to show us that he could be independent and initiate bold actions on his own in response to feelings he was experiencing. This was evidenced one evening when he ran away from the hospital after we had a disagreement in the art studio.

For the four years that I was employed at the hospital, we continued to work together closely. After leaving, I saw him once a week for four years in an expressive therapy group that we held at the Addison Gallery of American Art. These therapy sessions allowed us to maintain our relationship, and I was able to engage him with a number of new expressive therapists who were participating in the group as trainees. The weekly sessions also allowed us to sustain his artistic expression, but as time went on, it appeared that the development of his ability to relate to others became more important than the drawing of pictures. He was also personally interested in relating closely with the other staff; so we involved him more in drama, movement, and activities focused on interpersonal communication. It seemed that the visual arts were associated with his relationship with me, and he was not as motivated to paint with other people. Each of his new relationships thus developed its own rhythm and communication style.

However, we observed that without the daily attention I gave him at the hospital he began to regress somewhat in the institution. I was able to interest other therapists in working with him, and they have continued many of the rituals and activities that we did together. To this day there are expressive therapists at the hospital that I communicate with in an effort to help them relate effectively with this man and to help me maintain my relationship with him.

As a result of our work together, I was able to confirm my belief that art therapy can involve activities that range from helping this man appreciate the aesthetic component of shaving in the morning, to relearning how to ride a bicycle, to riding through a forest and discussing what we see, hear, and feel, to artistically enacting the emotional conflicts that brought him to the hospital over twenty years before, to sharing feelings about how he is feeling about developing relationships with other people, beginning to communicate again with his family, and so forth. Our work together over the past ten years has involved so much that I have not been able to describe here. What I have decided in evaluating our relationship is that our accomplishments first grew from a shared interest in art, which began to change his image of himself. The visual arts provided a *transitional* mode of interacting with another human being in a context that demanded more of him than the perfunctory patterns of institutional life. As other modes of relating developed, we maintained out work in the visual arts but interacted in many different ways. This case taught me that what withdrawn institutionalized patients need desparately is *attention within a caring relationship.* They need another person to begin to take an interest in *their total life process.* This is dramatically absent in our mental health institutions for severely disturbed people. As we began to make real progress within our relationship, my goal was to help him extend his trust and capacity to communicate to his family and other people within the hospital. I discovered that changes in his behavior were perhaps largely due to my perseverance rather than skill. I believe that he also experienced genuine enjoyment within our expressive therapy sessions, and he simply found that there were some things in life that were worth coming out of himself to experience. Another crucial factor within our relationship was the effort we made to work outside of the institutional environment, which placed so few expectations on him to express himself and relate to other people. I believe that it was not possible to delineate where his supposed psychosis began and ended in relation to what I perceive as the psychosis of the large mental hospital environment, which is one completely cut off from the realities of life outside and incapable of helping individual patients to lead creative and independent lives. No matter how dedicated and skillful individual staff members were, they were still forced to work within the psychosis of an environment that rarely supported their efforts.

While working as an expressive art therapist within a state hospital setting, I had a number of similar interpersonal experiences where growth within the medium of visual art precipitated development within the whole person and furthered the development of the therapeutic relationship. I also discovered that the process of giving attention and feelings of concern to another person within a creative and mutually fulfilling relationship tended to be the single most important aspect of our work together. The value of techniques and experiences in arts therapy is not to be denied, but the major and most important ingredient in all forms of psychotherapy is the interpersonal relationship and the quality of feeling transmitted to the other person. The arts are so valuable because they extend and enrich the emotional process in therapy. I have found in my own work that one of the greatest dangers facing the arts in therapy field is the excessive concern with *techniques and methods*. I believe that new technical methods are valuable in psychotherapy only if they are introduced with full respect for the primacy and ever present process of feeling and relating.

Another man, who was age fifty-six and who was for thirty-five years a state hospital patient, began his involvement in expressive art therapy on a much higher functional level. After two years of work in developing his artistic skills and his general self-image, he left the hospital to live in a community residence. It has now been six years since he left, and he continues to maintain himself outside the institution. As in the previous case, this man's intelligence and aesthetic sensibility were first made manifest through art. When we began to work together, he was completely dependent on the hospital, and this institutionalization was his major emotional difficulty. He could not conceive of living anywhere else. The thought of leaving the hospital was very frightening, and he would begin to act inappropriately whenever that possibility was suggested to him. He resisted all therapeutic programs and spent his days wandering about the hospital grounds.

It was this wandering that first brought him to the art studio. He joined our open studio sessions by standing off to the side and observing the various art activities. He would not participate in our group art therapy sessions and began on his own initiative to draw with pencils and watercolors in an isolated corner of the studio. His first picture was of a stereotypic Christmas scene that he drew over and over again, as many as fifty times (Fig. 28). He then went on to repeat numerous mandala designs, varying them slightly as he went along. During a session some months later, I observed a picture he was drawing of his pack of tobacco. The picture was quite interesting, and I could see that he had the potential to begin drawing from nature. I supported this new direction in his art, and he went on to draw personal representations of commercial designs and artworks painted by well-known artists (Figs. 29, 30, and 31).

Figure 28.

Figure 29.

Figure 30.

Figure 31.

This process of responding to the art of others was a transitional stage, yet his work was consistently original and uniquely expressive. As he became more confident and spontaneous in his drawings, I encouraged him to begin to focus his attention on real objects and people in the studio. The process of drawing other people was an important social event for him. He was in control of the flow of interaction, people were attentive and interested in his actions, and the eye contact, together with the general energy between him and the person that he was drawing, was quite intense. The drawings themselves were remarkably inventive and stimulating (Figs. 32, 33, and 34). He also produced a series of self-portraits, where he made the same kind of perceptual and emotional contact with himself (Fig. 35).

Within the art studio, he developed a reputation as a fine artist, and after a year and one-half of expressive art therapy, I began to exhibit his art outside the hospital in leading galleries. His art received significant critical attention by Boston's two major newspapers, and the public response to his work was enthusiastic and supportive.

Figure 32.

Figure 33.

Figure 34.

Figure 35.

All of the various aspects of the art therapy process helped to transform his self-image. He became more interested in life outside the hospital, and I would try whenever possible to take him with me on trips into the community. On a number of occasions, he left me unannounced and spent three to four days exploring the outside world before returning to the hospital. The staff supported these explorations, and we interpreted them as an indication of an interest in leaving the institution. After two months of preparation, he did leave the hospital.

As with the case described before this one, the art therapy process stimulated a more complete and total development of the self. What I feel must be emphasized is that, although significant, *the process of these two men in art therapy was but a part of the total psychotherapeutic process.* Because of their permanence and "visibility," the end products of visual art therapy can overshadow the ongoing process of the relationship. I do not wish to imply that the creations of these men in the visual arts were hierarchically more significant than their expression in the other sensory modalities or that any form of art can be separated from the total interaction patterns of human relationships. The process of writing this book has helped me to abandon any bias that I may have once had toward a particular medium of expression. I realize that a case study that I may have presented to an art therapy audience could be cast in a different light were I to emphasize the kinesthetic, aural, or poetic aspects of the relationship. All of the sensory modalities manifest themselves in each clinical case, and what is needed is increased sensitivity on the part of the therapist to the many forms of communication taking place within every relationship. It seems to me that it would be a clinical omission to overlook them. I understand now that my previous publications stressing one modality more than others were conceived in response to the expectations of my audience, whose values were very specialized and did not emphasize the integration of the arts.

This integration of all modes of expression and interpersonal activity tends to occur naturally and nearly effortlessly when working with children. The young child's expressive faculties have yet to go through the socialization process, which separates and isolates them from one another. For me, psychotherapy is a form of dramatic enactment, and this philosophical orientation has been an outgrowth of my experience with children. Six-and seven-year-old children have contributed enormously to my understanding of how the arts work together in therapy. *The different art forms merge into the greater totality of the psychotherapeutic relationship, which provides me an example of how life and art can be completely unified through human consciousness.* I do not wish to suggest that art and life can be integrated more effectively in psychotherapy than within other spheres of human activity. What I wish to emphasize is that my personal attitudes toward the separation of the arts were changed as a result of my work with children. Because of the spontaneity and expressiveness of most children, I have been able to act in a more *responsive role* with them than with adults, who generally need a much more structured approach to artistic activity. Many adult clients demonstrate this openness, flexibility, and self-initiative, but these tend to be an exception to the rule. The children have, in this regard, helped me to have a better understanding of what adults are lacking in their expressive behavior.

One of my most instructive experiences with children evolved around a relationship that I had with a six-year-old boy. This child was not considered emotionally disturbed, but he experienced considerable conflict and anger in relation to the death of his father in Vietnam when he was only four months old. This child's art, storytelling, movement expressions, and fantasy enactments consistently dealt with themes of war and death. In this respect he taught me a great deal about how children today are consistently acting out ancient mythological themes. He was a very bright child with an active and imaginative intellect. I was able to meet periodically with his mother throughout our work together, and our mutual assessment was that the loss of his father confronted this child with emotional realities that most young children do not face. This consequently gave him an unusual philosophical depth. At the beginning of the first grade school year, when all of the other children were expressing how they wanted to learn more about dinosaurs and how to read, he told the teachers that he would like to know more about "God and war."

I began to work with him while exploring the use of the expressive art therapies within a public school. In my first visit to the classroom for the purpose of observation, he walked up to me and introduced himself and immediately showed an interest in me. As it turned out, the teachers were considering him as a referral for expressive therapy because they felt that he could benefit from a relationship with a man and that he needed an ongoing expressive outlet for his feelings. Although he was doing well in school from an academic standpoint, he would attract attention to himself by pushing other children and interrupting discussions. He consistently wanted to control group process through disruption of the flow of activity. The teachers felt that an expressive art therapy relationship with me would not only allow him to vent aggressive feelings but would give him the kind of concentrated attention that he needed.

For the first two months of our work in the school year, we worked alone within the informal environment of his classroom. It was an open space with many different activities taking place simultaneously; so we were able to blend into the more general flow of classroom activity. Our work together was geared toward drawing, storytelling, and building a relationship. Within this short period, he openly discussed, on his own initiative, his feelings about his father's death and immediately developed a fatherly transference reaction toward me. My feelings of countertransference were equally strong because he very much resembled my own son. Within this first stage of our relationship, we were able to share and deal with the source of his emotional conflicts, and it appeared that it would be more helpful to him if we could begin to work within a small group setting, where attention could be focused on the behaviors that caused his difficulty in the classroom.

At this time we invited two other six-year-old boys to join us in our weekly sessions. One of the children was also fatherless, and the other's father was absent from the home as a result of a divorce. When the two boys joined us, we began to have our meetings in a room adjoining the classroom, where we could freely express ourselves with musical instruments and engage the whole body in forceful dramatic enactments and movement experiences.

I will continue to focus my attention on the child whose father died in Vietnam and summarize his development throughout the year within both individual and group sessions. Although my intent was to bring together three boys who were perhaps all feeling similar feelings of loss in relation to their fathers and whom the teachers (who were female) felt could benefit from an ongoing relationship with a man, he was the only one of the three who directly expressed feelings about his father, and this was done largely within our one-to-one sessions. Within the group sessions, I believe that he was continuously dealing with his father's death and absence through the means of mythological and fantasied enactments ranging from *Star Wars* and outer space battle pictures to personal dream imagery and heroic adventure stories. Over the course of the year, the expressive art therapy process did not precipitate dramatic changes in his behavior, but it did provide him with a regular means of communicating and expressing feelings. Through an integrated arts approach, he was able to experience fully, relate to, and share the intensities of his emotions.

In our first sessions together in the classroom, he drew a picture of his family, without any direction from me, and as he worked with his felt tip markers, he told me, "I like markers, but I like you best. . .because you're a man. I never saw a man before, except when I was a baby." He then described the figure that he was drawing as his father and told me that he wanted me to get to know his friends so that they could come and ask me to play with them. I was very impressed with the first session because he was able to control the flow of our interpersonal process, and he was immediately able to articulate the feelings of transference that he had toward me.

In our next meeting, he spoke of how he dreamed of marriage and of how people get married "because they want to see their baby so much. They want to see how he looks, how cute he's going to be. They want to see him because they think he's important to them. . .At night parents fear that their children will die." In our third session he once again articulated feelings about the death of children and parents. "I'm going to worry about if a baby is sick and dies. . .if there is someone you love the most, sometimes I like someone and they die and then those people who are killed don't feel so well. . .people who are dead are dead and can't do anything about it." I asked him a few minutes later that if he could change anything what would it be? He replied, "I would be God so I could be anything."

In our subsequent sessions he continued to draw picutres and tell stories about death and "killing." He said, "Nobody wants to be dead, nobody wants to be dead, nobody will be dead. . .I don't want to be dead, but I am dead. Webs will come on my grave. Nothing makes any sense." In these first meetings with me, he was not only dealing with the loss of his father, but as is commonly the case with the death of a parent, he was experiencing his own mortality. I believe that he was role reversing with his father in trying to understand what it feels like to be dead and to miss children and family. I think that he affirmed his own existence by fantasizing how his parents would miss him if he were to die. In these sessions and throughout our year of work together, he also tried to understand the significance of death, its meaning, and why people kill each other. He would not only role play his father during battle enactments, but he would also take on the role of the person, or people, who killed him.

Although he exhibited great strength in sharing these feelings, his fear was persistent from week to week, and there were only one or two sessions during the Christmas season when he did not deal with death in his art. At times his imagery was quite ominous. For example, in one of our earlier sessions he began to draw a picture of a box and said, "The box is going to get my brother and me. Everything will be different. We will have to live in it. It is dark." Our first two months seemed to be a period of catharsis for him. In addition to revealing his fears of death, he was able to describe why he gets into trouble in the classroom. "I didn't get enough attention. I really want it when I do not get it. I get angry and hurt kids because they don't give me attention. . .so I trip them. Fathers get attention, sons don't. Babies always get attention." It appeared that at times he almost resented the attention that his dead father got, while he is left with no response. The reference to babies getting attention is consistent with the baby-like behavior that he often exhibited at school and at home in order to get attention.

Figure 36, one of the first pictures that he drew with me, demonstrates how all of his creations ultimately relate to the theme of death. He began the picture as a tree house and went on to draw vines growing all over it. He said, "The vines are bad for wood. They kill it." He then told me, "It was a perfect day when we met. I have fun with a man like you. It's all new." He then turned his tree house into "a candy house with a witch in it at midnight." After this he initiated a dramatic enactment and described how "the biggest star is a magic star. It makes every wish come true. It makes you rich and kills the witch." After this statement, he drew a witch helicopter on the left side of the picture and told me that his father flew jets and helicopters when he was in the war. While I was tying his sneaker at the end of the session, he kept saying, "Killing is terrible."

Figure 36.

His more diffuse feelings and expressions about war and death were most focused in a series of pictures that he drew during a session after we had been working together for a month. His first picture, Figure 37, was one of his typical *Star Wars* images. This session and others that followed showed how what might appear to be stereotypic imagery often has very personal significance. *Star Wars* as a mythology of life and death, war and peace, good and evil, heroes and villians, etc. helped him to explain the cause and meaning of his father's death. My work with this child has helped me to see the mythological value of images and enactments that on first glance seem to hide personal revelation through the use of cultural stereotypes. The sequence of pictures and dramatic enactments that he created in this session seemed to help him to clarify and articulate the feelings that he had about his father's death, and afterwards he did not have as great of a need to talk directly about his father. In response to Figure 37 he described how "the ships are fighting. They're getting killed. I feel scared. My dad went on a battle cruiser, something stupid, he got killed. There was this bad guy in front who wanted to kill my father. He said, 'Go forward,' and my father got killed by the spaceship." In this picture there is a complete integration of the *Star Wars* mythology and his father's death.

Figure 37.

He went on to describe his feelings about the picture. "I'm in a fight because I do not know anything about my dad. I love spears because they're tough. I want to know more about him. I want to be a hero."

As the session progressed he did two fantasized pictures of his father as an elevator man at a shopping center. He went on to create a fourth drawing (Fig. 38), which started out as a picture of dinosaurs. At first I thought this might be a stereotypic covering up of the feelings that he had started to express about his father, but as he verbally dramatized what the picture represented, it was again demonstrated to me how important it is to reserve hasty judgments about apparent stereotypes. "This is a picture of dinosaurs and my father. My father is getting all the dinosaurs. They have hearts. [All of the picture was drawn with blue except for the hearts, which were colored red.] He's getting the bones for dogs. The big dinosaur is going to chomp him. He's going to get killed. He's picking up his body. My father was holding a book, but he dropped it. He just ate my dad. The dinosaur says that tastes cool, but should I have eaten him or not? My father opened the dinosaur's jaw and got his parachute, and got free, and jumped down. He hollered help. That's his pants, shirt. . .his pants are slipping off. Now he's getting so close to the other dinosaur."

Figure 38.

This was a truly remarkable enactment of his father's death. He utilizes the mythological structure of a hero being over-whelmed by forces beyond his control. The battle can be likened to Ahab and the white whale and other universal themes. Like Jonas being freed from the belly of the whale, his father escapes, but this resurrection is only temporary, as he confronts the finality of death by falling into yet another dinosaur. In this picture he also attributes feelings of ambivalence to the dinosaur after "he" ate his father.

Figure 39 is typical of a series of subsequent pictures in which he acts out frantic battle scenes without directly speaking about his father. "It's a rocket ship getting ready to blast off. It's in trouble because it's going to explode and there's a mini–ship on the nose that they'll get into. The bad ship (on the left) is going to kill them because bad guys hate good guys. They're going to laser them. The bad guys are going to win. They always do. They

They have more stuff. The bad guys ruined the whole ship because they just wanted the gold door. People fight for babies, bad stuff, and everything. People kill each other."

Figure 39.

In Figure 40 he drew a series of graves and introduced Jesus as the mythological hero. "I'm making graves all bent over. It is very interesting for you to learn about. I'm going to add Jesus. He's got arrows pointing into him. These little men, little ants [note mythological parallel to Gulliver] are trying to kill him and put him into the biggest of the graves. I am thinking all the way back in time. They stabbed him with a knife in the heart. He's dead, but he's in your mind all of the time." I asked if there was a reason for his death, and he answered, "Yes, he was trying to kill them, so they killed him. . .If people want to make war, they can. The spaceship [left side of picture] is trying to kill the ants, but they're too small, and it got Jesus, the god, by mistake." In this picture and the accompanying dramatization, he is beginning to come to grips with the realization that his father was an equal partner in the life–death struggle and that both sides were perhaps trying just as hard to kill each other. He also introduces the possibility that the hero may have been killed by mistake.

Figure 40.

He dealt with this theme again in the following session and made a picture that he described as, "A captain from long, long, ago like my dad. He sometimes wrecked his life himself. He used bombs to wreck other ships, and they bombed his ship. The iron face killed my dad. It's a metal ball type ship, and everything bounces off it. But this isn't my dad. Here's his grave. I'm going to make his grave. He's dead. The man who killed my dad is floating away."

In a later session that we began with movement and dramatic enactment to the theme of "under," he began his movement expression with yet another mythological enactment of death with the evil force embodied in the form of a snake. He told the following story about Figure 41: "The bad guys threw a ball down into the sea and put a snake and tarantulas into it. They wanted to kill people who went diving and would eat the poison by mistake. That's my uncle swimming. If he was Superman he could see what was inside the ball. He's going to die, not in real life but in the picture. It's interesting to me. Everybody likes to know about dead people. They go to the graveyard and pray and draw pictures of how they died. I like it when they were alive, but they are dead now. The people who are left alive hurt themselves because they're so angry. They want to be with those dead people."

Figure 41.

After this picture he began to become more closely identified with the hero. In Figure 42 he is the one who kills the snake who is about to kill the queen. His most forceful, aggressive, and violent enactment came in the following session, where we began by letting the children take me along with them in their movement dramatizations, and they could do with my body what they pleased. I believe that I served the purpose of taking on the role of the evil monsters that he constantly confronts in his pictures, and the real physical contact with me intensified his emotion. He drew Figure 43 afterwards and described it to me. "In my picture you're deadly, a giant. I have wires connecting your brain to mine. I am taking your memory to know what you were back in time, to know who you killed. I want to take all of your brain. The army is shooting at you because you're deadly. You're wicked angry because we are attacking you. You picked up the general and chewed him up and spit him out with his guts and all. I got hold of all the cannons and pressed all the buttons. They went mad. I knew everything you do. I knew everything you do. The best way to kill him is to pull down his pants in front of a firing squad. I know everything you do."

Figure 42.

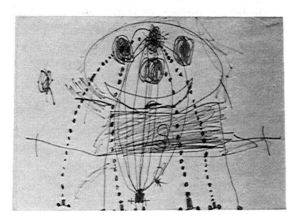

Figure 43.

In this picture and in Figure 44 that he drew in one of our final sessions, he is assuming control and power over a variety of mindless forces. He said that he was drawing monsters over and over again "because I have to get it out of my mind. Then I don't think of it anymore." In Figure 44 he is completely victorious over the evil forces and portrays himself in a massive representation of muscles and blood. "The grizzly wants to kill people and Godzilla comes along and all the people cheered for him and raised a flag. They shouted for him, and he made trees fall down on the grizzly. He breathed fire on him."

Figure 44.

With that final session we ended our year of work together. I received a phone call from his mother two months later during the summer, and she asked if I could see him again because he appeared to need the regular outlet for his feelings that was provided during the expressive therapy sessions. She said that during the year he was able to express his feelings with her, whereas in the past he would contain them. From time to time he would have uncontrollable emotional outbursts. We met, and he said that he missed me, and I said the same to him. At the end of our session he summed up our work together in a statement that I cannot improve upon: "It's good to get your feelings out. You tell people how much you feel so they'll understand and share their feelings with you. You're supposed to let feelings out so other people will know how you feel. Life doesn't just belong to you but to other people too."

With many children and adult clients, I have observed how in addition to allowing for the enactment of emotional dramas the visual arts provide the opportunity to create sensually pleasing objects. I would like to describe a ten-year therapeutic relationship that I have had with a woman in her midthirties whose approach to art is oriented toward experiencing beauty. This woman is a serious artist whose creative expressions have consistently been the most stable part of a difficult life. Two years ago she left a state hospital environment, where she had lived for her complete adult life, to live in a community residence. During her childhood and adolescence, she lived in a variety of schools and clinical settings for emotionally troubled children and had therefore spent her entire life within mental health institutions. In this particular case the woman, whose name is Priscilla Hathaway, would like to be mentioned by name so that she may receive the recognition that she deserves for her artistic achievement.

Priscilla is active in all forms of artistic expression. In addition to her work in the visual arts, she writes poetry, composes music, and dances with great enthusiasm. I will focus my attention here on her painting, with which she has been deeply involved since adolescence. Priscilla first became committed to art while attending a therapeutic school, which emphasized creative expression in its curriculum. Although her art was supported during her schooling, she received little formal training. She became aware of the more general world of art by reading art history books, and she is particularly drawn to the work of Van Gogh, Gauguin, and Georgia O'Keefe. Within her paintings Priscilla has created a bright and vivid world of color and sensual action that contrasts sharply to the austere state hospital environment that she lived in when creating her art. Her pictures are often religious, and they enact universal mythological themes of physical and divine love, good and evil, deliverance from suffering, and the glorification of human beings and the family. She would regularly describe to me how she could not have love and happiness within the institution setting and therefore created it for herself in her pictures.

Priscilla has referred to her pictures as her children and says that the artistic process for her is characterized by both struggle and fulfillment. "When I start a picture I'm afraid that I'm going to fail or goof up. But when the picture is halfway through, I begin to enjoy it. I start to see that this goes here and that goes there, and so on. It's like a mother carrying a child in her womb. She never knows whether it will be born deformed or a beautiful, healthy baby."

Figure 45, which Priscilla calls "The Kiss," is a very conscious sublimation of her desire for a close relationship with a man. "This is a symbol of my starvation for a man in my life. A man to love, and to be friends with, and to have me, and give me his all. No man ever loved me in this world, so I turn to men in artwork."

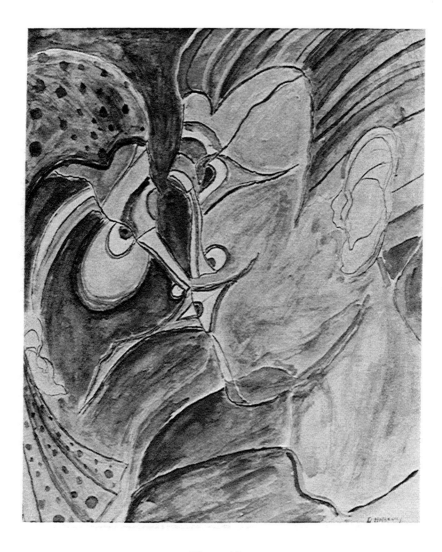

Figure 45.

In response to my question as to why she made art, Priscilla shared this statement with me: "When I make art, I forget my pain, and I feel closer to artistic men and women and to the Lord, who is the first creator. . .artists are special people because they are always creating beautiful things for others to see. Art is for me an escape from one world into a more perfect one. . .art helps me

Figures 45, 46 and 47 courtesy of J. M. Snyder, Addison Gallery of American Art.

to feel relieved from my feelings of guilt and self-abuse. When I
create new shapes and forms I feel a sense of accomplishment. It
makes me feel important and just as good as the next person. . .
art gives me a sense of freedom. My mind is not captivated by the
worries of the world when I am working. I think art is God's
world. . .when I am sad, I can look at one of my pictures and see
beauty. . .when sharing my art with others, I feel important,
secure and among friends. I do not want to spend my whole life
locked up in a mental institution. I am the master of my own decisions when making art."

Priscilla's art has repeatedly served as a means of escape,
and she consciously uses creative activity to find freedom and
beauty within herself during periods when these feelings are conspicuously absent in her relationships with other people. Now that
she is living outside of the state hospital, art continues to play a
primary role in her life. The process of creation and the pictures
that she produces help her to deal with feelings of loneliness and
isolation from other people. At the same time, her reputation as a
fine painter has dramatically strengthened her self–esteem. Prior
to her leaving the hospital, we were able to exhibit Priscilla's
art in galleries, at universities, and at professional association
meetings across the United States. The support and attention that
she received helped her to begin to place more value on herself,
her life, and her sense of what she has to offer to other people.
Because of the time she spent within various psychiatric institutions and the resulting negative effects on her self-image, Priscilla
needed the concrete reinforcement that she received from other
people through her art. People would send her letters, poems, and
other communications, which were in themselves an important
form of therapy, perhaps more important than I realized at first,
because Priscilla was for the first time consistently receiving the
message that she had much to give to people outside of the institution and that they would respect her for her art. Over the years
that we had worked together, she was always insecure, and from
time to time she was very confused about how other people were
perceiving her. Her art served as an aesthetic antidote to these
sometimes overwhelming emotions.

Figure 46 is a picture that expresses her feelings about childhood and community. She created the picture while living within

an urban psychiatric hospital, and she described how during her own childhood she briefly felt the feelings of happiness associated with the picture. Figure 47 is one of the hundreds of drawings and paintings that she has done describing mental hospital environments. In this particular picture, she is trying to transform the bleak and harsh exterior of the hospital into a world of vibrant color and forms. In other pictures she would direct her art toward observing people in the hospital. Figure 48 is a portrait of a man who worked with us everyday as a client in the art therapy studio, and Figure 49 is a self-portrait expressing her passion for music. Love for her mother and "all of the beautiful women in my life" is the subject matter of Figure 50. Figure 51, which she calls "Conspiracy," portrays men planning to deceive and kill Christ. Her pictures also create beautiful and pleasant imaginary places, such as those shown in Figure 52 and Figure 53. I believe that Priscilla's deepest longing is expressed in Figure 54, which represents a family enjoying each other by the shore where a boat symbolizes deliverance and escape from the cruel and painful world of inner emotions and conflict.

Since I have known Priscilla, her art has been completely self-initiated and self-sustained. In my relationship with her, I believe that I am perceived as a fellow artist who has a deep appreciation for her art as a symbol of her total self. Prior to my meeting Priscilla, her art was of interest to staff members at the hospital, but they would refer to her pictures as a representation of psychotic imagery. They felt that since she had many personal difficulties, her art was but another manifestation of psychopathology. Because they were so negatively conditioned by pathological approaches to art, it was difficult for the staff to perceive the intelligence, strength, and imaginative depth of Priscilla's expression. Throughout my work with her, I have tried to fill her role expectations of my being an artistic colleague. This role has actually come quite easily in that the seriousness and originality of Priscilla's expression inspired me on an aesthetic level. Her art would stimulate my personal creative expression, and I would often share my work with her. Over the years of our relationship, we have been able to interact and communicate with each other through the visual arts, and this interpersonal exchange has served as a source of ongoing artistic motivation for both of us.

Figure 46.

Figure 47.

Figure 48.

Figure 49.

Figure 50.

Figure 51.

Figure 52.

Figure 53.

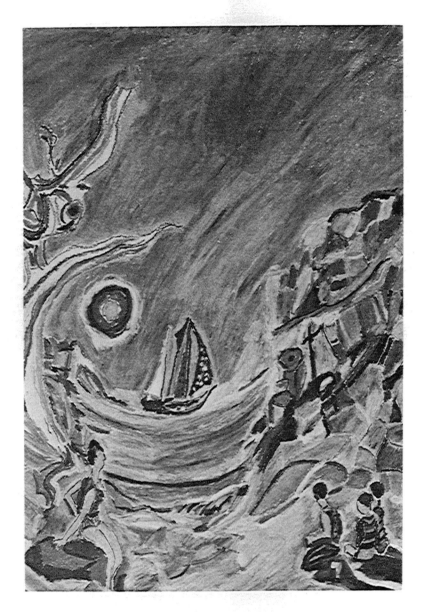

Figure 54.

In our work, Priscilla was able to carry on a relationship that emphasized her artistic strengths and made her feel very important. No matter how disturbed she might have been on a given day, she could always develop a sense of control, order, and personal meaning through her art. It was thus an absolutely dependable form of communication. Priscilla took great pleasure in my continuous excitement about her art, and she felt that our relationship evolved around, and recognized, her most personal inner imagery. As we continued our work together in art, and as her trust in me developed, I found myself taking on a new role as her primary therapist and friend. Our artistic relationship became the focal point and central axis of her life. I became involved in all aspects of her treatment program while she was in the hospital and have served as a consultant to her since she left to live in the community. We discovered that it was very appropriate for Priscilla to center her life and her future plans around art. With her talent and commitment to the creative process, she can continue to grow and expand as an artist and be secure in the realization that she can continue to make a rich and valuable contribution to the lives of other people while finding her personal fulfillment in art.

Priscilla asked me to be sure to include her poetry in this book. She creates poems with an intensity equal to her visual art. The subject matter of her poems and pictures is consistent, and they tend to reinforce one another. Her poetry is also strikingly visual and her poem "City Child" offers an appropriate conclusion to this chapter on visual imagery as well as a passionate beginning to the following chapter on drama, with the poem reinforcing my belief in art as dramatic enactment.

City Child
The lonely city is stained with dust.
The cold wind blows in from the sea.
The wind cries out: Come! Oh come, warm daughter
Sweet, with an angelic face.
Blare your golden fiery trumpet!
Sing the blues in every lonely city street.
Give the soiled workmen soul food.
They sing low with strong, stout hearts.
Tired babes are crying by the market sides. . .
I sigh: yes God, I notice them.

A fat flock of speckled pigeons,
Feathers as soft as the wings of butterflies
Are stirring the torn papers with flapping wings. . .
I sigh, deep inside: God grant me wings!
I long for the end of the road, where paradise begins.
A new land, stirred by the fire of love's allegiance;
the fire of poetic artists, friends of whom I once
Chanting, hailed like soft-caped royal deities,
Like kings and queens of another world, the
Land of creativity, the blood roots of sweet sensitivity.
That love star of infinity. The Union of grand liberty.
I listen to the trumpeteers play their silver trumpets.
Their music makes me want to cry. Their music makes me
Long to soar. Their sweet wild tunes make me long to
Rest my tired head on my departed mother's lap again.
The clapping of the people's hands makes me want to draw
Forth a lover. So mad are my desires, so starved is my
Passion. But I stand alone. Is this really my freedom?
Is the city dwelling my prison? Low I join the gathering
Crowds anyway. . .like a sad, sweet-eyed wanderer. I let the
Music of ceremony flood my longing heart. The young, dark-haired,
Black-eyed mothers hold the children, starry-eyed, in their arms
Like doves with deep throated breasts, full with the beauty
of fertility. The image of their love, like a satin veil,
Soothes my broken lovesick spirit. For a short time, the wind
Swirling the papers tugs at me and I hear my own thoughts cry out:
Little woman, who are you? The city stands erect like God.
The city lies chained to the hearts of men.
The wayward tide is the fateful way of life.
Vain men mock, vain men walk on.
City child, my city child,
Where are your friends?

Chapter 9

DRAMA

. . .for it is only when the intellect has wrought the whole of life to drama, to crisis, that we may live for comtemplation, and yet keep our intensity.

— William Butler Yeats

RAGEDY and all aspects of drama are propelled by unpredictable events, broken expectations, and tensions between the polarities of feelings. Theatre has grown from conflict and the upsetting of the normal balance of daily life. Thus, dramatic tension intensifies the experience of life by immersing our feelings in the eternal contradictions of self-consciousness. As Eugene O'Neill has said, "Self awareness, reason and imagination have disrupted the 'harmony' which characterizes animal existence." Drama confronts and expounds upon human illusions, projected masks, false ideals, unconscious aggressions, suffering, death, loneliness, and all of the emotional conflicts that surface in psychotherapy. Both therapy and drama are an affirmation of life, a "symbolic celebration" of human vitality through which the person *enacts* existential struggle while providing a structure in which struggle has meaning and value. True spontaneous drama created from the everyday lives of people is inherently therapeutic, while psychotherapy is essentially a process of dramatic enactment.

Theatre began as a therapeutic process in early cultures, and during the high points of classical Greek drama, the theatre served as a form of social therapy for the entire community. Public enactments enabled people to experience a spiritual rebirth by immersing themselves in tragedy. Through both drama and therapy we attempt to confront the dichotomy of the emotions, and through an awareness of, and acceptance of, the precariousness of emotional realities, we create a systematic sense of the dynamic organization and purpose of human life.

In my work I have come to see all forms of psychotherapy and expressive art activity as dramatic enactment. The art of theatre is an all-encompassing form of self-consciousness and expression. It has no boundaries other than the limitations of human imagination. Drama gives an artistic structure, which helps to clarify our perceptions and feelings, and psychotherapy can renew and expand itself by identifying more with theatrical continuities. Because of the control the medical profession has had over the mental health field during the twentieth century, society has been conditioned to look to places other than art for healing experiences. Otto Rank believed that therapy is a "philosophical" process and that the person in stress needs a "world view" together with "belief," increasingly so as self-consciousness faces doubt, loneliness, and moral alienation in the modern world. Rank was critical of Freud's narrow mindedness, which he felt could be attributed to the "medical ideology" in which he grew up. It would appear that medically oriented psychotherapy is often successful in spite of itself because the person has faith and believes in the values of scientific technology. Even in its more medical forms, psychotherapy involves relationships between people wherein dramatic conflicts are often enacted on an unconscious level in that, whenever people are together to share the stories of their lives, there is drama.

The ancient continuities of tragedy offer an alternative to medical notions of psychopathology in explaining human misfortune and suffering. Tragedy to me is a superior mode of understanding life because it is based on principles of action, struggle, and intervention. Rather than adopting the passivity and dependence of medical theories of behavior, the tragic protagonist confronts the eternal tensions between opposites in a never ending search for, or what might be described as a dream of, fulfillment. As soon as the tragic tension is lost, life loses its dynamic quality, and we see the kind of passivity and extinction of vitality so prevalent in contemporary emotional disorders. Tragedy realizes that there will never be perfection in the human realm, and there will always be struggle as people grow toward an understanding of the self and its inevitable conflicts. I believe that excessive reliance on scientific explanations for behavior weakens our resolve to engage the forces of tragic tension actively, which are not only sources of discontent but which also provoke our most creative, and deeply human, activity. With the acceptance of tragedy, there is an important lesson for psychotherapy.

DRAMATIC ENACTMENT AND PSYCHOTHERAPY

> *Why, from highest height*
> *To deepest depth below*
> *Has the soul fallen?*
> *Within itself, the Fall*
> *Contains the Resurrection.*
>
> — Ansky, *The Dybbuk* [1]

Dramatic enactment deals with tension and tragedy through physical action. In *The Poetics,* Aristotle proclaims that "life consists in action, and its end is a mode of action, not a quality." The use of intellectual analysis in therapy has its place but also its limitations. Our reasoning powers must be balanced by faith in intuition, emotion, and *action.* Within the dramatic enactment there is the same evaluation of motives, confrontation of illusions, and search for self-knowledge that takes place within traditional verbal psychotherapy, but through artistic action, the dichotomies of intellect and emotion, tension and release, together with self and non-self, are united. The ambiguities and contradictions of daily existence are not necessarily *resolved* by the enactment process, but by acting them out, we accept the inevitable conditions of life tensions. Through drama we move and express conflict, we transform our struggles into a form that is conveyed to ourselves and to other people, and we experience the total catharsis and release that can be obtained only through the enactment, which draws upon the full expressive powers of the organism.

---

[1] From S. Ansky, *The Dybbuk: A Play,* 1972. Courtesy of the Liveright Corp., Subsidiaries of W. W. Norton Co., Inc., New York, New York.

Dramatic enactments generally function within mythological systems that give meaning and structure to life. Joseph Campbell believes that neuroticism comes from the social decline of myth as a form of spiritual support. "The prime function of myth and rite is to supply the symbols that carry the human spirit forward" (Campbell, 1949, p. 11). The client in contemporary therapy is the embodiment of the "hero" in ancient mythological and dramatic systems or the "antihero" of modern literature. The psychotherapeutic process is an explicit enactment in a physically present form of the personal and social conflicts that were in the past projected onto heros. As we have come to understand the psychodynamics of projection, the focus of the existential and spiritual drama has become the individual person, family, and community. Yet, the fundamental enactment of the hero remains intact with the goal being "the unlocking and release again of the flow of life into the body of the world" (Campbell, 1949, p. 40). As in psychotherapy and theatre, the mythological hero "is the man or woman who has been able to battle past personal and local historical limitations to the generally valid, normally human forms" (Campbell, 1949, p. 11).

Dramatic enactment gives tangible form to a person's sense of being. Drama is thus a mode of validating the reality of private perceptions as well as interpersonal feelings. When the enactment becomes universal, it is transformed into a culturally accepted mythology. Campbell feels that "myths are public dreams. . .and dreams are private myths." The myths of a society are group dreams "projected from the personal–collective vision of a seer" (Campbell, 1972, p. 118).

The enactment of dreams is the point of origin for not only myth and drama but also psychotherapy. Within shamanic cultures the dream is a "journey of the soul." Spirituality, magic, conceptualizations of the soul, of a life other than that of our material waking existence, and the world of imagination originate in the dream. The process of dreaming expands consciousness through the transcendence of the time and space realities of conscious thought. Transpersonal modes of being and the life of the soul are revealed through the dream.

Aboriginal cultures attributed sickness to a loss of soul. During dreams certain aspects of a person's soul leave the body and enter again upon awakening. Shirokogoroff, in describing shamanic practices of the Tungus, reports that the absence of the complete soul could be harmful. Within certain healing enactments, the shaman will enter a dream state or actually go to sleep in order to enable the soul to leave the body and go in search of the missing soul of the sick person. Dreams must have been at times very frightening to aboriginal people in that they were the first indicators that there were events taking place in their lives that were apparently not directly related to the continuities of material existence. The only way that they could release these fears and communicate their feelings to others was through the full dramatic enactment of the dream. Mythological systems were subsequently created to give meaning to dream life, with myths evolving from the repeated and common dreams of the community. Dreams can be equally frightening today when feelings that we repress and deny emerge with full vitality in the dream, while the controls of the conscious mind are relaxed. Therefore, dream enactment as a means of making the experience tangible and developing some sense of control over, and communication with, our dreaming consciousness is as vital today as it was within shamanic cultures. What unites shamanic and psychotherapeutic enactments is a deep respect for the dream and a desire to understand its message.

Gésa Róheim believes that "the fundamental mechanism of the dream is the formation of a double, the dream image or the soul" (Róheim, 1979, p. 155). The enactment and journey of the shaman evolves directly from the dream. In this respect, sleep and theatre and psychotherapy suspend inhibiting dimensions of temporal reality to allow us to penetrate deeper into the more emotional, nonlinear, and transcendent realms of feeling. Drama has, in this respect, always been a means by which we ritualistically and symbolically bring together the different planes of existence. Anthropological evidence clearly shows that there is a very ancient and consistent pattern to emotional disorders. Róheim describes how aboriginal societies universally attributed dreams to the "wanderings of the soul," and how disease was caused by the "abduction of the soul." The shaman rose into prominence as the person who went in search of the lost soul. Róheim believes that there is a universal "basic dream" that involves the *flying* ascent into the sky or the descent into the lower regions of the world. All anthropological observers note how the shaman passes through a hole to reach the spirit worlds, and as noted in an earlier chapter on shamanism, these dream characteristics have appeared regularly in my clinical work as an expressive arts therapist. Psychoanalytically oriented theorists such as Róheim attribute the symbol of the hole to the uterine opening, and the passage is, to them, a return to prenatal existence. The shaman is thus reenacting, but at the same time reversing, the birth drama. The hole might be related to other bodily openings and passageways — the mouth, nose, ear, navel, etc. — while more spiritual people might connect the shaman's passageway with the eye, the sun, or the moon. What is significant for our purposes here is the reality that this, and other rites of passage, are consistently present in the enactment process as it manifests itself in shamanism, theatre, and psychotherapy.

Whatever the origins of shamanic symbols of enactment, the parallels between ancient theories of dream analysis and psychotherapy are remarkable. I see in these varied traditions a continuous belief that psychological disturbance is related to a disassociation between the person's soul (feelings) and the more general structure of the personality. As in contemporary descriptions of schizophrenia, different parts of the self are *split* from one another, and the cohesion of the personality is *shattered.* In all societies, the afflicted person, who is not able to deal with these difficulties alone, is in need of a person (shaman or therapist) who can help in reuniting the fragmented or "lost" dimensions of the self. In all cultures the healing process is achieved through enactment. Dreams, images, and fantasies are acted out and revealed so that the client and the shaman may begin to understand the nature of the problem. Only through dramatic action can we physically confront memories, dreams, and imaginary events and begin to reintegrate them into our lives. The power of drama lies in engaging disassociated feelings through emotional enactment. We thus act out and *become* the double image of the dream, the different and conflicting parts of our personalities, and through the process of dealing with these tensions, which are at times irresolvable, we achieve an experiential integration on the same emotional level where the difficulty lies. Through enactment we resurrect and *live* our emotional struggles and share them with other people. The process is strengthened by group involvement, through which other people sanction and encourage direct communication with the emotions. Drama maximizes the healing power of the group.

In western society, theatre has been the link between shamanism and psychotherapy. For thousands of years, drama, more than any other art form, has served society as both a means of emotional catharsis and as a mode of interpreting and giving value to life. All of the arts, as they are integrated into theatre, have made their respective therapeutic contributions. Theatre is preeminently a social and communal art. As a form of group therapy, it gave a sense of emotional order and support to members of the community in that it provided them with a means of acting out and gaining control of their greatest fears and emotional dilemmas. Perhaps more than any other artists, the actor, playwright, and director deal with the emotions in a way that closely parallels the role of the psychotherapist. Beginning psychotherapists have, in my opinion, an unconscious sense of the dramatic nature of their roles. They must engage another human being within a prescribed space and time and create an environment in which there can be a communion of thought, emotion, and expression. Both the psychotherapist and the client feel that they will be functioning within roles when interacting with one another, while within certain therapeutic processes, the changing and reversing of roles will be encouraged. Beginning therapists often feel a sense of nervousness, as the actor does, when intuitively grasping the reality that they must become skillful in helping themselves and other people to enact their life dramas, within the psychotherapeutic relationship. Like the actor, the therapist must develop concentration skills as well as a variety of personal techniques for actualizing this interpersonal process. Yet, when the exclusive concern of training is the acquistion of methods and techniques, there is a denial of the primary art and spirit of psychotherapeutic drama.

Róheim described how, in addition to "the journey of the soul," another common characteristic of both Siberian and North American shamanism is the *symbolic battle*. Within shamanic enactments, battles take place between animals that are transformations of the shaman as well as tangible manifestations of the malevolent spirits in nature. The shamanic battle is a dramatization of the conflict within the person. The battle motif is a universal phenomenon in both theatre and therapy. In theatre there is the ancient tragic tension between the opposites of life and death, good and evil, light and darkness, pleasure and pain, parent and child, shadow and persona, and what Yeats described as the will and the mask, the self and the antiself, the creative drive and fate. Within psychotherapy there is a similar symbolic enactment of the battle between opposites with the terms being revised – *eros* and *thanatos,* the conscious and unconscious mind, id and reason, underdog and top dog, good parents and bad parents, present and past, etc. As I have shown in the previous chapters, the psychotherapeutic art experience invariably involves the enactment of these tensions and primal conflicts through dance, drama, music, poetry, the visual arts, and storytelling. All forms of emotionally charged art are essentially enactments that engage the different senses. The enactment theory of art in this respect provides a rationale for the complete reunification of the artistic process and healing. All of art has a potential to realize the process of emotional enactment fully, and to the extent that artists choose to explore the basic nature of the self, the other, and nature through their expression, they are engaging in shamanic drama.

Consciousness is in its essence a form of enactment. Dreams dramatize the tensions and joys of daily experience as they relate to our individual and collective past, and within our thoughts, we are always either acting out imaginary dramas of how we relate to life situations or engaging in the real life interplay of roles and interactions. Our distinctive human ability to be conscious of behavior is the source for both thought and drama. Psychotherapy and theatre intensify the process of enactment by making us more aware of its ongoing flow. This is achieved primarily through the creation of a spatial and interpersonal context, which is separate from the instrusions of various obstacles to introspection, contemplation, and self-expression that are presented in daily life. Theatre and therapy use a number of different conventions that transform one's life space into a sacred meeting ground. Through the focusing of consciousness any artistic or daily activity can take on dramatic and deeply personal qualities. A woman in her early seventies who makes quilts in a small wood-frame farmhouse in Texas described quilting as an expression of how she saw the world.

> You can't always change things. Sometimes you don't have no control over the way the things go. Hail ruins the crops, or fire burns you out. And then you're just given so much to work with in a life and you have to do the best you can with what you've got. That's what piecing is. The materials is passed on to you or is all you can afford to buy. . .that's just what's given to you. Your fate. But the way you put them together is your business. You can put them in any order you like. Piecing is orderly. First you cut the pieces, then you arrange your pieces like you want them. I build up the blocks and then put all the blocks together and arrange them, then I strip and post to hold them together. . .and finally I bind them all around and you get the whole thing made up. Finished. (Cooper and Buferd, 1977, p. 20)

In relating therapy to drama, I do not wish to increase the mystique of psychotherapy and further alienate healing from everyday life processes. On the contrary, the dramatic consciousness can help us to appreciate the significance of the simplest qualities of human interaction more fully. My goal is to heighten appreciation of what people convey about themselves within the perfunctory patterns of their lives as well as within emotionally charged relationships with other people. If one accepts the fundamental dramatic strain of psychotherapy, then it becomes essential to think in terms of training therapists to deepen their understanding of role theory as well as to strengthen their ability to enact different roles within the psychotherapeutic process. Traditional psychotherapy has explored this issue through its concern with transference and countertransference, but expressive art therapy training goes further in perceiving the therapist and client as co-participants in dramatic action. Rather than becoming completely separate from the client's action for the purpose of objectivization and analysis, the therapist generally becomes involved in the person's drama. By personally relating to the client's enactment the therapist strengthens and intensifies the sharing process. The case studies that I have described in previous chapters demonstrate the dramatic component of all expressive therapy enactments.

Dramatic interactions between therapists and clients can take place in all art mediums. For example, a graduate student whom I was training demonstrated to me how interactional drawings are based on dramatic principles. He was working with a woman who in the past would always isolate herself from the group and work alone. Although this pattern was generally not a problem because of the seriousness of her art and her needs for intense concentration, her approach to art did reinforce the more pervasive egocentrism of her behavior. In a series of therapeutic sessions, the student began to interest her in interactional drawings. She was drawn to him because, in addition to his other personal qualities, he was a very capable artist. They began their first interactional drawings together, with him completely following her lead. She was much more concerned with initiating her own expressions rather than responding to his. However, as he related to her colors and forms, she increasingly began to feel and enjoy his presence. He described how "when we started to work together we saw how our styles and interests could interrelate. This comparison helped her to define herself and her identity." It was important for her to see him enjoying himself with her, and their interactional synchrony further motivated her expression.

As they progressed in their first collaborative picture, their styles began to coordinate with one another. Each of them described how they learned something new and expanded their art by responding to the other. The collaborative pictures developed into a therapeutic enactment of cooperation and shared creation. As the series of pictures continued, she encouraged him to initiate drawings, and she would respond. This was a totally new behavior pattern for her. They were also aware of the kinesthetic and physical dimensions of their work together. He said that "this physical contact allowed her to be more open. We were responding to each other's tempos and kinesthetic patterns. I have done collaborations with other artists, group murals with psychiatric patients and conversational drawings with children, but they would usually involve a process of taking turns. With her, everything was simultaneous. The collaboration made us even more aware of our interpersonal process since communication was sensory as well as verbal. Everything was so tangible and we were able to express what we were dissatisfied with and we helped each other whenever we got stuck" (excerpted from a conversation with Ron Hueftle, 1978).

Even this case example, where communication between the two people was largely through the graphic medium of drawing, supports Rank's definition of psychotherapy as understanding the meaning of an interpersonal experience while in the process of having it. The drama of psychotherapy is largely focused on both acting out, and reflecting upon, the human exchange. The different arts allow for the expansion of the enactment process into varied modes of expression. With dance therapy, therapists and clients often show their sensitivity to another's movement by dancing in synchrony with the person. In addition to mirroring another's expression, dance therapy might involve the therapist in responding kinesthetically to a client's movement, and this might precipitate an ongoing exchange of feelings through movement. Instrumental and vocal sounds might be introduced to both acknowledge and intensify a person's expression. The same applies to music therapy where the therapist's participation can reinforce sounds made by the client. With the therapist joining in, a rhythm can be supported and carried beyond the point where the client might usually stop. Within these artistic enactments, the therapist becomes an alter ego, thoroughly sensitized to the client's needs, who provides added strength and external support while also facilitating the establishment of a therapeutic and artistic structure for the client's expression.

Our understanding of psychotherapy as dramatic enactment owes much to the work of J. L. Moreno.[2] In creating psychodrama, Moreno saw the oneness of theatre and therapy. He believed that, in relating to the dramas of everyday life, "we deal with drama at a level where the neat separation of the esthetic from the therapeutic is meaningless" (Moreno, 1973, p. 28). Moreno referred negatively to traditional drama as a "cultural conserve" and chided its "worship of the dead." His concern was a revitalization of both therapy and theatre through an artistic enactment of living process. He believed that identity is comprised of a collection of roles that manifest themselves in relation to

---

[2]The following passages are taken from J. L. Moreno, *The Theatre of Spontaneity*, 1973. Courtesy of Beacon House, Inc., Beacon, New York.

the momentary context. Through dramatic enactment he clarified these roles and helped people to increase their effectiveness as human beings by becoming more spontaneous, open, and dynamic in their varied roles. Moreno's practical and theoretical contributions to fusing artistic enactment with psychotherapy are vast. He responded to Freud's negativistic view of human motivation with a philosophy in which "spontaneity and creativity are regarded as primary and positive phenomenon and not as derivatives of libido or any other animal drive" (Moreno, 1973, p. 49). Moreno further distinguished himself from Freud in declaring that "the distinction between the conscious and the unconscious has no place in a psychology of the creative act" (Moreno, 1973, p. 42). Spontaneous expression brings about an interplay of all aspects of a person's being in which the enactment of the feelings of the moment liberate what Moreno would describe as the true and creative self. He describes the Theatre of Spontaneity as a place, the true symbol of which is the private home, where "the persons play before themselves. . .the same life again. The place of the conflict and of its theatre is one and the same. . .they re-experience it, they are master. . .the whole past is moved out of its coffin and arrives at a moment's call. It does not only emerge in order to heal itself, for relief and catharsis, but it is also the love for its own demons which drives the theatre on to unchain itself. . .this unfoldment of life in the domain of illusion does not work like a renewal of suffering, rather it confirms the rule: every *true* second time is the liberation from the first" (Moreno, 1973, pp. 90-91).

A forceful philosophical push like that of Moreno was essential to begin to bring theatre back into line with therapeutic enactment. Within Moreno's system, the individual is both playwright and actor within a personal drama. According to his philosophy, art must use the present material of a person's life if it is to create a process that has value. The idea was not necessarily novel in that classic lines, such as "All the world's a stage and all men and women merely players," had helped to make the integration of theatre and life a commonplace idea. One of Moreno's greatest contributions to theatre resulted from his vehement opposition to the traditional idea of creating art for the benefit of an audience. His approach to psychodrama achieves a major "role reversal" between the protagonist and the audience in that the primary value placed on psychodramatic enactment is the attentiveness to the needs of the actor. The drama is heightened by the extent to which the group is able to facilitate the actor's catharsis. The audience vicariously experiences these feelings, as in traditional theatre, but the sacredness of the context is intensified by the total spontaneity and honesty of the enactment, which is precipitated by the emotionally charged atmosphere created by the group.

From a practical point of view, Moreno introduced operational principles such as role reversal, doubling, sociometry, and therapeutic intervention techniques, which were to provide the stimulus for later psychotherapeutic systems such as Gestalt therapy. However, many of these subsequent developments have lost touch with Moreno's belief in spontaneity and creativity as the fundamental units of human life. Moreno's model of strong leadership has also been revised by therapists in an effort to give clients more control over the dramatic enactment. The psychodramatic leadership model has been criticized by some as involving too much control and intervention on the part of the director. Whenever it is possible in my own work, I try to engage the client as both playwright and director of the dramatic process. Yet, at the same time the great power of psychodramatic enactment is often due to the ability of the leader to direct and intensify the group process. The skillful leader will not appear to be intrusive, but as Moreno said, this person must have a grasp of the basic idea of the enactment and will be able to assist the protagonist in overcoming obstacles to expression. Problems encountered in psychodramatic experiences are often due to the resistance within groups. The group's ability to trust and support spontaneity is essential to dramatic enactment. The director's experience and knowledge of the emotional intensities of the enactment of feelings tends to have a critical effect in creating a trusting environment and a supportive structure for the dramatic process. Structure in this sense helps to free the expression of participants. The competent director not only helps the group to begin the enactment process but, most importantly, knows when to pull back and let the group take its own course. In *The Theatre of Spontaneity* Moreno describes the subtle nuances of how the director's judgment operates in relation to intervention and control within a group. "But without some measure and discipline the inter-play of even the most creative players may fail. Spontaneity work is so challenging to man's mental organization that it is wise not to invite failure to start with by methods of laissez-faire. It is as if reason, before the jump into the spontaneous drama takes place, goes cautiously ahead of it with its lamp of intuitive anticipation, draws a sketch of the possible terrain to be encountered with its barriers and traps, so that it can indicate the direction which the jump should take" (Moreno, 1973, p. 63).

Moreno's work in psychodrama has been adapted by other expressive therapists. Albert Pesso, who developed without being influenced by Moreno, explores the enactment process in movement. His terminology differs from Moreno's in that the "protagonist" becomes an "enactor," and this person rather than the "director" is encouraged to choose "accommodators" and to direct the course of the enactment through movement. Words are used by the accommodators only when given to them by the enactor. Thus, the accomodator tends to have less expressive freedom than the "auxiliary" in psychodrama, but Pesso would argue that this is necessary to focus maximum therapeutic energy on the emotional script as developed by the enactor. Pesso's therapist acts as a guide to the enactor who creates "positive" and "negative" accommodators (good and bad parents) who represent the polarities of feeling from the person's past that have not yet been acted upon or resolved. As in psychodrama, the person allows the impulses connected to past feelings to emerge into action. Psychomotor therapy, however, with its emphasis on parental conflict, is more closely aligned with traditional psychoanalytic theory than psychodrama.

Moreno's and Pesso's systems complement one another, and in my own work I tend to use whatever method seems to be called upon by the clinical situation. Dogmatic methods are of little value in psychotherapy, and they tend to alienate us from openly experiencing our own feelings and those of our clients. What we need is an ever expanding integration of art and therapy, which will transcend the limitations of technical systems and terminology and, in so doing, knowingly unite our work with the universal and eternal myths and beliefs that manifest themselves in all historical epochs and all geographic regions of the world.

In addition to what has been discussed here, there are many other ways of approaching dramatic enactment in therapy. For example, dramatic dance allows the dance therapist to relate to the broad spectrum of psychotherapeutic issues through the body. Dance as emotional enactment continues an ancient continuity of art where the content of feelings, fears, and conflicts is made tangible and expelled through the body. Within an integrated arts context, attentiveness to the dramatic enactments of dance can increase the significance of gestures and movements that are made in conjunction with other modes of expression as we consciously and unconsciously act out inner feelings through our bodies.

In previous chapters, I have also demonstrated how instrumental and vocal sound, as well as poems and visual artworks, can be used for the purpose of enactment. I have tried to make the enactment of feelings the connecting link between the arts in therapy. All of the case materials discussed have, in one form or another, supported the enactment principle.

Dramatic action provides a basic aesthetic unity to the therapeutic process in that drama gives value to confusion, struggle, and emotional contradiction, and it does not oversimplify experience. Opposites are allowed to exist alongside one another, and they are accepted as part of the reality of life. This sense of artistic order is a source of hope and validation for both the therapist and the client. Through dramatic enactment, we try out different roles and, within a safe structure, confront those aspects of our personality which we fear and keep hidden during everyday life. According to Yeats, we are most completely ourselves when we are living and acknowleding these hidden parts of the personality: "the other self, the antiself or the antithetical self. . .comes but to those who are no longer deceived, whose passion is reality." People who are living out those personal deceptions and idealized self-images are themselves acting. However, their dramatic enactment is one of emotional subterfuge rather than truthfulness.

In psychotherapy the theatrical experience prepares people to act more effectively and honestly in their lives. In encouraging total expression in all art modalities, psychotherapy is bringing theatrical evolution to a point where artistic enactment again serves the purpose of healing. Dramatic and therapeutic processes mediate between the individual human being and the conflictual forces of the self and nature. Neither artistic nor psychotherapeutic methods claim to eliminate tension completely, since that would involve extinguishing the primal life force that brings pleasure and meaning as well as pain and disillusionment. Psychotherapeutic enactment gives value to personal struggle just as the artist affirms life through the creative integration of contradictory emotions. The opposites are bridged within the person through the process of artistically acknowledging their existence.

CONCLUSION

I N this book, I have tried to show how the artists of our culture can teach us about the healing qualities of the arts. As Eugene O'Neill proclaimed, "Authors were psychologists you know, and profound ones before psychology was invented." The greatest value of the artist's insights rests in the fact that they are heated in the fire of human passion and in living life fully. The same applies to what I have learned from children and adults making art in therapy. Because of its dependence on traditional psychology, the mental health field often presents itself as a despirited technical system of categorizing and "managing" people. The arts will not only expand the range of communication and sensibility within psychotherapy, but they will connect contemporary healers and clients to their ancient past. The continuity of art healing practices throughout the ages has convinced me that the modern artist-therapist has more in common with the aboriginal shaman than the medically trained therapists, whose methods are more often than not antithetical to the artistic process. Not least among the healing powers of the arts is their ability to bring therapists into closer contact with their personal feelings and expressive needs. The therapist who is ignited with the emotion of art will not only be useful in projecting this commitment to others but will be that much more attuned to the expressions and inhibitions of clients. As D. H. Lawrence put it, "we are transmitters" who stimulate others to create art and life.

Psychotherapy, like shamanism, is a process of "empowerment." In this regard, all art is therapeutic and shamanic. What distinguishes the expressive art therapist is an extraordinary commitment to acting as a "transmitter" of the artistic consciousness for those people who have lost or who have never achieved a sense of personal power. I speak of power in terms of a belief that the greatest, and ironically the most available, source of strength is the value-giver in each of us that can ascribe personal meaning to virtually anything. All people are potential alchemists of the spirit in that the transformation of one form of consciousness into another is the essence of art. The expressive arts therapist is a person whose life is committed to transmitting this power to create consciousness within each moment. We are artistic alchemists and twentieth century shamans who have discovered that in a time of emotional estrangement the arts offer a very old and predictable hope in sanctifying life through creative enactment.

BIBLIOGRAPHY

Allen, Robert, and Krebs, Nina: *Psychotheatrics: The New Art of Self-Transformation.* New York, Garland STPM Press, 1976.

Alvin, Juliette: *Music Therapy.* New York, Basic, 1975.

Alvin, Juliette: *Music Therapy for the Autistic Child.* London, Oxford U Pr, 1978.

Arnheim, Rudolph: *Art and Visual Perception.* Berkley and Los Angeles, U of Cal Pr, 1954.

Arnheim, Rudolph: *Visual Thinking.* Berkley and Los Angeles, U of Cal Pr, 1971.

Barron, Frank: *Creativity and Psychological Health.* Princeton, New Jersey, D Van Nostrand, 1963.

Berlyne, D. E.: *Conflict, Arousal and Curiosity.* New York, McGraw, 1960.

Blinderman, Abraham: Shamans, witch doctors, medicine men and poetry. In Leedy, Jack J.: *Poetry the Healer.* Philadelphia, Lippincott, 1973.

Brown, Norman O.: *Love's Body.* New York, Vintage Books, 1966.

Campbell, Joseph: *The Hero with a Thousand Faces.* Bollingen Series XVII. New York, Pantheon, 1949.

Campbell, Joseph: *Myths to Live By.* New York, Viking, 1972.

Cassirer, Ernst: *The Philosophy of Symbolic Forms.* New Haven, Yale U Pr, 1970, vol. 1, 2, and 3.

Chaiklin, Harris (Ed.): *Marian Chace: Her Papers.* Columbia, Maryland, American Dance Therapy Association, 1975.

Cofer, C. N., and Appley, M. H.: *Motivation: Theory and Research.* New York, Wiley, 1964.

Condon, W. S., and Ogston, W. D.: Sound and film analysis of normal and pathological behavior patterns. *J Nerv Ment Dis, 143:*4, 1966.

Copper, Patricia, and Buferd, Norma Bradley: *The Quilters: Women and Domestic Art.* Garden City, New York, Doubleday, 1977.

Costonis, Maureen Needham: *Therapy in Motion.* Urbana, Illinois, U of Ill Pr, 1978.

Czaplicka, M. A.: *Aboriginal Siberia.* Oxford, Oxford U Pr, 1914.

Einstein, Albert: *Relativity: The Special and the General Theory.* Translation by Robert Lawson. New York, Crown, 1967.

Eliade, Mircea: *Shamanism: Archaic Techniques of Ecstasy.* New York, Pantheon, 1964.

Festinger, Leon: *A Theory of Cognitive Dissonance.* Evanston, Illinois, Row, Peterson, 1957.

Frank, Jerome: *Persuasion and Healing: A Comparative Study of Psychotherapy.* Baltimore, The Johns Hopkins Pr, 1961.

Freud, Sigmund: *The Interpretation of Dreams.* New York, Basic, 1956.

Freud, Sigmund: Leonardo Da Vinci. In Strachey, James (Ed.): *The Complete Psychological Works of Sigmund Freud.* London, Hogarth, 1968, vol. XI.

Gaston, E. Thayer (Ed.): *Music in Therapy.* New York, Macmillan, 1968.

Harlow, Harry: Motivation as a factor in the acquisition of new responses. In Jones, Marshall (Ed.): *Current Theory and Research in Motivation.* Lincoln, U of Nebr Pr, 1953.

Hoffman, Lois Wladis: Early childhood experiences and women's achievement motives. *J Soc Issues, 28* (2), 1972.

Jaques-Dalcroze, Émile: *Rhythm, Music and Education.* London, Dalcroze Society, Hazell Watson Winey, Ltd., 1973.

Jung, C. G.: *Psychological Types.* New York, Harcourt, Brace, 1923.

Jung, C. G.: *Memories, Dreams, Reflections.* New York, Pantheon, 1963.

Jung, C. G.: The spirit in man, art and literature. In Adler, G. et al (Eds.): *The Collected Works of Carl G. Jung.* Princeton, Princeton U Pr, 1966, vol. XV.

Kagan, Jerome: Motives and development. *J Pers Soc Psychol, 22:*1, 1972.

Knill, Paul: *Intermodal Learning in Education and Therapy.* Cambridge, published by the author, 1978.

Köhler, Wolfgang: *Gestalt Psychology.* New York, Liveright, 1970.

Kris, Ernst: *Psychoanalytic Explorations in Art.* London, Intl Univs Pr, 1953.

Kubie, Lawrence: *Neurotic Distortion of the Creative Process.* New York, FS&G, 1961.

Laban, Rudolph von: *The Mastery of Movement.* London, MacDonald and Evans, 1947.

Laban, Rudolph von: *A Life for Dance.* New York, Theatre Arts, 1975.

Leedy, Jack, (Ed.): *Poetry Therapy.* Philadelphia, Lippincott, 1969.

Leedy, Jack (Ed.): *Poetry the Healer.* Philadelphia, Lippincott, 1973.

Lerner, Arthur (Ed.): *Poetry in the Therapeutic Experience.* New York, Pergamon, 1978.

Lewis, I. M.: *Ecstatic Religion: An Anthropological Study of Spirit Possession and Shamanism.* New York, Penguin, 1978.

McKenna, O. J. and McKenna, T. K.: *The Invisible Landscape.* New York, Seabury Press, 1975.

McNiff, Shaun: Video art therapy. *Art Psychotherapy, 2* (1), 55-63, 1975.

McNiff, Shaun: Motivation in art. *Art Psychotherapy, 4:*3-4, 1977.

McNiff, Shaun: The art therapist as artist. *Ninth Annual Conference of the American Art Therapy Association,* Los Angeles, California, 1978.

McNiff, Shaun: Truman Nelson: An interview. *Minnesota Review,* Spring 1978.

Meyerhoff, Barbara: Balancing between worlds: The shaman's calling. *Parabola, 1* (2), 6-13, 1976.

Michel, Donald: *Music Therapy: An Introduction to Therapy and Special Education Through Music.* Springfield, Thomas, 1976.

Montagu, Ashley: *Touching: The Human Significance of the Skin.* New York, Columbia U Pr, 1971.

Moreno, J. L.: *Psychodrama.* Beacon, New York, Beacon Hse, 1946, vol. I.

Moreno, J. L.: *The Theatre of Spontaneity.* Beacon, New York, Beacon Hse, 1973.

Naumburg, Margaret: *Dynamically Oriented Art Therapy.* New York, Grune, 1966.

Neihardt, John: *Black Elk Speaks: Being the Life Stroy of a Holyman of the Ogalala Sioux.* New York, PB, 1975.

Nordoff, Paul, and Robbins, Clive: *Music Therapy in Special Education.* New York, John Day, 1971.

Nordoff, Paul, and Robbins, Clive: *Therapy in Music for Handicapped Children.* New York, St. Martin, 1971.

North, Marion: *Personality Assessment Through Movement.* Boston, Plays, 1975.

Olson, Charles: *Selected Writings.* Edited by Robert Creeley. New York, New Directions, 1966.

O'Neill, Eugene: Personal communication with Arthur Hobson Quinn, 1925.

O'Neill, Eugene: In *The American Spectator Yearbook.* New York, 1934, pp. 166-167.

Nietzsche, Friedrich: *The Birth of Tragedy and the Case of Wagner.* Translated by Walter Kaufmann. New York, Vintage Books, 1967.

Park, Willard Z.: *Shamanism in Western North America.* New York, Cooper Sq, 1975.

Pesso, Albert: *Movement in Psychotherapy: Psychomotor Techniques and Training.* New York, New York U Pr, 1969.

Priestley, Mary: *Music Therapy in Action.* New York, St. Martin, 1975.

Prinzhorn, Hans: *Artistry of the Mentally Ill.* New York, Springer-Verlag, 1972.

Rank, Otto: *Psychology and the Soul.* Philadelphia, U of Pa Pr, 1950.

Rank, Otto: *The Myth of the Birth of the Hero and Other Writings.* Edited by Philip Freund. New York, Vintage, 1959.

Rank, Otto: *Art and Artists.* New York, Agathon, 1968.

Reich, Wilhelm: *Selected Writings: An Introduction to Orgonomy.* New York, FS&G, 1973.

Reichel-Dolmatoff, G.: *The Shaman and the Jaguar.* Philadelphia, Tempel U Pr, 1975.

Rogers, Carl: The actualizing tendency in relation to "motives" and to consciousness. In Jones, Marshall (Ed.): *Nebraska Symposium on Motivation.* Lincoln, U of Nebr Pr, 1963.

Róheim, Géza: *The Gates of the Dream.* New York, Intl Univs Pr, 1979.

Schloss, Gilbert: *Psychopoetry*. New York, G & D, 1976.

Shirokogoroff, Sergei: General Theory of Shamanism among the Tungus. *JRAS*, North China Branch (Shanghai), *LIV*. 246-49, 1923.

Slade, Peter: *Child Drama*. U of London Pr, 1954.

Spolin, Viola: *Improvisation for Theatre*. Evanston, Illinois, Northwestern U Pr, 1963.

Stanislavski, Constantin: *An Actor Prepares*. New York, Theatre Arts, 1976.

Villoldo, Alberto: The magical path of the shaman. *New Age, 4:*11, May, 1979.

Waters, Frank: *Book of the Hopi*. New York, Ballantine, 1969.

Way, Brian: *Development Through Drama*. London, Humanities, 1967.

White, Robert: Motivation reconsidered: The concept of competence. *Psychol Rev, 66,* 1959

Whithead, Alfred North: *Process and Reality: An Essay in Cosmology*. New York, Humanities, 1929.

Whorf, Benjamin Lee: *Language, Thought, and Reality*. New York, MIT Pr and Wiley, 1956.

INDEX